WRITING THE
LEGAL RECORD

WRITING
the LEGAL
RECORD

LAW REPORTERS
in
NINETEENTH-CENTURY KENTUCKY

KURT X. METZMEIER

UNIVERSITY PRESS OF KENTUCKY

Scholarly publisher for the Commonwealth,
serving Bellarmine University, Berea College, Centre College of Kentucky,
Eastern Kentucky University, The Filson Historical Society, Georgetown College,
Kentucky Historical Society, Kentucky State University, Morehead State
University, Murray State University, Northern Kentucky University, Transylvania
University, University of Kentucky, University of Louisville, and Western
Kentucky University.
All rights reserved.

Editorial and Sales Offices: The University Press of Kentucky
663 South Limestone Street, Lexington, Kentucky 40508-4008
www.kentuckypress.com

Library of Congress Cataloging-in-Publication Data

Names: Metzmeier, Kurt X., author.
Title: Writing the legal record : law reporters in nineteenth-century
    Kentucky / Kurt X. Metzmeier.
Description: Lexington, Kentucky : University Press of Kentucky, [2017] |
    Includes bibliographical references and index.
Identifiers: LCCN 2016042786| ISBN 9780813168609 (hardcover : alk. paper) |
    ISBN 9780813168623 (pdf) | ISBN 9780813168616 (epub)
Subjects: LCSH: Law reporters—Kentucky—Biography. | Law
    reporting—Kentucky—History.
Classification: LCC KFK1726.C68 M48 2017 | DDC 347.769/016—dc23
LC record available at https://lccn.loc.gov/2016042786

This book is printed on acid-free paper meeting the requirements of the American
National Standard for Permanence in Paper for Printed Library Materials.

Manufactured in the United States of America.

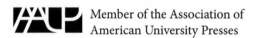 Member of the Association of
American University Presses

CONTENTS

Illustrations follow page 106

INTRODUCTION

Whoever bestows a thought on the humble reporter? Their names may be as familiar in our mouth as household words, but this familiarity is too usually attended by its well-known offspring. . . . Indeed our abstract idea of a reporter is rather that [of] a book than of a man. Whoever thinks of Bingham, for example, as a human being? There he is, alive and well, and ardently discharging his duties . . . but he is never present to our mind's eye in that character: if his name is mentioned, an octavo volume, naturally of a pale complexion, but sallowed and enbrowned by time and use, presents itself to the imagination.

—"Reports and Reporters," *Albany Law Journal* 3 (1871): 222

Dusty, dun-colored, and ponderous, the law report is the defining artifact of the legal profession. But while the modern version is the product of a regimented and relentlessly uniform system created by that quintessentially midwestern entrepreneur John B. West, the early Kentucky law reports were anything but uniform. In stark contrast to the bland efficiency of the West reporter system, these eponymous state reports shared neither style nor format nor even a uniform size. The early Kentucky law reports were extensions of the personalities of their creators, an individualistic group of rising young lawyers, future and former judges, aspiring politicians, and enterprising journalists. These men, commonly called "law reporters," collected the opinions of the court by taking notes as the judge read them aloud or by making copies of the handwritten decisions from the papers of the judge or the clerk of the court. They selected the best opinions, annotated and indexed them, and then arranged to have them printed and bound. In the beginning, the authors financed their efforts by subscription, and the costs of publishing often outweighed the profits from sales. Later they acted as contractors, depending on promised sales to the state

1

to subsidize publication. It would take eight decades and seventy-seven volumes before legal publishing was mature enough to change law reporting from a sideline of working lawyers to the official business of a state agency, and still longer for it to become the staple of a national commercial publisher.

The history of these reporters is not confined to the history of legal publishing; it also informs the legal history of the United States. When the American Revolution ended, the citizens of the new republic had to determine whether to continue the "common-law" legal system or create a new one. The common-law system was based on an ancient body of judge-made law that was constantly augmented and expanded by new printed decisions of appellate courts as they grappled with new issues and circumstances. At a time when some democratic voices were calling for a justice system without lawyers and decrying the common law as a remnant of royal servitude, the early law reporters helped create a new common law inspired by the law of England but fully grounded in the printed decisions of American judges. In doing so, they not only preserved and promoted the common law but also made real the idea of federalism implicit in the new Constitution. Thus, in a real way, these pioneer lawyers used their pens to mark out the boundaries of the law, just as their contemporaries marked out the boundaries of the American frontier.

After the Revolution, Americans were ambivalent about the continued adherence to the English common law. Some wished to push it into the sea with the departing redcoats, not just as an expression of nationalism but also because they believed it embodied conservative Tory values that were in direct conflict with democracy and republican values. As the Boston pamphleteer Benjamin Austin asked in 1786, "Why should these States be governed by British laws? . . . Can the monarchical and aristocratical institutions of England be consistent with the republican principles of our constitution?" His critique grazed the subject of this work when he mourned, "Is it not melancholy to see such numerous volumes, brought into our Courts, arranged in formidable order, as the grand artillery to batter down every plain, rational principle of law?"[1] Others, however, were convinced that the common law protected hard-won liberties. James Wilson, in his 1790 *Introductory Lecture of the Study of Law in the United States,* argued that the common law was the form of jurisprudence that most perfectly expressed the social contract the American republic was founded on. In the common law, he suggested, "the stream of authority run[s], from the most early periods, uniform and strong in the direction of the principle of consent—consent, given originally—consent, given in the form of ratification—and, what is most satisfactory of all, consent given after long, approved, and uninterrupted experience. This last, I think, is the principle of the common law. It is the most salutary principle of obedience to human laws that ever was diffused among men."[2]

For many lawyers, legislators, and judges, there was a readily apparent way to absorb the common law into the new republic and animate it with the consent of the governed. They proposed to build a thoroughly American legal system on the foundations of the English common law, expanded and clarified by state statutory law, but made native most of all by the published decisions of American judges. To these men, the common law was a living system that had far more to do with American judges than with dusty English law books. The instrument of this transformation would be the American law reporter, collections of written opinions of republican judges. Of course, the preeminent role of the case reporter in legal literature was not foreordained. At the time the US Constitution was ratified, abridgments, legal treatises, and legal manuals (some native, but many of British origin) were equally widespread sources of common-law precedents. However, by the mid-nineteenth century, it was clear that state and national American case reporters had taken the leading role in providing authority for legal rulings—perhaps reaching their apex in 1890, when Christopher Columbus Langdell decided to put the analysis of case reports at the center of legal education at Harvard Law School.[3]

In Kentucky, the move to native case reporters was not subtle. In 1808, the state legislature decreed that "the reports and books containing adjudged cases in the Kingdom of Great Britain" that had been decided "since the 4th day of July, 1776, shall not be read or considered as authority in any of the courts of this commonwealth."[4] This was not a mere pronouncement of an abstract principle; the Kentucky courts rigorously enforced the law, leading to a dramatic debate before Kentucky's highest court in 1808. The argument would involve two of Kentucky's earliest court reporters—one serving as counsel and the other reporting—as well as a future US Supreme Court justice and a young Henry Clay, whose legal renown was already established, though his political fame was still in the future.

The scene is described in the reports of Martin D. Hardin (very fortuitously, because he was the only Kentucky reporter who fully recorded oral arguments). The case of *Hickman v. Boffman* brought together the leading members of Kentucky's bar.[5] The attorneys representing the appellant (the person seeking to reverse the decision of the lower court) were James Hughes, the author of Kentucky's first law reports, and Clay. The appellee (the party defending a favorable decision) was represented by John Allen, whose brilliant law career was cut short when he was killed at the battle of River Raisin in the War of 1812, and Charles A. Wickliffe, a future governor. The three-judge Court of Appeals was equally distinguished. It had just lost its chief justice, Thomas Todd, to the US Supreme Court. Its current chief, Ninian Edwards, would later relocate to Illinois and serve as one of that state's first two US senators and its third governor. Edwards's associate justice Robert Trimble would replace Todd on the US Supreme Court in 1826; his colleague John Boyle would serve two decades on the court and another as US district court judge for Kentucky.

Appellate cases were decided at the time by oral arguments. While arguing a point of law, Clay casually picked up a copy of the third volume of *East's Reports,* first published in 1805, to illustrate a point—an action that quickly drew an objection. "I do not read or rely on the opinions or decisions in 3 East," Clay protested, but use it only to show "what other [pre-1776] books . . . which are authority" contain but "which we have not at this place." "I would use a newspaper in the same way," Clay pleaded. "This is no more a violation of the act than it would be to use books reported but reprinted since 1776."

Allen responded by arguing that the statute was clear and that the "prohibited" books "should not be used at all." Hughes rebutted this dogmatic reading of the law, arguing that "there are many books which are not authority but ought to be read and used for the sound and clear reasoning they contain." He went further, declaring that if the law meant what Allen thought it did, the "legislature has no right to pass the law." "The mind of the judge should be free and unshackled," Hughes continued. Legislators "had no more power to pass this law than they would to prohibit a judge the use of his spectacles."

The court did not accept Clay's and Hughes's arguments. "I cannot doubt the power of the legislature on this subject," Chief Justice Edwards pronounced. "It was proper that some period should be fixed by law" after which English decisions would not be cited. "I cannot think any rights are withheld or impaired" by the law. Edwards was joined by Justice Trimble, who added, somewhat curiously, that it was clear the legislature wanted to prohibit the use of English books in Kentucky's courts and "thus cut off the importation of them."[6] While the prohibition later fell into abeyance, and it never stopped the importation of English law books, the case reflects the state's firm desire to create its own native-born law.[7]

If English law books were banned, what would take their place? Connecticut's

Ephraim Kirby had already shown the path. In 1789 Kirby published *Reports of Cases Adjudged in the Superior Court of the State of Connecticut*, the first volume of printed decisions of an American court. By the mid-nineteenth century, the reporting of cases would increasingly be undertaken by state agencies and national commercial publishers; however, the reports that sketched the main outlines of American law were created by individuals acting entirely on their own or assisted by thin state subsidies (though they retained control of all aspects of production). Called "nominative" reporters because their reports were named after them, these men forged a new American common law from carefully selected collections of decisions of the American judiciary.

Such a task was not one for mere functionaries. The early law reporters were leading lawyers, law professors, and sitting or retired judges of the highest state courts. They led troops in America's early wars, sat in both houses of the US Congress, and served in the cabinets of presidents. Many distinguished jurists served as law reporters. James Iredell, an associate justice of the US Supreme Court, published volumes of North Carolina reports early in his career. His frequent colleague on the Southern Circuit Court, US district court judge Thomas Bee, left a collection of admiralty decisions before his Charleston-based court that became the foundation of US maritime law. The early law reporters were scholarly and industrious lawyers who were passionate about creating a body of American case law. The judges they served with trusted them to select their most important decisions and to edit them responsibly.[8]

Kentucky's nominative reporters were typical of this breed. All were white men—both women and blacks were completely excluded from the legal system—and they shared Kentucky's pioneering tradition. James Hughes, the first, had practiced law in the state from territorial days; as a legislator, he had written its earliest property laws. Martin D. Hardin was born to pioneer stock, commanded troops in the War of 1812, and experienced the tragedy of losing his father and friends to war. Alexander K. Marshall, brother of US Supreme Court chief justice John Marshall, and his cousin John J. Marshall would help transplant Virginia's great legal tradition in the Bluegrass. George M. Bibb served as chief justice of the Court of Appeals of Kentucky, US senator, and secretary of the treasury before passing the last years of his life as one of the leading advocates before the US Supreme Court. Thomas B. Monroe spent a long career as a law professor and US district court judge before leaving his Kentucky home to serve as a legislator in the Confederate Congress and an adviser to rebel president Jefferson Davis. He would bury two sons with Confederate honors, but his brother and fellow law reporter Benjamin Monroe would take a different path, advocating gradual abolition through emancipation and African colonization. His own son, George, would win fame as a Union general. Other law reporters ran newspapers, served as judges, founded universities, and added fame to the state bar as advocates.

A New Commonwealth

With pomp and circumstance, the commonwealth of Kentucky inaugurated its existence:

> On the 4th day of June 1792, the day appointed by the Constitution for the first meeting of the first Legislature elected for the state of Kentucky, Isaac Shelby Esq., the Governor elect, arrived in Lexington from his seat in Lincoln County, to enter on the duties of his office. He was escorted from his seat in Danville by a detachment of the Lexington troop of horse, and was met a few miles from town by the county Lieutenant, the troop of horse commanded by Capt. Todhunter and the Trustees of the town. The Light Infantry commanded by Capt. James Hughes, received him at the corner of Main and Cross streets with military honors. After attending the Governor to his lodgings, the Horse and Infantry paraded on the public square, and fifteen rounds alternately, and then gave a general discharge in favor of his excellency.[9]

General Shelby, a distinguished Revolutionary War veteran, took office after a procession led by the Lexington Light Infantry, commanded by James Hughes, a respected attorney and the first reporter of the decisions of the Kentucky Court of Appeals. Present at its creation, Hughes and his fellow law reporters would help write the legal history of the new state, case by case, volume by volume. Kentucky's law—property law, the law of wills and estates, contract law, evidence rules, and the principles of equity—would take shape in the carefully compiled, edited, and indexed half-calf volumes of the state reports named for these men. James Hughes, Martin D. Hardin, George M. Bibb, Alexander K. Marshall, William Littell, Thomas Bell Monroe, John James Marshall, James G. Dana, Benjamin

Monroe, James P. Metcalfe, Alvin Duvall, and W. P. D. Bush have become mere names on book spines and legal citations—eclipsing the flesh-and-blood men who published them. This book resurrects them from their dusty tombs in the footnotes of mostly forgotten cases.

The Reception of the Common Law

The new state would retain the common law it had known as a territory of Virginia. In many ways, the legal history of Kentucky had begun years ago, in the courts and legislature of colonial Virginia and in the legal institutions of England. Kentucky's common-law system (and when lawyers speak of the common law, they mean both a way of making law and a body of law) was ancient in origin yet relatively modern in its structure. At its simplest, the common law consists of the written legal opinions of courts, ancient and modern, which create a chain of precedents stretching back over centuries. Each new case, in theory, reaffirms, refines, or expands these precedents.

The mythic origins of the common law can be traced to the Norman Conquest of England. As the story went, the lawyers sent to arrange for the extraction of wealth from William's new subjects encountered a patchwork of legal systems left by previous conquerors and rulers. Focused on the orderly collection of tax revenues, the king's men did not set out to create a new system of law; they merely collected those customary laws thought to be common throughout the domain to act as a legal lingua franca. Then, as these laws were applied over the centuries, the king's judges added refinements, and gradually a robust body of law arose.[10]

Of course, this simplified version straddles the line between overgeneralization and mythology. The common law competed for years with other legal principles, especially the canon law practiced by ecclesiastical courts, but common-law lawyers and judges defeated those rival forms with a combination of hardball politics and the intellectual tour de force of common-law judges such as Sir Edward Coke. In fact, citations in early reporters show that the common law beloved by early Kentucky lawyers was mostly the law of the relatively recent seventeenth and eighteenth centuries, not that of any Norman successors. More important, the decisions of those earliest judges had long ago evaporated in the mists of history because, until the thirteenth century, no one had thought to write them down, and when they finally did, their reasons were entirely different from the motives of current law reports, and they took a much different form. It would take the creation of a new figure, the case law reporter, to fix those decisions in printed texts and allow the common law to become recognizable to the men who leaned on the bar of Kentucky's early courtrooms.

English Law Reporters

The early printed records of judicial decisions were far different from today's West reporters. Although the yearbooks of the late Middle Ages preserved bare descriptions of cases, they were formulated not to describe the law but to illustrate oral arguments between lawyers over common-law "writs," the written forms requests for legal relief had to take. Likely devised at first to train lawyers, early yearbook entries did not even bother to record the results of cases. Some made it into print, but the genre died out in the early sixteenth century. However, in the wake of these yearbooks came an individual who would, for a time, cut as large a figure as the judge: the law reporter, whose collections of decisions eventually achieved the same authority as collections of statutes. These law reporters, by the mere act of recording courts' decisions and the reasons judges decided as they did, greatly advanced the common law. By adding other features such as reports of the advocates' arguments, marginal notes, citations, and indexes, they created a living apparatus for a text-based system of law.[11]

Like many fruits of the print revolution, law reports started as handwritten manuscripts, created purely for personal use. Most lawyers kept commonplace books where they recorded notes on cases they had argued or seen argued in court. Like absent law students, lawyers occasionally borrowed the notes of other attorneys and copied them. The notebooks of older attorneys were transcribed by their clerks and the law students in their chambers. The printing press offered the opportunity to publish these books, and in 1571 Edward Plowden prepared his manuscript notes to be set in type. *Plowden's Reports,* as they would be known, set a template for successors. For the first time, they used the names of the parties to head and thus title the case, originating the practice by which cases are known today (e.g., *Dred Scott v. Sanford, Roe v. Wade,* and *Steelvest, Inc. v. Scansteel Service Center, Inc.*). Plowden also set the standard whereby the reputation of a leading attorney added to the prestige of the reports. However, in an era when there was little respect for authors' rights, that did not prevent Plowden's success from spawning a number of poor imitators. London's Grub Street pressmen procured defective manuscript copies and attached the names of the leading attorneys presumed to have kept them. Said Plowden:

> Having lent my book to a very few of my friends, at their special instance and request, and but for a short time, their clerks and others, knowing thereof, got the book into their hands, and made such expedition by writing night and day, that in a short time they had transcribed a great number of the cases, and especially of the first, contrary to my own knowledge and intent, or of those to whom I had lent the book; which copies at last came to the hands of the printers, who intended (as I was informed) to make a profit of them by publishing them. But the cases being transcribed by clerks and other ignorant persons, who did not perfectly understand the matter, the copies were very corrupt; for in some places a whole line is omitted, and in others one word was put for another, which entirely changed the sense; and again, in other places spaces were left where the writers did not understand the words; and divers other errors and defects there were, which, if the copies so taken had been printed, would have greatly defaced the work and been a discredit to me.[12]

Obviously, the tradition would not have continued if all law reports were poor plagiaries, and by the mid-seventeenth century, many of the better ones carried authority.

However, it was in the eighteenth century, the age of enlightenment, when law reporting intersected with a period of intellectual reform on the English bench to create the most influential reports—ones that would influence the development of law both in Britain and in its fractious colonies in North America. The pinnacle of this era of law reporting occurred when Sir James Burrow published cases of the Court of King's Bench during the time William Murray, First Earl of Mansfield, was sitting as chief justice.[13]

Like many lawyers, Burrow collected manuscript notes on cases, including those before the King's Bench. He decided to publish them after "continual interruption and even persecution by incessant application for searches into my notes, for transcripts of them, sometimes for the note-books themselves (not always returned without trouble and solicitation)."[14] In doing so, he set a high standard. As one recent commentator asserts, *Burrow's Reports* "established the modern pattern of what a law report should contain: the reporter's statement of the facts, a summary of the arguments of counsel, and the court's judgment."[15] John W. Wallace, the great historian of law reports, went further, observing that *Burrow's Reports* may "fairly be called works of art," with "case, arguments, and opinion—going out to the bar separate in form as distinct in nature, each from the other; each complete in itself, but having, one with all, exact and reciprocal adaptation, and presenting so a full, harmonious, but never redundant whole."[16]

Burrow was one of the four reporters (the others being Cowper, Douglas, and Lofft) who captured the opinions of Justice Mansfield. Thus, his reports were highly sought (and cited) by admirers of the opinions of the modernizing jurist. Mansfield is best known for his ruling in *Somerset's Case,* where he held that common law was abhorrent to the institution of slavery, which could be maintained only by statutory law; he called slavery "so odious, that nothing can be suffered to support it, but positive law."[17] However, his reforms of the common law are what made him so popular with early American lawyers. Mansfield supported the appropriate application of equity in common-law courts, an innovation adopted by many colonial courts, including those in Virginia and later Kentucky. Moreover, Mansfield sought to nudge the courts away from mechanically following precedents whose rationales were no longer relevant. "As the usages of society alter, the law must adapt itself to the various situations of mankind," Lord Mansfield wrote in 1784, three years before the United States fashioned a new political society in Philadelphia.[18] To many American lawyers, the common law was vaguely ancient and concretely the law of Mansfield's eighteenth century. When one analyzes early American law reports, these English reports from this era were cited most often.

The First American Reporters

While American lawyers were happy to use English law books during the colonial era, after the Revolution, they sought native precedents suitable for the new republic.[19] Many of the early state constitutions had provided for native appellate courts even before the Revolution was over. The federal Constitution declared that the "judicial power of the United States shall be vested in one Supreme Court" and gave it appellate jurisdiction. Although some judges in colonial America had followed the English practice and issued opinions orally from the bench, many states required that judicial opinions be written and lodged in the records of the court. In

1785 Connecticut adopted a statute that required the judges "in all matters of law by them decided, or writ of error, demurrer, special verdict or motion in arrest of judgment, each one to give his opinion seriatim, with the reasons thereof, and the same reduce to writing."[20] By the middle of the nineteenth century, this Connecticut statute had become the norm.

Whether early appellate courts issued their opinions orally or in written form, they were issued publicly. Even before the first American reporter was set in type, lawyers were writing cases down and circulating them in manuscript form. Thomas Jefferson took notes of law cases he witnessed and collected manuscripts on other lawyers.[21] Judges also kept notebooks, called bench books, that contained copies of decisions rendered during their time on the court. Benjamin Tappan, a judge on the Ohio Circuit Court of Common Pleas, published a volume of reports based on his bench books.[22] Despite the fact that lawyers were seeking and copying manuscripts of local court decisions, it took time for the first state opinions to be printed because publication was not "commercially feasible."[23] Publishing at this time was funded mostly by the author and supplemented by subscriptions—an early crowd-funding method whereby potential buyers promised to buy the volume once it was published. With just over a dozen state court systems, a publisher looked at the potential market; for instance, a volume of Delaware law reports would most likely be purchased only by lawyers in Delaware, and a set of Virginia reports would be bought mostly by Virginia lawyers. (These fears of limited demand were largely borne out; all the pioneer American law reporters lost money.)

According to historian of American legal publishing Erwin C. Surrency, it "is yet to be resolved" whether Ephraim Kirby's *Connecticut Reports* or Francis Hopkinson's *Judgments in Admiralty in Pennsylvania* (both published in 1789) was the "first volume of reports to be published in America." However, there is no dispute that Litchfield lawyer Kirby is the father of nonspecialty state law reporters.[24] Kirby outlined the hopes that would animate other law reporters of his era: "When our ancestors emigrated here, they brought with them the notions of jurisprudence which prevailed in the [old] country." The English common law was a sound legal system, he said, but one "not fully operable to our situation." When the Connecticut legislature required appellate judges to "render written reasons for their decisions," it was a "great advance . . . but half performed." What was needed, Kirby argued, was the publication of these cases "showing the true grounds and principles of the decision." This, he averred, "would in time produce a permanent system of common law." Unfortunately, the state had not seen this benefit, and it offered little "prospect of private advantage" for an individual preparing such a collection of state law reports. Kirby undertook the endeavor as a "sacrifice" to "advance the common interest" of his "fellow-citizens."[25]

Others followed Kirby in pioneering this new American system of common law. Alexander J. Dallas published a follow-up to Hopkinson with his *Reports of Cases Ruled and Adjudged in the Courts of Pennsylvania* in 1790. (His second volume included US Supreme Court decisions rendered at Philadelphia—then the capital—and would later be renumbered as "1 *U.S. Reports*.") The Supreme Court of Vermont's decisions from 1789 to 1791 were published in 1793 by former chief justice Nathaniel Chipman; a copy was found in Kirby's library when it was sold in 1804. In 1798 Elihu Hall Bay published decisions of the South Carolina courts from 1783 to 1796.[26] Of course, among these pioneers was James Hughes of Kentucky. All of them grappled with the same hardships and difficulties: acquiring manuscripts; editing them and adding headers, marginal notes, and indexes; finding reliable printers; and, ultimately, financing their endeavors.

Among these issues, the most common complaint of early law reporters involved finances. Although issues over copyright arose later, in these early years, those rights were nearly worthless in the face of production costs. The first step toward a satisfactory financial model occurred after the first law reporters published well-reviewed but money-losing volumes. The bar and judiciary recognized both the value of these reports and the difficulties of publication. They began to lobby the legislature, a body made up mostly of lawyers. But actual publication by the state was impossible. In this era, only a handful of government employees toiled in state capitals, and even the governor handled his affairs himself or with the assistance of an aide he paid from his own funds. The solution, modeled on existing arrangements to print state statutes and legislative journals, was a governmental promise to the designated reporter to purchase a sufficient number of copies to make the endeavor worthwhile. (In several states, these state-purchased volumes were distributed to the legislators—a nice perk for those voting to approve such an arrangement.) The offer came with some strings (mostly to keep costs down), but the details were largely left to the reporter. This was neither a straight subsidy—the volumes had to be delivered, and the state paid close to market price for them—nor a monopoly. Nonetheless, it provided a known factor on which a business plan could be constructed. It is true that these laws often named "official" law reporters, but it was the certainty of future sales, not the title, that was important. These reporters remained private businessmen, responsible for all aspects of production and dependent on privately sold copies (printed in addition to the number required to fulfill the state contract) to make a profit.

The early American law reporters quickly began to change the nation's concept of legal authority, substituting the opinions of their own state judges for those of Blackstone and Mansfield as the source of decisional authority. Legal historian Elizabeth Gaspar Brown has analyzed briefs filed in court cases in the Territory of Michigan from 1808 and 1828, tracking the change from arguments based on purely English precedents to those significantly based on American judicial opinions.[27] An analysis of early Kentucky law reports shows the same development. The citations to authority in Hughes's and Sneed's reports are almost exclusively to English sources. However, even in Sneed's reports, judges were beginning to reference cases they had decided in earlier sessions (even though they knew those cases were unpublished). In the reports of Hardin and Bibb, Kentucky cases were cited regularly among the citations to English legal authorities. By the time Ben Monroe's reports were published, citations to English cases were rare.

Kentucky Law Reporters

HISTORY OF THE KENTUCKY COURT OF APPEALS

An introduction to the collective biography of the reporters of the decisions of the Kentucky Court of Appeals should include a brief history of that court. However, in some ways this is a circular task, because ultimately, the best source for the early history of the court is the law reports published by these reporters. A fire in 1865 destroyed the papers of the Court of Appeals, and secondary sources can shed only so much light. The most valuable insights can be teased out of the three earliest and most idiosyncratic reports. The reports of Hughes and especially Hardin convey the spirit of oral argument to such a degree that it is sometimes possible to get a snapshot of the court in operation. The volume called either *Sneed's Decisions* or simply *Decisions* is less a classic law report than a clerk's record book set in type. Although its inadequacy for legal use would be cursed at the time, this thin volume provides the court historian with a glimpse of the types of materials lost in the Frankfort fire.

Another window into the operations of the Court of Appeals—or at least a fun-house mirror image—is found in the proliferation of written invective during the mid-1820s, when Kentucky had two competing appellate courts (the Old Court–New Court controversy is covered in detail later). With competing clerks and their deputies fighting one another in the streets, and with new penny newspapers springing up on both sides, a bright, distorted light was shined on every aspect of what was usually the doughtiest branch of government—falling on everything from where its records were stored to the quality of courtroom furniture.

The courts of Kentucky were not created from a blank slate. In its years as a district of Virginia, Kentucky had a court system consisting of local trial courts, a district appellate court, and access to distant appellate tribunals in the home state. Many Kentuckians had practiced law in these and other Virginia courts, and several had served in the Virginia legislature. George Nicholas, one of the framers of Kentucky's constitution, served in the House of Delegates for many years and, along with his good friend James Madison, had supported Virginia's ratification of the federal Constitution as a member of the 1788 convention called for that purpose. Future Kentucky governor Christopher Greenup was born in Fairfax County, Virginia, and moved to the Kentucky Territory in 1781, where he practiced law and represented Lincoln County in the Virginia House of Delegates. Thomas Todd was born in King and Queen County, served in the Revolutionary War as a teen, and returned to Lexington, Virginia, to attend college, read law, and learn surveying before moving to frontier Kentucky. He would later serve on Kentucky's Court of Appeals and the US Supreme Court, being appointed to the latter from a list that included his friend James Hughes, whom he had encouraged to publish Kentucky's first law reports. Even the younger generation would be connected to the mother state. Future presidential aspirant and lion of the Senate Henry Clay was born in Virginia in 1777; as a youth he served as secretary for George Wythe, a signatory of the Declaration of Independence and a delegate to the Constitutional Convention that met in 1787. Clay read law with Wythe, who was then sitting as chancellor of Virginia, and was admitted to practice law in 1797, just before relocating to Lexington, Kentucky.

The 1792 state constitution created a "supreme court" to be "styled [on] the Court of Appeals." The organization of this court and the establishment of trial courts were left to the discretion of the legislature. This high court was to sit in the capital city (then Danville, but Frankfort by the time of the court's first session) and was given "appellate jurisdiction" over civil matters and "original and final jurisdiction in all cases respecting the titles to land" still pending in Virginia courts, including those before the Supreme Court for the District of Kentucky. Judges of the Court of Appeals held their offices "during good behavior"; they could be impeached or, if there was not "sufficient ground" for impeachment, removed "by address," an alternative procedure by which the legislature, by a two-thirds vote in both houses, could order the governor to remove them. In its 1792 organization law, the legislature created a "Court of Appeals" consisting of three judges appointed by the governor and confirmed by the General Assembly, as well as a system of lower courts.

The new Court of Appeals was situated in the capital city of Frankfort and met for two or three sessions for most of the nineteenth century before eventually settling into a year-round schedule. It was assisted throughout the antebellum era by a slender staff consisting of the clerk of the court and his young tipstaves, a group largely anonymous to history until the New Court–Old Court controversy, when they took on the role of extra muscle in the battle between the clerks of the two courts. Until midcentury, the court took only those appeals issuing out of civil cases; a grievant from a criminal matter could only seek a pardon from the governor.[28]

THE IMPORTANCE OF WRITTEN OPINIONS

From its origin, the Court of Appeals was required to put its opinions in writing. The 1792 constitution mandated that the ruling majority "state on the records the whole merits of the case, the questions arising therefrom, the opinion of the court thereupon, and a summary of the reasons in support of those opinions." Moreover, any dissenting judge was asked to deliver an opinion in writing. The majority was not required to offer a single opinion; based on the language of the constitution, the judges could have issued a number of separate (or seriatim) opinions, as was done in the English appellate courts, but after a few experiments with multiple opinions, the court settled on a single opinion as the most efficient means of managing its docket.

The Kentucky constitution also required the parties to state the "material parts" of their complaint or defense in writing. From indications in the early reports, especially *Sneed's Decisions* (which are, in essence, a record ledger set in print), it appears that until 1823, this did not mean a full-blown modern legal brief but instead a brief outline and, perhaps more important, a list of authorities.[29] This is not surprising; in an era long before Westlaw or even the photocopier, lawyers lugged law books to court, which is why these books were always prominently marked with their owners' names. If the authorities cited were presented in writing, the court (and the other party) would be able to assemble the books (from various sources) and check the authorities the court was being asked to follow. Early on, some individual attorneys had impressive legal collections, but it would be a few years before publicly accessible law libraries were established.[30] Even so, the *Hickman v. Boffman* case, mentioned earlier, offers a glimpse into the unwieldy mechanics of arguing case law while handing around law books.

THE EARLY DEVELOPMENT OF KENTUCKY LAW REPORTERS

What set Kentucky's nominative reports apart from the government-published and commercial reports that succeeded them was the men whose names graced them; they were responsible for collecting the written opinions of the court, selecting appropriate decisions to include, editing the handwritten documents, copying them into a clean hand that could be easily read by the typesetter, inserting marginal notes and footnotes, indexing the typeset work, compiling a table of cases, overseeing the printing and binding of the reports, transporting them to customers in the legislative and executive branches, and then marketing and distributing copies to private customers. The earliest reporters faced great hardships, but even with the benefit of their predecessors' experience, a more sophisticated publishing and printing industry, and government subsidies, later reporters still had a significant task.

The roots of Kentucky's first law reports followed a typical eighteenth-century pattern. As James Hughes argued his cases before Virginia's Supreme Court for the Kentucky District, he kept notebooks of the property cases that were his specialty. Later, he continued the habit during his attendance at early sessions of the new commonwealth's Court of Appeals. At some point, he decided to publish them and sought subscribers to ensure a successful venture. Despite this effort and praise for their quality, Hughes's reports were a financial bust. The subscribers kept moving west, and he lost "several hundred dollars." Hughes had created an appetite for state law reports, but the risk was too great. In 1804, the legislature ordered the clerk of the Court of Appeals, Achilles Sneed, to print the order book of the court for the period beginning where Hughes's reports had ended.[31] This satisfied nobody, and in 1808 the legislature enacted a law allowing the Court of Appeals to "procure" reports and to certify a "reasonable allowance" to compensate the person so contracted.[32]

The Court of Appeals "procured" Martin D. Hardin, who created an admirable volume of reports. More than any other Kentucky nominative reports, Hardin's adhered to the model set out by the best English law reports. Unfortunately, because of the "backwardness manifested by the legislature," he had to wait until 1809 to get legislative approval to print his first volume, which finally came out in 1810. Although he had collected enough material for a second volume, by then, Hardin was in no mood to prepare another. Five years passed before the legislature contrived a scheme with the necessary specificity to lure a competent attorney to assemble and collect reports. The 1815 law created the position of reporter of decisions of the Court of Appeals, appointed by the governor and approved by the state senate. Sadly, the thrifty legislature was not interested in emulating Burrow; it mandated the omission of all arguments of counsel.[33]

In 1832 the legislature repealed the 1815 law and all prior laws, taking the appointment of an official reporter out of the hands of the governor and senate and giving it to judges of the Court of Appeals. The court was to choose someone to arrange for the publication of its opinions; this person would be guaranteed "one dollar for every page, including tables and indexes," upon the delivery of 250 copies of each volume certified by the judges as meeting "their approbation." This would remain the legislative authority for nominative reporters until the practice was discontinued in 1879.

METHODS AND PRACTICES OF KENTUCKY LAW REPORTERS

The earliest Kentucky reporters admired the great eighteenth-century reporters such as Burrow and Plowden, but because of costs, legislative purchasing mandates, and the reduced circumstances of frontier Kentucky compared with London, they were forced to construct a simplified model. Only Hardin accomplished the archetypical reporter with detailed reports of the advocates' oral arguments and the judicial opinion and with lavish marginal notes highlighting the key legal points. Nonetheless, within these constraints, they created law reports that compared favorably to the best of America's case reports.

Our understanding of the operations of the Kentucky law reporter and the courts is hampered by the fact that most of the Court of Appeals' records were lost in a fire on November 21, 1865. "This morning between three and four o'clock the alarm of fire was sounded when the citizens hastened to the spot from whence it proceeded and it proved to be the building adjoining the State-house," wrote a correspondent for the *Cincinnati Daily-Enquirer*. "The fire originated in the office of the clerk of the Court of Appeals, and before it could be subdued, the devastating element" destroyed that office and those of the secretary of state and the governor, "at which point, by the extraordinary exertions of a few willing and energetic spirits, the fire was subdued." Leslie Combs, the clerk of the Court of Appeals, sent a letter to Governor Bramlette, detailing the tragedy. He began by explaining: "Ever since I have been in office, I felt the rooms I occupied were in imminent danger of the terrible calamity which has just befallen us, and have therefore repeatedly called the attention of the Legislature to the subject; but my warnings were disregarded." He continued: "It was almost as combustible as a powder magazine, with every part full [of] papers and books—all around the fire place, as well as elsewhere in open cases and on shelves some in bundles, and some necessarily loose in pigeon holes. No safety anywhere against even a spark of fire." Combs then listed the damage: "All the books, records, and papers in the building, public and private, were burnt. The loss to the state in incalculable—to me most ruinous," he reported mournfully. He had reviewed the surviving court records, including "about seventy cases under submission and the records and briefs" that were in the hands of individual judges. "I think I shall be able to supply eighty or ninety other records by copies given out to attorneys," he noted, and "many of those used by the reporter (Judge Duvall) were removed to the court room named, for his convenience, some weeks since, and are safe."[34] Except for these few files, all unpublished manuscript opinions, docket ledgers, minute books, briefs, and orders were lost.

For the earliest law reporters, simply acquiring written opinions was among the most difficult tasks. In *Hughes's Reports,* it appears that notes of orally delivered opinions were used for the earliest cases. Later, the decisions came from the judges themselves, likely handwritten copies. A careful reading of *Sneed's Decisions,* and hints from controversies over judicial records in the 1820s, indicates that court papers were indifferently managed, so it might have been a chore just to round up the relevant opinions. Moreover, as opinions were handwritten by a variety of individuals, preparing a readable copy for the printer was the first task. The fire has robbed us of direct evidence, but records from other states suggest that while lawyers learned in their apprenticeship to write clearly, judges wrote quickly and often left uncorrected errors for the reporter to fix.

Also lost in fire (and the dust of time) is any clarity about how the reporters selected the opinions to reproduce. As Lewis Dembitz (uncle of US Supreme Court justice Louis Dembitz Brandeis) noted in his *Kentucky Jurisprudence:* "Even since 1808, it seems to be [the] rule and custom of the court to give only such opinions out for publication in the printed reports as they thought to be of public interest. Sometimes, also, they withheld opinions from publication on the ground of feeling some doubt as to the correctness of the result arrived at."[35] Unpublished opinions were filed in the clerk's office, described in case law, and occasionally cited by commentators. Littell's *Cases Selected from the Decisions of the Court of Appeals of Kentucky* presumably came from a much greater mass of "cases which the court had not ordered to be published" (hence the word "selected" in the title).[36] Careful analysis of Littell's work pulls back the curtain a bit more; the 437 decisions published there were omitted from ten volumes, but the bulk of them were from the four official reports previously published by Littell himself. Moreover, it is obvious why the judges decided not to publish them; most are less than half a page in type. This explains why selection was necessary. Law reports were expensive to produce, and the Court of Appeals had no discretion in the cases it was asked to review. If the appellant paid the court fees, the court had to take the case—even if the legal issues were easily resolved by settled precedents and the decisions added little to existing law. (Although the court decided that these cases were not something the legislature and other government subscribers should pay for, Littell apparently saw a commercial opportunity and published the reports using his own funds.)

Often, judges only alluded to the authorities they used to decide cases, so reporters had to clarify this practice and decide how to format these citations. In some cases, they added their own annotations, using different formatting to distinguish them. The citation of precedents was likely assisted by the advocates, who submitted written briefs or lists of authorities they planned to cite in oral arguments. While this may have been done voluntarily at first, a rule adopted in the spring term of 1823 required that "no cause shall be argued or submitted to the court for a decision, unless the counsel or parties, on each side, shall, in convenient time before the hearing or submission, furnish the court with a brief statement in writing, of the points of law relied on, and a citation of such appropriate authorities in support thereof, as they may wish to use."[37] These lists helped the parties and the bench assemble the books they would need to consult during arguments, but they must have been helpful to the reporter as well. (Descriptions of early appellate cases include lawyers arguing over tables stacked with law books.) Some early reporters decided that the procedural history of many cases was obscure, so they summarized this in marginal notes. As the reporters assembled cases into a manuscript, they noticed connections between these cases and those in prior reports and added them in the margins. (Later reports have fewer marginal notes, likely because the judicial opinions submitted to the reporter were more polished and cited their authorities.)

Having prepared a manuscript for a volume of reports, the reporter next had to have it printed. Early reporters established (or, more frequently, built on preexisting) connections with Kentucky's earliest printers and publishers. This relationship was critical to the reporter's success; the printer's speed and quality were important in terms of meeting obligations to both public and private customers. Historically, the law press of Kentucky was intimately entwined with the newspaper. An early Lexington settler reflected the symbiotic relationship between the law and the press in a 1790 letter to an eastern newspaper: "The form of a regular republic is already assumed, we have our parson and our printer, our academy and our court of justice."[38] John Bradford, the state's first printer, published Kentucky's first legislative acts and journals from the presses of the *Kentucky Gazette,* the first newspaper in the commonwealth. The *Gazette*'s Lexington office also served as a bookstore and a print shop. Bradford was a civic leader who encouraged the cultural development of Lexington; he joined with friends John Breckinridge, Thomas Todd, and James Hughes to found the Democratic Society of Lexington, an early manifestation of the spirit that would lead to the Jeffersonian Democratic-Republican Party. Law books shared the shelves with religious texts, making up the bulk of Kentucky's early imprints.[39]

Not surprisingly, when Hughes sought to publish his reports, he turned to his friend Bradford. But in later years, the bulk of law reports (and legislative publications) was printed by the publishers of the partisan newspapers located in Frankfort. Those papers fought fiercely each year to be designated the legislature's official printer. Little is known about what they did to win the contract to print law reports, but the nominative reporters usually had strong ties (often of a political nature) to the Frankfort press and close relationships with individual editors. Future law reporter John J. Marshall took up his pen in support of the Old Court for the *Spirit of '76,* while Thomas B. Monroe provided literary support for the insurgent court (before becoming its law reporter). James G. Dana's able advocacy as editor in chief of the *Frankfort Commentator* for both the Old Court and the 1828 presidential campaign of John Q. Adams contributed to his successful tenure as law reporter (and perhaps to the high quality of the volumes printed on the *Commentator*'s presses). Later reporter James P. Metcalfe took a brief turn as a political editor for the *Frankfort Yeomen,* which later published his reports. W. P. D. Bush, who owned a Louisville newspaper, was the first law reporter to use a Louisville printer, the well-respected John P. Morton & Co.

While overseeing printing was the most important production task for law reporters, it was not the only one. Legislative contracts required that reports be bound, and early printers did not offer that service. Reliable bookbinders with the ability to handle relatively large jobs were sometimes hard to find, as Alexander K. Marshall (the only reporter to operate out of the Frankfort-Lexington-Louisville triangle) would discover. Moreover, once bound, the books had to be transported to the buyers, both public and private. At a time when paved roads were unknown in the state and transport was by horse and mule, the books' safe delivery to the Kentucky secretary of state was likely followed by many a celebratory glass of claret at Weisinger's Tavern.

POLITICS, THE COURT OF APPEALS, AND KENTUCKY LAW REPORTERS

Though unelected for Kentucky's first six decades, the state's appellate court judges did not—or could not—avoid politics, and they were inevitably pulled into the periodic controversies that roiled the state. Sometimes individual judges were involved because of their own political stances, alliances, or prior actions. In other cases, the court was caught up because of its unpopular decisions. The men who served as law reporters did not avoid these battles; indeed, in many cases, they were right in the thick of them.

The first controversy that nipped at the bench was an issue bequeathed to it by Virginia, involving tangled land titles. Virginia had granted papers to veterans of its militia that allowed them to claim land in the Territory of Kentucky, but the holders of these land warrants had to properly occupy, survey, and record deeds to this land to acquire a clean title—something that rarely occurred as flawlessly as the law envisioned. The case of *Kenton v. McConnell* forced the Court of Appeals to examine how a land commission had attempted to resolve title issues from 1779 to 1780. Its 2–1 ruling cast doubt on the land titles of many Kentuckians, so the Kentucky legislature summoned the authors of the majority decision to explain themselves. Citing judicial independence, the two judges, George Muter and Benjamin Sebastian, refused to attend a legislative hearing on the matter. This further inflamed the legislature, which voted to censure them (after failing to line up the two-thirds vote required to remove them by address). State senator Alexander Bullitt of Jefferson County called for changes to the state constitution to give the legislature the right to review and overturn judicial rulings.[40] But the controversy soon cooled; the constitutional convention of 1799—chaired by Bullitt—made only minor changes to the judicial branch.

The next storm that hit the court was an outgrowth of the pre-statehood period. Before the commonwealth was established, Kentuckians were preoccupied with ensuring access to the Spanish port of New Orleans, where, before the steamboat defied the flow of the Mississippi River, most of Kentucky's agricultural products were sold or exported. Kentuckians were suspicious of faraway easterners and feared they would trade away or cause a blockade of this vital lifeline. The Spanish crown tried to take advantage of this anxiety and gave leading westerners secret cash payments. Most of the takers banked the Spanish coin and then did what they wanted, but years after statehood (when the Spanish were gone and US diplomacy had assured access to New Orleans through the Louisiana Purchase), politicians found it profitable to "discover" these subsidies (whose existence was an open secret) and use them as a political cudgel to drive rivals from the political sphere. The so-called Spanish conspiracy affair began in 1806 when Humphrey Marshall, who hoped to revive his dying Federalist Party, accused several Democratic-Republicans of treason, among them federal district court judge Harry Innes and Kentucky Court of Appeals judge Benjamin Sebastian. The ensuing controversy affected many future law reporters, including the court's clerk Achilles Sneed and William Littell, who was recruited to write propaganda for Innes. Sebastian was forced to resign, but the affair soon fizzled out.

However, it was Kentucky's rickety financial system, based on undercapitalized banks and the custom of Kentuckians standing surety for friends (and political supporters), that led to the Court of Appeals' greatest existential crisis—a political affair known as the Old Court–New Court controversy. This would split the judicial system into warring factions and create permanent political divisions that would eventually lead to the formation of the Democratic and Whig Parties. In 1819, the global economy shaped by the Napoleonic Wars lurched into peace, creating monetary dislocations throughout the American financial system. In Kentucky, the sparseness of hard currency on the frontier had led to the heavy use of unregulated bank notes and personal loans backed by surety arrangements to provide the liquidity necessary for growth. What passed for economic wisdom in that era led the US Bank to call in debts. This started a chain reaction of collapsing private and state banks and legal proceedings against farmers to force them to pay back bank loans. The local leaders who had cosigned the loans also faced ruin. Creditors seeking payment attempted to foreclose on the property of debtors, leading to political resistance. In states like Kentucky, candidates who promised relief to debtors were easily elected to political office.

Pro-relief candidates in Kentucky won control of the lower house of the General Assembly in 1820 and, with support in the senate, began passing measures to stop foreclosures. Creditors filed suit, claiming these laws violated both the federal and state constitutions. The Court of Appeals agreed, declaring in 1822 that the legislature had violated the constitutional right to contract. Relief supporters were outraged and channeled that anger into the 1824 elections, winning the governor's race and majorities in the legislature. Using what it perceived as its constitutional power to determine the exact form of the state's appellate court, the legislature voted to abolish the old Court of Appeals (effectively removing its judges) and to create a new appellate court in its place. This prompted a dramatic standoff between the New Court and the Old Court, as the latter denied the legislature's right to replace it. The new panel ousted Sneed, clerk of the Old Court, and had its officials break into Sneed's office to seize the records in his custody. In addition to Sneed, past and future law reporters were in the midst of the controversy. A former reporter, George M. Bibb, helped draft some of the relief laws. James G. Dana denounced the presumptuous new tribunal from the pages of the *Commentator* and launched barbs at Thomas B. Monroe, who was collecting the New Court's opinions in what would be its first and only volume of reports. But as the economy improved, the political atmosphere moderated. Old Court adherents regained the legislature in 1825 and restored the old judges to their benches by repealing the reorganization law. The most fervent members of the two factions would later head the political forces behind the formation of the Democratic and Whig Parties. Bibb was elected to the US Senate as a Democrat, and Dana poured his editorial venom on that party's standard-bearer, Andrew Jackson.

Amazingly, the Court of Appeals' reputation revived quickly as Kentucky continued to grow and prosper. The opinions of its judges were regularly cited in national treatises and by the appellate courts of many states. Particularly prominent was George Robertson, who served from 1829 to 1843 and 1864 to 1871; he also taught law at the prestigious Transylvania College Law Department for a quarter of a century.[41] The Court of Appeals had recovered to such an extent that the constitutional convention of 1849 spent relatively little time on it. The real focus of that convention and the resulting 1850 constitution was making state offices elective. A fourth judge was added to the court, and the legislature was charged with dividing the state into four districts. A judge representing each district was to be elected for an eight-year term; those elections would be staggered so that one judgeship was on the ballot every two years. The judge with the shortest time before reelection would be designated the chief justice. The clerk of the Court of Appeals was also made an elective office, with a term of four years. Soon, these august officials would be stumping for votes at barbecues and political rallies throughout their large districts.

The one other innovation was that the legislature was empowered to grant a right to appeal (via a writ of error) for a person convicted of a criminal offense. Until the legislature approved such a right in 1852, circuit court decisions were final. The practical result was that lawyers faced different procedural rules and sentencing practices from circuit to circuit. In some circuits, free black men could testify in court; others allowed only whites to do so. Lawyer-delegates to the 1849 convention also noted that crimes punished with a whipping in one court might warrant the death penalty in another. Delegates reasoned that the right of appeal would lead to a more uniform application of the state's criminal law, and after 1852, appeals of criminal cases began to fill the pages of the law reports.

One issue the Kentucky Court of Appeals mostly avoided but its reporters could not was slavery.[42] Many of the law reporters owned slaves, a few of them hated the institution of slavery, and several joined the national debate over its extension. That debate ended up being settled by a Civil War. At least two of the reporters, James Hughes and William Littell, owned no slaves and counted themselves among the early supporters of abolition. Littell would be despised and mocked for his harsh, satirical critique of the peculiar institution. Based on the US census, as well as published wills, eight reporters (Hardin, Bibb, A. K. Marshall, J. J. Marshall, T. B. Monroe, B. Monroe, Duvall, and Bush) were among Kentucky's slave owners. Most held only a few household slaves, but A. K. Marshall's Mason County plantation was the harsh habitation of many African Americans in permanent bondage.

The peaceful resolution of the issue of slavery attracted much interest in border-state Kentucky. One law reporter, Ben Monroe, grappled with it as a Presbyterian elder and as president of the Kentucky Colonization Society, which sought to gradually emancipate Kentucky's slaves and resettle them in Africa. George Bibb's father, the Reverend Richard Bibb, went beyond theory and actually freed and provided funds for his slaves who wished to settle in Liberia (and emancipated the rest at his death). Such half measures did not ward off the Civil War, which divided the law reporters as it did others. Thomas B. Monroe resigned as a US district court judge at the onset of war and was elected to the Confederate Congress. He lost two sons to the rebel cause, while his brother Ben's son George fought on the Union side.

John J. Marshall, whose brother-in-law was the abolitionist candidate for president in 1856, was the father of a Confederate general. As the war progressed, Kentucky's loyalty to the Union was always in question; two law reporters, Bush and Duvall, were often counted by federal officials as "rebels-at-home."

These men were pioneers of legal publishing, pathfinders of a uniquely American law, and founders of the state legal profession. As such, their lives offer valuable insights into the legal history of Kentucky and of the United States. By resurrecting the law reporters from their dusty graves in the rare book rooms of law libraries, we can take advantage of their services as local guides to the legal past.

1

THE BARRISTER

James Hughes (d. 1818)

James Hughes, *A Report of the Causes Determined by the Late Supreme Court for the District of Kentucky, and by the Court of Appeals, in Which the Titles to Land Were in Dispute [1785–1801]* (Lexington: Printed by John Bradford, 1803).

The legal system of the new state of Kentucky was born in 1792 amid a thicket of thorny disputes over confused land claims, uncertain boundaries, and unsettled law. Into this wilderness stepped James Hughes. As a legislator, he drafted laws to reform the muddled property laws inherited from Virginia; as an attorney, he litigated the myriad land cases that clogged the new commonwealth's courts. While waiting to have his own cases heard in the Kentucky Court of Appeals, he took detailed notes on the other cases before him. To these accounts, he added notes for his own arguments and similar notes from his friend George Nicholas. From these scraps of foolscap, Hughes fashioned the first case reporter for the state of Kentucky, known as *Hughes's Reports*.

The finished quarto volume was beautiful, filled with detailed engravings by the artful silversmith who would later design the seal of the commonwealth of Kentucky. Alas, the splendid tome was a spectacular financial bust. Like many similar projects financed by subscription, it fell prey to the state's volatile population; pledged buyers either moved west, chasing the expanding frontier, or experienced the cruel change of fortune so frequent in those days. Nonetheless, Hughes's volume struck a path that would be followed by others.

The career of Kentucky's first law reporter spanned the state's transition from a frontier territory of Virginia to a thriving new commonwealth. Little is known about James Hughes's early life. Some of his contemporaries reported that he had been born in England and immigrated to the Kentucky Territory in his youth, but that story is unproved and appears unlikely. His date of birth is also unknown, but at his death in 1818, he was counted among the generation of George Nicholas (1754–1799) and John Breckinridge (1760–1806).[1] Referred to as a "barrister" by his contemporaries, there is the faintest possibility that he received his legal training in one of London's Inns of Court. However, he is not listed among the Americans at the Inns of Court meticulously documented in 1924 by E. Alfred Jones, and that fact would have been noted in Hughes's obituaries, which provide the most solid account of his life.[2]

What is somewhat clearer is that he was likely a soldier in the Revolutionary War, serving as a private on the Virginia Line. For this service he was awarded land warrants to be perfected in Kentucky. His move to Kentucky, presumably from Virginia, is suggested by his admission to the Lincoln County bar in 1788.[3] At the time, Lincoln County was huge, representing more than one-third of Kentucky, and it contained the thriving town of Stanford. Hughes appears as a lawyer in early records throughout Kentucky's Bluegrass region, and he is likely the same James Hughes who signed a petition from Kentucky landowners to the Virginia legislature, dated September 9, 1791, asking for more time to return land surveys to the register's office in Richmond.[4]

Hughes spent a large part of his productive life in Lexington. In 1788 he helped organize the Lexington Light Infantry, and in 1789 Lieutenant Hughes was promoted to captain and given command.[5] By the mid-nineteenth century, the unit was mostly known for its smart uniforms and crisp parade drills (both of which soon wilted in the gun smoke and gore of the Civil War), but back in the 1780s, the still potent threat of Shawnee raiders gave the Light Infantry a real purpose.

In 1793 Hughes was elected trustee of the city for the first time; he would be returned to office four more times and in 1795 served as chairman.[6] He was also active in the city's social and cultural affairs, supporting the building of a public library and encouraging the growth of educational institutions as Lexington transitioned from a frontier outpost to the "Athens of the West."[7] Under Hughes's eye, and often with his active assistance, Lexingtonians opened theaters and bookstores and founded literary and political societies. The state seminary grew into Transylvania College, the most prestigious educational institution west of the Allegheny Mountains.

Hughes also represented Fayette County in the Kentucky House of Representatives from 1793 to 1797 and from 1801 to 1803.[8] His legal acumen and drafting skills were well recognized, and in 1796 he was asked to help "amend and reduce into one the several acts dealing with the law of descents."[9] Later that year, he oversaw the organization of all the laws of Virginia regarding land titles into one comprehensive act.[10] In 1801, when confusion arose over which other laws of Britain and Virginia were still in force in Kentucky, Hughes headed a committee to make that determination.[11]

Politically, James Hughes embraced the democratic ideals of his friends George Nicholas, John Breckinridge, and John Bradford, publisher of the *Kentucky Gazette*.[12] Hughes, Breckinridge, and Bradford joined with brothers Robert and Thomas Todd to found the Democratic Society of Kentucky, which advocated the end of slavery, fought for free navigation of the Mississippi River, and supported the presidential campaign of Thomas Jefferson.[13]

Despite his political and civic activities, Hughes was best known to his contemporaries as one of the state's foremost lawyers and legal scholars. He was counted among the leading appellate lawyers of his day.[14] In 1811 Hughes moved to Frankfort, where he continued to apply his considerable forensic skills in the state capital.[15] He was a widely recognized expert in property law and was especially adept at navigating the tangle of land titles that Kentucky inherited from its time as a territory of Virginia. The Old Dominion's colonial and republican governors had dispensed land patents willy-nilly to veterans of the French and Indian War and the Revolutionary War. The patents did not convey the land itself but only the right to enter, survey, and record claims to unclaimed land. If any of these steps were faulty, the title would not be perfected. This, along with questionable surveying practices, the rare use of permanent boundary markers, and chicanery by some land speculators, resulted in a mess of overlapping claims that filled the new state's courts with litigants.[16]

As a legislator, Hughes had helped rewrite Kentucky's land laws to alleviate some of the problems. However, much of the damage had already been done, and title cases from the state's founding years clogged the court dockets.[17] Hughes would spend many hours arguing the land claims of his clients before the Court of Appeals, Kentucky's first court of last resort. He was not blind to the advantages his vast knowledge gave him in the "great game" of land speculation and soon acquired significant landholdings around the state.[18]

Respected in his time, James Hughes would be unknown in ours if not for his single volume of law reports, which inaugurated case law reporting in the common-wealth of Kentucky. Covering the years 1785 to 1801, the reports recount judicial decisions in the numerous land cases that clogged Kentucky courts before and after statehood. In many of the cases, Hughes was also an advocate; in others, he made good use of the time he spent listening to colleagues argue their cases while waiting for his own matters to come before the court.

In the preface, Hughes notes that the work "was undertaken by Thomas Todd and the author jointly." Knowing that the project was going to be expensive, the two men agreed to "join in the expense and risk," partially funding the book by subscrip-tions. A "different arrangement" was later made, and with Todd's assent, Hughes published the work at his own risk.[19] It seems that Todd and Hughes remained friends, so it is possible that Todd's elevation in 1801 to the Court of Appeals caused him to withdraw. Todd was later named chief justice of that court in 1806, and in 1807 President Thomas Jefferson appointed him to the US Supreme Court.[20] Or it is possible that Todd was just a shrewder investor; in the preface to his own law reports, Martin D. Hardin says that Hughes lost a lot of money on the book, which discouraged the publication of law reports for nearly a decade.[21]

The large, crown quarto volume published by Hughes was 236 pages, exclusive of front matter, and contained 41 plats masterfully engraved by prominent Lex-ington silversmith and artist David Humphreys.[22] In 1792 the state legislature had paid Humphreys twelve pounds sterling to create Kentucky's first state seal. He was given the vague instructions that it should show "two friends embracing, with the name of the state over their heads and around about the following motto: United we stand, divided we fall."[23] Humphreys's version depicted two men in formal dress; only later did one of them acquire the frontier garb and coonskin cap now found on the state seal and flag.[24] Humphreys was also responsible for engraving the maps in his friend Robert B. McAfee's memoir of the War of 1812.[25] Today, Humphreys's silver work is much more highly regarded than his book engraving.[26] However, his plats for *Hughes's Reports* are beautiful and include whimsical details such as the depiction of an American bison. The cost of the engravings themselves, as well as the cost they added to binding, may well have contributed to the volume's lack of financial success.

The reports were printed by Hughes's friend John Bradford, the state's pioneer printer and a leading publisher and patron of the cultural arts. In the late stages of Kentucky's push for independence from Virginia, the intrepid entrepreneur anticipated the need for a state printer, so he bought a press in Pittsburgh and transported it by raft down the Ohio River and then overland from Maysville to Lexington via the buffalo trace that would later become the Maysville Turnpike.[27] Bradford thus received the contract to print the acts and journals of the new state legislature when it began work in 1792. He was soon publishing the state's leading newspaper, the *Kentucky Gazette,* as well as many early law books, including the first collection of statutes.[28]

Sadly, few people have the opportunity to see the elegance of Hughes's original work, which is among the rarest of Kentucky law books. Most law libraries carrying *Kentucky Reports* have the 1869 "century edition" by Cincinnati publisher Robert Clarke & Company. Hughes's work, numbered as 1 *Kentucky Reports,* was reset by Clarke in a more uniform typeface, and the illustrations were reengraved to fit a smaller but more standard page size (22 by 14 cm, compared with the 20 by 25 cm original). The reconfiguration dramatically changed the pagination, and the Clarke volume ballooned to 458 pages.[29] The plats were crudely simplified, and sadly, Humphreys's bison—along with a lot of useful detail—was lost.

In 1807 Congress added a seventh Supreme Court justice to represent the new western states and preside over a new circuit court for Kentucky, Tennessee, and Ohio. President Jefferson considered three candidates: Hughes, fellow Kentuckian John Boyle, and George W. Campbell. At one point, Hughes was the leading candidate, but friends of Campbell, a sitting member of the US House of Representatives, organized a groundswell in Congress. Jefferson was less than enthusiastic about letting a congressman campaign himself onto the Supreme Court. Ultimately, he decided that nominating Hughes's friend Thomas Todd, who was also a well-known and popular congressman but had not actively campaigned for the position, was a good compromise.[30]

Jefferson may have cooled on Hughes after the latter observed that republican principles of civil liberty had been trampled in the rush to prosecute Aaron Burr for treason. Writing to his friend Judge Harry Innes, Hughes worried that mere allegations were being treated as "evidence of the actual existence of a rebellion." He noted, with no small degree of prescience, "It now infrequently happens that, transported by the indignation arising from an attempt to destroy a free Government its friends, by measures they take to defend and support it, sap those principles on which it was founded."[31] While Jefferson was focused on his dangerous and disloyal vice president, Hughes was well aware that Kentucky Federalists like Joseph Daviess and Humphrey Marshall were attempting to use Burr's prosecution to attack leaders of the state Democratic-Republican Party, including many of his friends.

Hughes's first volume of cases would be his last. No doubt he decided that the practice of law, land speculation, or even a game of cards with his friend Henry Clay was a better gamble than law publishing.[32] After a long and successful legal career, Hughes died in 1818 and was mourned by his contemporaries and by his fellow members of the Kentucky bar. The Lexington bar passed a resolution in tribute to Hughes, resolving that the legal community would "for one month wear black crepe on the left arm."[33] But he would forever be remembered for the beautiful squarish volume that started case law reporting in Kentucky.

2

THE REPORTER WHO WAS NOT

Achilles Sneed (1772–1825)

> Achilles Sneed, *Decisions of the Court of Appeals of the State of Kentucky, from March 1st, 1801, to January 18, 1805, Inclusive* (Frankfort: n.p., 1805).

Hughes's decision to cut his losses after his financially unsuccessful venture in law reporting left a vacuum in Kentucky legal literature. In response, in late 1804 the state legislature ordered the clerk of the Court of Appeals to prepare an accounting of that court's decisions from his order book.[1] The clerk was Achilles Sneed, who had succeeded his friend Thomas Todd in 1801. (Todd, who had dropped out of Hughes's ill-fated law publishing venture, once again narrowly avoided becoming a law reporter.) Forced onto the list of law reporters by the General Assembly, the unfortunate Sneed would later be dramatically ousted from his post as a result of another legislative fiat—one that would leave the windows of his office shattered, along with his career as a judicial officer.

Despite his long career as a court official and businessman, only the barest facts are known about Achilles Sneed. He was born in Caroline County, Virginia, in 1772, one of six sons and one daughter of Israel Sneed (1744–1787) and Mary Crutcher (1744–1792). Sneed and all his siblings apparently migrated to Kentucky sometime in the 1790s.[2] He made an early appearance in the pages of the *Kentucky Gazette* in February 1797, as an agent for a man selling land,[3] and he is listed as a property owner on the Franklin County tax rolls for 1800.[4] He married the former Sarah "Sally" Stewart in 1800 in Frankfort, where he would make a family and a career.[5]

Sneed mostly avoided electoral politics, and there is no evidence that he stood for any office other than a term as a trustee of the city of Frankfort. He became involved in the political dustup that happened years after the so-called Spanish conspiracy. In the 1780s, when the Articles of Confederation governed the new American state, westerners were very concerned over Spanish control of the Mississippi River and the vital port of New Orleans, which was the only route to export their crops. When it appeared that their desire for guaranteed access to the port of New Orleans was being ignored in treaty negotiations with Spain, many Kentuckians began to explore a separate deal with Spain, even if it meant breaking with the Confederation. Several, including the adventurer General James Wilkinson, took secret payments from Esteban Miró, the Spanish governor of Louisiana.

Nothing ultimately came of these vague intrigues, but years later in the mid-1800s, when Wilkinson's part in yet another western plot with Aaron Burr came to light, a loose coalition of Kentuckians who were dissatisfied with the current political establishment raised the charge of treason against persons alleged to be associated with the old conspiracy. This group included outsiders of every stripe, ranging from the ultra-Federalist Humphrey Marshall to the future debt relief advocate and Jackson Democrat William T. Barry. At one point or another, all three judges of the Court of Appeals were accused, and one, Benjamin Sebastian, ultimately resigned after admitting he had taken a Spanish pension. Marshall's newspaper, the *Frankfort Western World,* included Achilles Sneed in its attacks, although it marked him as only a "lackey."[6] Sneed, who likely was a Virginia teen when Wilkinson was plotting with Miró, was probably only guilty by association.

We know little of Sneed's early venture into the law profession, such as with whom he read law or when he was admitted to the bar, but he is listed as an attorney in documents from the early 1800s.[7] His early efforts were in business rather than the law. In 1798 Sneed helped establish the Kentucky Vineyard Society.[8] Two years later, he and a partner promoted a venture to build a bridge over the Kentucky River at Frankfort.[9] In 1807 he helped establish the first Bank of Kentucky and served on its board of directors until its charter was repealed in 1822.[10] Nonetheless, Sneed made a career as the clerk of the Court of Appeals. Appointed in 1801, he would serve until his death in 1825.

The first section of the legislature's Act Concerning the Promulgation of the Opinions of the Court of Appeals directed the clerk to "make a fair transcript of all decisions" of the court "in which the case is stated, and the reasons of the court are given at large" for the period from March 1801 to April 1805. Upon completion, the clerk was directed to deliver the manuscript to the public printer, who would print the reports "with all convenient dispatch" and deliver to the secretary of state one copy for each of the judges of the circuit courts, each judge of the Court of Appeals, and another copy to be deposited in the clerk's office of each court in the commonwealth, "for the use of said courts, free for the inspection of all persons who may wish to [do so]."[11] In 1804 there were nine geographically defined circuit court districts in Kentucky,[12] each with a judge and a clerk; three Court of Appeals judges; and county court clerks in each of Kentucky's forty-four counties,[13] for a total of sixty-six copies. The printer was not barred from printing extra copies for sale, which he most certainly did. Nonetheless, the print run was small, and like *Hughes's Reports,* copies of *Sneed's Decisions* are extremely rare today.

Section 3 of the act provided for payment of the clerk: two cents for every twenty words. The resulting volume has 414 pages, each containing about 375 words, for a total of 155,250 words. Sneed would have been paid about $155 under this formula, or $3,000 in 2014 dollars.[14] Interestingly, section 2 of the act directed the governor to buy a copy of *Hughes's Reports* for each of the circuit courts, "provided that no person, except the judges, and they only during term time, shall be permitted to take the book out of the clerk's office." If Hughes had received this kind of support earlier, he might not have lost so much money.

History does not record Sneed's views regarding the publication of his order books, but it appears that he either resented the additional work or, more likely, felt constrained to do no more than what was specified in the act. The completed work, usually known as *Sneed's Decisions,* is very compact and has no frills such as syllabi or headnotes that might explain the terse orders he printed. The legislature clearly did not authorize these features, and the format of each entry indicates that Sneed scrupulously adhered to the requirements of the act.

Having discharged his duty by delivering his manuscript to the public printer, Sneed competently fulfilled his other duties as clerk for another two decades. He also continued to pursue his interests in business and in the development of Frankfort, serving on the charter board of trustees of the Kentucky Seminary.[15] If these had been Sneed's only marks on history, he might have "ranked among the most eminent men of the state" at the time of his death, but he would have soon joined such men in obscurity.[16] However, his small role in the dramatic upheaval known as the Old Court–New Court controversy would enshrine Sneed in the permanent record of Kentucky's early history.[17]

The national economic crisis known as the Panic of 1819 hit Kentucky particularly hard. Notes and bills issued by independent banks served as currency in the cash-poor frontier states; when the value of those notes, and those of the state bank, dropped far below par, the disruption left many Kentuckians in debt. The state legislature considered several relief measures, including a law staying sales of land for debt and other legislation forcing creditors to accept state bank notes at fixed values. In 1823 the constitutionality of these measures was taken up by the Court of Appeals in two cases: *Blair v. Williams* and *Lapsley v. Brashear*.[18] It ruled that the Kentucky debt relief laws were unconstitutional under the contract clauses of both the US and Kentucky constitutions. The pro-relief forces were outraged, and after the election of a sympathetic governor and narrow pro-relief majorities in both houses in August 1824, the legislature passed the Court Reorganization Act on December 24. This act abolished the "Old Court" and created the "New Court"—the Supreme Court of Kentucky—which was expected to validate the relief act. The reorganization measure was quickly signed by Governor Joseph Desha.

New Year's Day 1825 greeted the city of Frankfort with a deep foreboding. The political atmosphere was charged with emotion, and there was a palpable fear of violence. Several newspapers had sprung up to weigh in on the Old Court–New Court issue, and they dealt in personal attack rather than dispassionate debate. On January 10 Governor Desha appointed the four judges of the New Court, as provided for in the reorganization act: William T. Barry as chief justice, and associate justices James Haggin, Robert Trimble, and Benjamin W. Patton (Patton died before the court met and was replaced later that year by Rezin Davidge). The Old Court of Appeals met at its traditional time on the fourth Monday of January, with Achilles Sneed serving, as he had for years, as its clerk. The Old Court did nothing to suggest that it accepted its abolition, but it quickly adjourned until the fall term to see how the public would respond to the reorganization act in the August legislative elections.

The New Court was scheduled to meet in February. Its supporters moved the furniture of the Old Court into the senate chamber, where the panel planned to meet. Although Sneed did not know it yet, the New Court's judges had already decided to appoint a fiery populist, Francis P. Blair, as court clerk. Given the situation, it was a bold but perhaps necessary choice. Authority would not simply settle on the New Court by virtue of legislative enactment; it would have to be seized.

Blair, a true believer who would later build the national Democratic Party as part of President Andrew Jackson's Kitchen Cabinet, was ready to provide the energy to secure the court's position.

However, Sneed was not prepared to give up the job he had held for nearly a quarter century. According to an explanatory account he later published, on February 2, the day before the New Court was set to open its first term, Sneed buttonholed judges Haggin and Barry and offered to serve as its clerk.[19] Haggin tried to put him off, saying they had not yet decided the matter, but suggesting that Sneed had "deserted" by serving the Old Court in January, a sentiment echoed by Barry. Pointing to the heading "Clerks" in a copy of Littell's *Digest of Statutes* he carried with him, Sneed countered that he had a statutory duty to serve the court; anyway, he argued, if the Old Court was a legal nullity, his service was purely a private matter. Barry sniffed that Sneed had been specifically warned not to do so, but Sneed denied receiving such a warning. The impromptu conference ended with Sneed giving the judges a letter formally requesting his reappointment as clerk.

On the morning of Thursday, February 3, Sneed next accosted Trimble. The judge was not particularly enthused to see him and told Sneed bluntly that the court had already decided to appoint Blair as clerk. Sneed went to the capitol, watched the New Court judges take their seats on the bench, and then retired to his home a couple of blocks away. Later, he "was informed, but unofficially," that he had been ordered to "render to F. P. Blair the books &c." of the Old Court. Sometime between nine and ten o'clock the next morning, Sneed received the official order; then, "forenoon," he received a summons to "appear and shew cause" why he should not be attached for not delivering the records. That Friday afternoon he appeared before the court with his counsel, John J. Crittenden. The court once again ordered Sneed to surrender the papers immediately, but it held over the charge of contempt until the next morning.

Later that Friday, Blair led a group, including his two tipstaves, to Sneed's office for the purpose of seizing the records. The office was in the home Sneed had built in 1820 on the corner of Clinton and Ann Streets, only a few blocks from the Old Capitol. Finding the door locked and the shutters closed, the group "pried off a shutter" and broke a window to get in and then carried off some—but, as it turned out, not all—of the papers.[20]

Saturday morning the court met to consider the contempt case against Sneed. Initially, Attorney General Solomon P. Sharp suggested dropping the case because

Blair's extralegal action had mooted the order, but as the inventory of loot from the clerk's raid progressed, the court soon realized it did not have all the records. Apparently, Blair had seized closed-case files rather than papers concerning open matters, which the court needed. Sneed's friend John J. Marshall urged the court to continue the case, given the absence of the defendant's attorney, but Crittenden soon arrived. Nonetheless, Judge Haggin was "anxious to go home," so the court agreed to resume the case on Monday. Sharp made out a number of interrogatories that Sneed was ordered to answer at the next hearing.

On Monday morning Sneed appeared before the court with answers to the interrogatories. Sharp had framed his questions with two purposes in mind. First, he wanted to prove his contempt of court case by getting Sneed to admit that his refusal to provide the records was based not on principle—because Sneed had implicitly acknowledged the New Court's constitutionality by applying to be its clerk—but on obstinacy or political reasons. Second, he wanted Sneed to reveal the location of the missing records. He and other court officials believed Sneed had removed the records before the break-in, possibly moving them to the premises of the Bank of Kentucky, which, though de-chartered, was still winding up accounts.[21]

Sneed responded to the interrogatories by explaining that he was not a politician and that when the court controversy arose, he had experienced much anxiety, not knowing which side would prevail. He had determined that the best course would be to preserve the integrity of the court's records by becoming the New Court's clerk. In response to the suggestion that he was unprincipled because he was refusing to surrender his records to the court now—when he would have gladly done so if he had become clerk—Sneed claimed that this misstated his stance. If Sneed had been named the New Court clerk, he argued, the records would have remained in his custody, in the same place they had always been, and they would have been securely maintained until the political question regarding the two courts had been worked out. He had tried to avoid taking sides, but when pressed, he acknowledged that he thought the abolition of the Old Court was unconstitutional—as was his removal. He had "grown old and grey headed" in faithful service to Kentucky's high court but had been removed "without offense on his part, without trial, accusation or any just cause."

Sneed's response to the alleged "missing records" was to turn the question back on Blair. He denied moving any records, asserting that except for the records taken during Blair's burglary of his home, they were all "in their usual place." He pointedly noted that it was impossible for him to answer the question of what was missing without a detailed inventory of what Blair had taken. He also noted that some papers relating to current undecided cases were still in the possession of the justices of the Old Court, a circumstance that was not unusual in the day-to-day operation of an appellate court. Blair had made no effort to recover those papers, as clearly the New Court's political position was not secure enough to harass men like Chief Justice John Boyle (a former congressman who reportedly twice refused appointments to the US Supreme Court),[22] William Owsley (a future governor), and Benjamin Mills.

Based on Sneed's claim that some of the papers were still "in their usual place," the court recessed and sent the sergeant with his tipstaves to Sneed's house, where they found the doors locked. They returned to request permission from the court to seize the documents, which was given "unhesitatingly." The band returned, forced the door, and carted off a "quantity of books and papers." Once this was done, the court ruled on the contempt charge. Chief Justice Barry, while admitting that Sneed had, for the most part, "acted conscientiously and according to his understanding of his rights and duties," did not believe Sneed's assertion that he had not moved any records, and he fined Sneed ten pounds. By all accounts, Sneed never paid this fine, and a few weeks later, on March 23, a Frankfort grand jury indicted Blair and his tipstaves Benjamin Hickman and Richard Taylor for breaking and entering Sneed's home and carrying off both court and personal papers.[23] Commonwealth attorney Charles S. Bibb declined to prosecute, and it appears that this ended the legal portion of the Sneed affair, although the case continued to be fodder for outrage by Old Court partisans. Blair's "violence" was regularly raised during the August 1825 elections, which gave Old Court supporters control of the lower house of the legislature.[24]

In 1826 the Old Court party triumphed completely in the August legislative elections, and by an act of December 30, 1826, the Supreme Court of Kentucky was abolished and its actions ruled a nullity.[25] However, Sneed was not around to enjoy the final triumph. The controversy must have been highly stressful for the clerk, especially coming on the heels of the failure of the Bank of Kentucky. He had died in his Frankfort home on September 18, 1825, less than a year after his dramatic ouster as clerk.

3

THE SOLDIER

Martin D. Hardin (1780–1823)

> Martin D. Hardin, *Reports of Cases Argued and Adjudged in the Court of Appeals of Kentucky, from Spring Term 1805, to Spring Term 1808, Inclusive* (Frankfort: Printed by Johnston & Pleasants for the author, 1810).

In 1808 the Kentucky legislature followed up on its experiment with government-sponsored case reporting by passing an act that allowed the Court of Appeals to appoint a reporter and to pay him a "reasonable allowance."[1] The court selected Martin D. Hardin, a respected young attorney who had recently represented Madison County in the state house of representatives. The scion of a distinguished pioneer family, the handsome Hardin would be an able law reporter and later an accomplished appellate advocate, but his native conservatism and moral inflexibility would hamper any sustained political career. Perhaps his greatest satisfaction was in carrying on his family's martial traditions and passing them on to later generations.

According to family lore, Hardin was descended from a French Huguenot who immigrated to America in the wake of the St. Bartholomew's Day massacre of 1572 and eventually settled in Virginia. That man's son (or grandson), named Martin, put down roots in Fauquier County and built a considerable estate. When he made a will in 1799, a year before his death, Martin had four daughters and three sons: Mark (born 1750), John (born 1753), and Martin (born 1757). Around 1765 the siblings relocated to George's Creek on the Monongahela River in western Pennsylvania. There, on June 21, 1780, John's wife, the former Jane Davies, gave birth to future law reporter Martin Davis Hardin. Shortly after this, the Hardin clan moved again, settling in Nelson County, Kentucky, near the town of Springfield.[2]

All the Hardin brothers were Indian fighters, but John distinguished himself as part of Virginia governor Lord Dunmore's 1774 war against the Shawnee and their Mingo allies, led by the celebrated war chief Hokoleskwa (known as Cornstalk by his white enemies). He fought in the Battle of Point Pleasant on October 10, 1774, when the Shawnee were defeated and forced to accept the Ohio River as the southern boundary of their lands. During the war, John Hardin became a close friend of Benjamin Logan, and the two would later fight alongside each other in three wars. In 1776 he joined the Continental Army as a second lieutenant in General Daniel Morgan's Rifles, and he was wounded at the Battle of Saratoga in 1777. In 1786 he and Logan led Kentucky militia forces against Shawnee raiders during the Northwest Indian War, often crossing the Ohio and striking deeply into Shawnee-controlled territory. Hardin was promoted to colonel for his exploits, and in 1792 President George Washington recruited him to negotiate a peace treaty with the Shawnee. Tragically for his family, including twelve-year-old Martin, John Hardin was killed by a group of Shawnee sent to escort him to the conference.[3]

The now fatherless Martin's formal education began at Transylvania Seminary in 1794 or 1795, where he made a lasting impression on his classmates. In a memoir of his college days, Robert B. McAfee recalls Hardin's serious and upright demeanor:

> Among those since distinguished were William Logan, Martin D. Hardin and John Marshall. Mr. Logan & Hardin only continued the First Session as they had been to school longer and were just completing their Education as I was beginning mine. There was one trait in M. D. Hardin, which I deem it my duty to relate, he was a youth of remarkable sober and regular habit, and with all very pleasant and agreeable, he was universally known & called by the boys "The Priest" and would always answer to that name without taking offence, our amusements were playing marbles, and Ball against the North end of the lot, and of course we would have frequent disputes & wrangles about our play, which were uniformly referred to the "Priest" Hardin [who] would hear the stories on both sides and then gravely decide it and such were the equity & justice of his decisions that I never knew an appeal taken from his opinion, but all instantly acquiesced, until he seemed at length really our rightful judge.[4]

Following graduation, Hardin studied law with George Nicholas, a friend of Thomas Jefferson and a giant of the Kentucky bar. Nicholas was a driving force for Kentucky statehood and almost single-handedly drafted the new state's constitution. In 1798 (perhaps while Hardin was still under his instruction) Nicholas pushed the Kentucky legislature to adopt a remonstrance against President John Adams's Alien and Sedition Acts. The document was written secretly by Jefferson and sent to Nicholas's friend John Breckinridge.[5] That November, the General Assembly adopted the "Kentucky Resolutions," a statement of republican principles that is generally considered the founding document of the Democratic-Republican Party.

Hardin was admitted to the Richmond County bar in 1801 (in the former county seat of Milford) and soon developed a successful practice in the new county seat of Richmond. In 1805 he was elected to the Kentucky house to represent Madison County. In 1807 the Kentucky Court of Appeals appointed Hardin its official reporter under the legislature's charge "to procure reports to be made of such decisions of that court, since its establishment, as should be deemed useful."[6] According to Hardin, the court "left to his discretion, the selection of the cases to be reported."[7]

When Hardin began his work, the state's law reports were in disarray. Given the financial failure of *Hughes's Reports,* no individual was willing to continue the endeavor "at private hazard," so in 1804 the legislature had directed Achilles Sneed to take up where Hughes had left off. Hardin considered Sneed's work "a bare transcript from the order-book," without an index or alphabetical table of cases, which "hid" the law "in obscurity and trash." If by some miracle a case could be found in the work, Hardin felt that, "by omission of the facts on which the court adjudicated," it "was too often calculated to mislead" rather than enlighten.[8]

Despite its flaws, Hardin decided to take up where *Sneed's Decisions* ended. "To have gone back would have added . . . more to the labor than the utility of the work." He started with cases decided in the spring term of 1805 and ended with the spring 1808 term. The decisions from 1805 through the spring term of 1807 were prepared from the "order-book of the court and the records filed." Being the reporter did not bar Hardin from practicing in the Court of Appeals, and beginning in the fall of 1807, he "took notes of the arguments of counsel" and incorporated them into his report when he "deemed it serviceable." Although he was forced to curtail the practice when he "found it was swelling" the size of the volume, these cases provide a unique window into Kentucky appellate practice at the start of the nineteenth century.[9]

A good example of Hardin's thorough treatment was an alimony case from 1807.[10] He detailed the early procedural matters, from the start of the case in the court of quarter sessions in Wayne County through a venue change to Adair County, and went on to cover the preliminary pleadings, the trial verdict, and the final petition to the court. Hardin then described the oral argument of the plaintiff's attorney, identified only as Allen (likely John Allen), and even included descriptions of two interruptions by Chief Justice Edwards and Justice William Logan. The defendant's arguments were also well summarized. Nearly four pages into the report, the court's two-and-a-half-page "opinion in writing" began.[11] While the legislature would bar later reporters from adding such arguments, those found in Hardin's reports are a hidden treat for historians of early legal procedure.[12]

Hardin's volume also included a wealth of indexing and annotation. In addition to the expected table of cases, there was a table of all cases cited. Each individual case was annotated with marginal notes summarizing the legal issues and giving full cites to statutes and cases that were often only alluded to in the court's decisions. Hardin aimed to be "careful throughout" to refer to prior Kentucky cases, "as far as they came within his knowledge," whenever they were supported or overruled by the cases he reported.[13]

Hardin's work received praise when it was published, but the date of that publication came far later than he expected. "The backwardness manifested by the legislature of 1808, to carry into effect the law of 1807," he complained in the book's preface, "was one cause of the work being so long delayed."[14] Not until early 1810 did the legislature allocate funds to print the work, and Hardin then found that printing and binding took more time than anticipated.[15] The published work was finally completed in late September 1810. Although he had taken notes of additional arguments and decisions in the meantime, he completed no second volume. Whether he had grown tired of the endeavor or had worn out his goodwill with the legislature with his cranky preamble is lost to history.

Hardin had returned to full-time legal work by 1812. Now a resident of Frankfort, he was once again elected to the Kentucky legislature, this time as Franklin County's member in the lower house.[16] He also took his place as a leading member of the Kentucky appellate bar. The published reports indicate that he appeared in 476 cases before the Court of Appeals from 1815 to 1826.[17] With war clouds looming in the United States, given the confrontation with Britain over its trade blockade and impressment of sailors, Hardin convinced family friend Isaac Shelby to run for governor in 1811. Shelby had been a distinguished soldier in colonial Virginia and had fought with Hardin's father in Lord Dunmore's War. During the Revolutionary War he had led a Virginia militia that played a pivotal role in the decisive Battle of King's Mountain. When Kentucky achieved statehood in 1792, the popular Shelby had been elected Kentucky's first governor. Expecting him to be an able war leader, Kentuckians elected him again in 1811.

In August 1812 Governor Shelby appointed Hardin as his secretary of state. Hardin's service was soon interrupted, however, by the declaration of war against Great Britain. The conflict was very popular with Kentuckians because they believed Britain had returned to its Revolutionary War strategy of arming Native Americans to attack the western frontier. Hardin raised volunteers in Washington County (near his first Kentucky home at Springfield) and from his current home in Franklin County. On May 18, 1813, Hardin addressed a group of volunteers in Frankfort and offered a litany of grievances against England, including its "insidious" commercial policies, the impressment of US seamen, and "the Indian murders daily committed on our defenseless frontiers."[18]

Hardin was commissioned a major in Colonel John Allen's First Kentucky Rifles. Both Hardin and Allen were married to daughters of Benjamin Logan, and the two men were "intimate friends," despite the fact that Allen was nine years older. The Kentucky volunteers were led at first by Major General William Henry Harrison, who had been appointed head of the Kentucky militia by Governor Shelby. They were to be part of a force sent to relieve Detroit from British forces and, if fortunes blessed it, invade Canada. However, once the US War Department organized the Northwestern Army, the popular Harrison relinquished command of the Kentuckians to General James Winchester, which caused some grumbling in the ranks. As Winchester's army continued its long march toward Detroit in August, provisions were low, and the many hardships of the march increased the troops' disaffection. Harrison, who had been given command of all forces in the northwest, arrived at the camp in the autumn of 1812, when morale was at its lowest. Allen's Kentuckians appeared to be in an especially sour and querulous mood.

Upon their arrival at camp, the troops were mustered, and both Allen and Hardin spoke to them, addressing the men in "very effective terms, and portray[ing] in a lively manner the confidence and expectations" of their fellow Kentuckians. The Kentucky officers "exhorted" the soldiers to endure "their privations with patience and fortitude." The popular Harrison then spoke to the ranks, and soon "shouts of applause" indicated that a tenuous harmony had been restored. With morale revived, Harrison divided his army and assigned the left wing, which included Allen's Kentucky Rifles, to Winchester.[19]

Sometime around this time, murmurs of disloyalty were heard about one of the US Army's Native American allies: Shawnee chief Johnny Logan. Born Spemicalawba, he had been captured in 1786 by Hardin's father-in-law Benjamin Logan. Captain Logan had raised him as a son, and Johnny became a boon friend of young Martin. Once he came of age, Johnny Logan returned to his tribe and became one of the Shawnee chiefs most sympathetic to the Americans. The accusations of disloyalty fired Logan's desire for vindication by glory, and he rashly set off with a small scouting party to harass British forces. He succeeded brilliantly (if ultimately pointlessly), ambushing an enemy detachment and killing both a British colonel and the chief of one of Britain's native allies. However, Logan was mortally wounded in the attack. Dying, he asked his old friend Hardin to arrange for his burial and to take care of his children. Hardin was detached to convey Logan's remains to his home village of Wapogkconata. There, he met with the elders to put his friend's affairs in order and likely to seek the continued loyalty of Logan's Shawnee band in the war.

In early November Harrison asked Winchester to send him two regiments to reinforce his right wing. Winchester had other ideas; he wanted to advance rapidly to Frenchtown, twenty-five miles from Fort Detroit, to secure Michigan and his own glory. Around November 15 Winchester dispatched Hardin to inform Harrison of his plan to "advance further and fix his camp at the Rapids" of the Raisin River. While Hardin was in Harrison's camp on November 20, Winchester took Frenchtown. Flushed with this success, Winchester failed to take prudent measures to secure the newly won position, and British forces successfully counterattacked on November 22. Winchester was captured early in the assault, and Allen was killed in furious hand-to-hand fighting. The defeated American forces surrendered to Colonel Henry Procter, who promised to protect the several dozen wounded prisoners; however, Procter's thin British force was unable to restrain the larger host of native troops, and more than sixty Kentucky militiamen were massacred.[20] The incident at Frenchtown inflamed Kentuckians at home. Meanwhile, the remaining Kentucky militiamen were integrated in other units or went home. With his regiment in tatters, Hardin apparently remained as a staff officer with Harrison, who went on to defeat the British at the Battle of the Thames. In November 1813 Hardin was among the host of dignitaries who feted the triumphant General Harrison at a dinner in Frankfort.

With peace restored, Hardin resumed his law practice in Frankfort. He remained close to the family of John Allen. When Allen's widow, Jane, died in 1821,
Hardin and his wife took in her daughter, Eliza Sarah Allen. In 1816 Governor
Gabriel Slaughter appointed Hardin to the US Senate to complete the term of William T. Barry. The appointment was unpopular, and Hardin was accused of being
a "Federalist." The attack had less to do with Hardin than with Slaughter's prior
appointment of John Pope as secretary of state. The "acting governor," as his critics
called Slaughter, had been elected lieutenant governor but assumed the governorship when George Madison died just weeks into his term. Although he had been
elected as a Democratic-Republican, Slaughter sparked a battle with radicals in the
legislature when he appointed his old friend Pope. Pope, though not an avowed
Federalist, had voted with the most conservative elements of that party when, as a
US senator, he had opposed the 1812 declaration of war against Britain.[21] That was
a highly unpopular position in pro-war Kentucky. Indeed, the Federalist Party's
antiwar stance rendered it almost extinct west of the Alleghenies after 1812, and
for years, the accusation of "Federalist" remained a potent taunt in battles between
factions of the dominant Democratic-Republican Party in Kentucky.

Hardin's political allegiance might have been a bit murky, but there is little
evidence that he was a Federalist. Indeed, the evidence suggests that Hardin spent
most of his career in the mainstream Democratic-Republican Party. In an 1807
letter, William T. Barry called Hardin "an agent" of General John Adair, whom he
accused of participating in Aaron Burr's allegedly treasonous western conspiracy.
Barry, who would wear a brace of pistols under his robe as one of the New Court
justices, had a conspiratorial mind-set and numbered Adair's superior, General
Andrew Jackson, among the many plotters. Nonetheless, all of Barry's imagined
plotters were solidly Democratic-Republicans, placing Hardin in that party's ranks;
Hardin's friend Adair, who was elected Kentucky governor in 1820, was solidly in
the liberal, pro-relief wing of the party. Moreover, Hardin's 1812 recruiting speech
repeated anti-British charges that were standard Democratic-Republican rhetoric
and anathema to Federalists. Nonetheless, the official *Biographical Dictionary of the
United States Congress* follows his critics in listing Hardin as a Federalist, perpetuat-
ing this ancient but now impotent slur into its third century.

Despite the temporary furor, Hardin's appointment was readily approved by
the Kentucky legislature, and he served in Congress from November 13, 1816, to
March 3, 1817. Returning home to Franklin County, he was once again elected to

the Kentucky house of representatives in 1818, serving as speaker from 1819 to 1820—another indication that the Federalist attack was groundless (although his old classmate McAfee, who represented Mercer County in the house, later remarked that the "Priest" was overly strict in his interpretation of that body's rules). In 1821 his Democratic-Republican politics were presumably secure enough for the party to entrust him as one of the presidential electors casting Kentucky's vote for the reelection of James Monroe.

In 1823 Hardin died at his Franklin County estate of Locust Hill at the age of forty-three and was buried on the grounds. Among the mourners was his son John J. Hardin, who would fall in the Mexican-American War. (John's son, also named Martin Davis, would later rise to the rank of brigadier general in the US Army during the Civil War.) In recognition of his contribution to Kentucky's history, Martin D. Hardin was reinterred in the State Cemetery in Frankfort, near the centrally located monument for the dead of the War of 1812. His grave is shaded by the towering cenotaph bearing the name of his old friend John Allen and the other casualties of Raisin River.

4

The Jurist

George M. Bibb (1776–1859)

> George M. Bibb, *Reports of Cases at Common Law and in Chancery, Argued and Decided in the Court of Appeals of the Commonwealth of Kentucky,* 4 vols. (Frankfort: Printed for the author by Johnston & Buchanan, 1815–1817).

Hardin's efforts had produced a fine volume in 1810, but by the time the legislature renewed its interest in case law reporting—some five years later in 1815—Hardin had long since moved on. For the first time, the legislature seriously addressed the task of creating proper incentives to promote high-quality case reporting. This convinced George M. Bibb, a former chief justice of the Court of Appeals, to take over as reporter. Bibb would set Kentucky law reporting on a steady course before returning to national life as a US senator, secretary of the treasury, and one of Kentucky's most active advocates before the US Supreme Court.

With at least two leading attorneys discouraged by the General Assembly's haphazard efforts, it was clear that if it wanted to attract a worthy candidate for the position of law reporter, the state needed a more long-term legislative scheme with clear objectives, a dependable plan for publication, and assurance that the new reporter would be paid. The legislature met this challenge on February 15, 1815, when it passed a law creating the position of reporter of decisions of the Court of Appeals. The official reporter would be appointed by the governor and approved by the senate. The law set out detailed specifications for the reports, including page length and paper quality: "It shall be the duty of said reporter, to publish the decisions of the said court, in volumes of about six hundred octavo pages each, to be printed in a good type, on good paper, with a complete alphabetical table of cases, and an index of principal matters, well bound in law binding and lettered."[1] The legislature also directed that the reporter omit the arguments of counsel "in all cases."[2]

The new reporter was instructed to pick up where Hardin had left off seven years earlier in 1808, which suggests that Achilles Sneed had improved the court's record keeping in the years since he had been ordered to print his bare order books in 1805. Also, whereas Hardin had included arguments of counsel—a not unusual choice in an era when written briefs were rare and appellate courts based their decisions on the oral arguments of counsel—the new law barred such extraneous material. This may have been merely a cost-containment measure, but it is likely that the legislature was trying to ensure that the authority of the court's decisions was not diluted by conflicting language in the arguments of the losing attorneys.

The new law also set out a rate of payment and, perhaps more important, an annual publication schedule. It directed that the reporter "shall, at least annually, finish and deliver two hundred and fifty copies" to the secretary of state, for distribution to various state agencies. For each copy, the reporter "shall receive as compensation a rate of five dollars for every 600 pages of printing contained therein—tables and indexes being taken into the calculation." The secretary of state was to examine these copies and certify them to the auditor of public accounts, who would issue a warrant for payment upon the governor's signature.[3]

The new law thus assured the reporter an annual income. Unlike Hardin, he would not have to wait years to be paid. The reporter was also awarded the copyright for his work, giving him the promise of additional income. Typically, the reporter would contract with the printer and binder to publish more than the required 250 books and sell the others to the private bar at a competitive price. The University of Louisville Law Library has a copy of the second volume of *Bibb's Reports,* which contains 677 pages; inscribed in ink inside the front cover is "$5.50 John B. Bibb." Of course, this Bibb was the brother of the reporter, so other private buyers may have paid a slightly higher price.

The success of the new law was evident when Bibb agreed to accept Governor Shelby's nomination to the position of reporter. On February 8, 1815, the Kentucky senate unanimously approved Bibb's appointment.[4]

Born October 30, 1776, just months after the signing of the Declaration of Independence, and dying April 14, 1859, on the precipice of the election of Abraham Lincoln, George M. Bibb's life neatly spanned the first period of American history. In a photograph from the studio of Mathew Brady—who would achieve fame for his documentation of the horrors of the Civil War—Bibb sits stolidly facing the camera, wearing the outdated knee breeches of the founding fathers. But it is somewhat deceptive to visualize Bibb as the faded old man in Brady's daguerreotype. He is better remembered as a vigorous man in a painting from his youth—a brilliant lawyer and respected judge who would help found the Democratic Party and serve as both a US senator and secretary of the treasury.

Bibb was born in Prince Edward County, Virginia, to a distinguished family. His father, Richard, was a clergyman of "great learning" who served as one of the first trustees of the Hampden-Sydney College and as a captain in the Revolutionary War. He was reportedly a descendant of Benjamin Bibb (1640–1702), a French Huguenot who immigrated to Virginia from Wales. Richard's father, John (1703–1769), was likely a grandson of Benjamin. John married Susannah, and they had at least five sons.[5] The oldest, William, was born in 1739 and would father the first two governors of Alabama, William Wyatt Bibb (1781–1820) and Thomas Bibb (1783–1839).[6] William Wyatt Bibb (then representing Georgia) and his cousin George M. Bibb would serve together in the US Senate.

Richard Bibb (1750–1839), the youngest son of John and Susannah, married Lucy Booker on September 28, 1775. One year later the couple had the first of their eight children, George M. Bibb. Bibb's middle name is a bit of a mystery, cited variously as Mortimer or Motier. One attractive theory might be that he was named after Gilbert du Motier, the Marquis de Lafayette, but the famous Revolutionary War hero did not set foot in America until June 13, 1777, several months after his putative namesake's birth. Still, Mortimer does not seem to be a family name, so the mystery remains. Richard Bibb joined the fight against the British as a captain in the Virginia militia; his son George's "earliest recollections were of the Revolutionary War."[7]

Bibb attended nearby Hampden-Sydney College in 1790 and 1791.[8] Named after two heroes of the English constitutional struggles for political and religious liberty, the college had been founded in 1775 and was strongly identified with the American Revolution. Patrick Henry and James Madison sat on its first board of trustees. Richard Bibb had been appointed a trustee in 1784 and might have been serving when his son attended.[9] The college took the University of New Jersey at

Princeton as its model—its first president was Princeton's 1769 valedictorian—so it is not surprising that Bibb decided to attend the New Jersey college in 1792.[10]

Although he matriculated for only one year (apparently receiving some credit for his work at Hampden-Sydney), Bibb fully participated in Princeton student life. He was admitted into the university's Cliosophic Society, which was noted for its debates on leading questions of the day; in fact, the society, which merged with its rival Whig Society in 1928, is still in existence today and boasts that it is the oldest debating society in America and the third oldest in the world (after those at Cambridge and Oxford). Questions from 1793 that were published in a history of the Cliosophic Society show that the group debated questions of both domestic policy ("Whether would it be more politic in America at present, to encourage extensive navigation or the cultivation of unimproved land?" and "Would it be politic in America to abolish slavery?") and foreign policy ("Whether is the British government justifiable in joining the league against France?" and "Whether would it be proper for the United States to observe the strict neutrality recommended by the President's proclamation with respect to the Belligerent powers of Europe?").[11] It is possible that Bibb first exhibited the talents that would make him one of the nation's leading appellate lawyers while debating a similar topic with one of his fellow students.

After graduating Princeton in 1792, Bibb attended William and Mary College for a time. Some biographies report that he received a degree there in 1795, and the school lists him among its notable alumni.[12] With a degree from Princeton in hand, it is likely that Bibb was there to take courses on the law in order to benefit from the college's excellent reputation in that area. George Wythe, the legal tutor of Thomas Jefferson, John Marshall, and Henry Clay, had been appointed professor of law in 1779 (the first such position in America), giving William and Mary the most prestigious Law Department in the United States. In 1798, after Wythe's retirement, St. George Tucker received the chair, using his time there to edit the respected American edition of Blackstone's *Commentaries on the Law* (1803).[13] Nonetheless, Bibb soon began to read law with Richard N. Venable, a Prince Edward County attorney who was serving alongside Bibb's father as trustee of Hampden-Sydney College. Bibb was admitted to the Virginia bar toward the end of the 1790s.[14]

Bibb likely practiced law in Virginia for only a short time. His father had moved to the thriving Kentucky town of Lexington in 1789, and sometime in the late 1790s the young lawyer joined him there. He married Mary Tabb Scott, the daughter of future governor Charles Scott, on May 19, 1799.[15] Bibb quickly established a legal reputation in Lexington and the surrounding counties. Benjamin Hardin, a leading attorney in midcentury Kentucky, met Bibb in 1804 at the circuit court session where Hardin was admitted to the bar. "At the April Circuit Court in Madison County," he recalled, "I became acquainted with William T. Barry, Samuel Woodson, George M. Bibb, John Pope, and William Owsley. I was humble and obscure. These gentlemen paid me some attention." Bibb, he remembered, "was in his twenty-ninth year. Coming from Virginia in 1798, the interval of six years had sufficed to raise him to the front rank of his profession." Hardin later noted, "I remember what Judge Bibb told me when I received my license"; he said, "It is not enough to get a license from the judge, you must also get one from the people."[16]

In 1805 Bibb was appointed circuit judge, replacing Buckner Thruston, who had been elected to the US Senate.[17] Bibb's political career started modestly when he ran unsuccessfully for US senator in 1806 against Henry Clay, a move that may have been designed largely to get his name out. Shortly after that loss, he was elected to replace Clay in the Kentucky house of representatives.[18] It is possible that Bibb's rise was assisted by his association with Freemasonry. Likely first initiated in Virginia, he served as grand master of the Grand Lodge of Masons of Kentucky from 1804 to 1808.[19] In March 1807 Bibb was appointed US attorney in the Kentucky district, replacing Joseph Hamilton Daviess, the Federalist who had tried unsuccessfully to get a Kentucky grand jury to indict Aaron Burr.[20]

In 1808 Bibb was appointed to the Kentucky Court of Appeals to replace Felix Grundy, who had resigned to make his fortune in Tennessee. The next year, on May 30, 1809, he was nominated by the new governor, his father-in-law Charles Scott, as chief justice of the court. Although he served less than two years, the always prolific Bibb authored 126 decisions, most of them while sitting as chief justice.[21] These decisions were eventually published in the first volume of *Bibb's Reports*. His opinions were regularly cited in the years that followed, both in Kentucky courts and in legal treatises nationwide.

Bibb resigned in November 1809, after the court's fall term, to seek his fortune in the frontiers of western Kentucky. His father, the entrepreneurial Richard Bibb, had left Lexington to run a salt mine in Bullitt County and represented that county in the lower house of the Kentucky legislature in its 1803 session.[22] The elder Bibb had since moved to Russellville in Logan County, and by 1820, he had built the Palladian-style town home that still stands as a museum. Logan County was one of the centers of Kentucky's experience with the Great Revival or Second Great Awakening in American Christianity. This may account for the fact that the Reverend Bibb is described as an Episcopalian in Virginia but became a leading Methodist minister in Kentucky.[23] Although he was a slave owner, Richard Bibb later became convinced that slavery could not be reconciled with Christianity and was an early member of the movement to emancipate the nation's slaves and return them to Africa—a desire he incorporated into his last will and testament. Nonetheless, at this point, Bibb was still a businessman at heart and served as president of the Russellville branch of the Bank of Kentucky.

George Bibb became reacquainted with his father and his brothers John and Richard, and he made friends and political allies among the other settlers in Kentucky's frontier. Russellville was the center of a distinct region that was markedly different—both agriculturally and culturally—from the central Bluegrass. Better suited for plantation farming than the rest of the state, southwestern Kentucky was more in tune with the Deep South than any other part of the state. When Kentuckians wished to form a separate Confederate government during the Civil War, they met at Russellville. Bibb's later political career would reflect these attitudes.

In 1810 Bibb was elected to represent Logan County in the Kentucky house of representatives. In March 1811 he secured enough votes in the Kentucky legislature—perhaps by adding his new friends from western Kentucky to his former allies in the Bluegrass—to win election to the US Senate. Bibb replaced Henry Clay, who had decided that a seat in the lower house of Congress would be a better place to pursue his goal of getting the United States to declare war on Britain. During its struggle with France, Britain's high-handed activities on the high seas had offended US honor; more important, its diplomatic alliance with Indian tribes in the Northwest had threatened the security and thus hampered the economic growth of western states like Kentucky. The charismatic Clay was immediately elected Speaker of the House and transformed the office into a tool to pursue his war aims. He was joined by John C. Calhoun, whom Clay appointed to chair the House Foreign Relations Committee, and other like-minded young congressmen from the South and West. Bibb joined the "War Mess," a group of young war hawks who lived in the same boardinghouse on New Jersey Street and included Kentuckians Bibb and Clay and Calhoun, Langdon Cheves, and William Lowndes from South Carolina.[24] The only senator in the group, Bibb assisted the cause as best he could in the less energetic upper chamber. Although the House was clearly the moving force in the pro-war coalition, Bibb was part of Clay's strategic center, as the senator's well-informed letters to his friend John J. Crittenden attest.[25] Bibb and Calhoun would become close friends during the effort, a relationship that would blossom when both men served in the Senate during the Jackson era.

Bibb's analytical and drafting skills may have been enlisted to write the declaration of war. On May 21, 1812, he wrote to Crittenden: "[The] manifesto of the causes of war is in preparation. The declaration is preparing. The President is preparing an official communication."[26] On June 1 President James Madison sent a message to Congress asking for a declaration of war. On June 3 Calhoun's committee released its report, entitled "Report or Manifesto of the Causes and Reasons of War with Great Britain," which strongly supported a war resolution. The manifesto included many of the grievances that concerned Kentuckians. The West's primary concern was Britain's alliance with Indian tribes in the Northwest, but Kentucky newspapers confirm that national honor was also an important factor. The same proud Kentuckians who would duel at the slightest provocation were chafing at the indignity of British impressment of American sailors. The resolution declaring war was passed on June 18. When the news that Madison had signed the war resolution reached the inhabitants of Mrs. Dowson's boardinghouse, they were just beginning their noon meal around the large circular dining room table. "Clay spilled his soup on his buff waistcoat as he jumped to his feet to shout." The reserved Calhoun gave Clay a hug, as the "hot-spirited young War Hawks stamped out a boisterous Shawnee war dance around the big table."[27]

With the war under way, Bibb returned to Kentucky after the Senate adjourned in April. He resigned his office on August 23, 1814, and left the capital well before it was burned by the British on August 25. But it was poverty, not redcoats, that Bibb feared. He needed to strengthen his family finances and was soon arguing cases before the Kentucky Court of Appeals. However, he found an even steadier source of income when Governor Shelby appointed him reporter of the Court of Appeals. Bibb's appointment was easily ratified by the state senate, but he had some hard work ahead of him; in addition to preparing for the January 1816 term, he needed to make up seven years of reports. He did have some advantages. First of all, he had served on the Court of Appeals for two of those years and was the author of many of those decisions, drafts of which he retained in his personal papers. Also, former reporter Martin D. Hardin was still living in Frankfort, serving as Governor Shelby's secretary of state; he would likely be amenable to turning over some of the work on his unfinished second volume for a reasonable financial arrangement. Moreover, it is clear that during his long tenure as clerk, Achilles Sneed had enhanced the office's record keeping, retaining copies of written opinions as well as improving his order book. By this time, judges had begun to write polished decisions with a careful eye toward eventual publication, and they had become more diligent in filing them with the records of the court.

Bibb's first volume of decisions was published in 1815. In the introduction he noted that, whatever their merit, the legislature had mandated that the arguments of counsel were not to be reproduced, and he cautioned, "The very limited encouragement heretofore given in this state to the publication of the decisions of our courts, is a warning to the reporter to contract his cases within the narrowest permissible limits." He observed that, even with his "great ability and indefatigable energy," James Hughes had not recovered his expenses, and Martin D. Hardin still had unsold copies of his work, "although executed with fidelity and ability."[28] Bibb had carefully measured his task and planned to avoid his predecessors' fate.

Nonetheless, the four volumes of reports Bibb published between 1815 and 1817 are among the state's best. Each volume's apparatus was limited to a single table of cases, but Bibb's scholarly marginal notes more than make up for this legislatively mandated economy. The reports themselves are accurate and exhibit a refinement attributable more to the quality of the judges than to that of the reporter—although, as the first volume contains many of Bibb's own opinions, that role is often indivisible.

Despite Bibb's prudence in the rest of the reports, the scholarly (and opinionated) former judge could not help using the front matter of the first volume to lay out his philosophy of the law and society, the role of jurisprudence in a democracy, the dangers of popular prejudice against lawyers and judges, and—somewhat incongruously—how to properly register and sustain a land claim in Kentucky. In his dedication "to the people of Kentucky," Bibb discusses the importance of published court decisions, a reasonable statement in a collection of such decisions. He then moves quickly to establish those decisions as an independent source of law: "The mind of ingenuity is not stationary," Bibb notes. The progress of men leads to new forms of property, new contractual issues, and other societal concerns that the law must address. "New rules to regulate these must be made either by statute," which, Bibb notes, must be interpreted by courts, "or by the judges, from analogy and the equity of the old laws." So, Bibb concludes, "the decisions of the courts are not less operative than the acts of the legislature" and "ought therefore be as public."[29] Bibb next moves from this firm ground to a more contentious subject by arguing against the comprehensive codification of all laws, as advocated by some reformers, comparing such a code to slavery. "The spirit and inevitable effect of such a code may be abridged to one sentence," he almost cries from the page: "Humble your persons before a despot, render up your lives and property at his will and the pleasure of his ministers!!!" His argument is clearly aimed at certain early-nineteenth-century reformers who saw codification as a democratic measure to take the law out of the hands of lawyers and judges and put it in the hands of the people. Bibb goes on to argue that a "multiplicity of laws is inseparably connected with political and civil liberty." The tension among the legislature, the executive, and the judiciary preserves that liberty because it is a protection against corruption in one of the branches. "The Constitution is on *paper,* and *men* are the agents" on which its success depends, but the "wisest plans will fail . . . when fools and knaves are chosen to execute them." He then defends the judiciary, another target of democratic reformers, arguing that the rich are "not [as] likely to suffer from a weak judiciary as men in middling and lower circumstances." A strong judiciary is in fact a check on the rich and powerful who, without its protections, would be free to prey on the weak. "Favor and influence are the never failing attendants on riches," Bibb argues, and they can be countered only by "a court superior to such influence." He follows with a defense of the legal profession, which was a popular target of abuse. "Do not cherish prejudices against lawyers as a class," he pleads. "They have in all free governments the friends and supporters of liberty." The multiplicity of lawsuits comes from confusing laws, and critics should concentrate on electing better legislators to reform such laws. He concludes with a paean to the law and its role in a free government and assures the reader that "the thoughts I have herein ventured to publish are not original to me." They are, he insists, the ideas of men "whose benevolence embraced the human family, whose bosoms glowed with a holy enthusiasm for liberty." These are the thoughts of men who "attracted the jealous eye of arbitrary power" and those who died as "martyrs to the cause of freedom." They were, Bibb modestly suggests, the ancestors and founders of American liberty.

Bibb's elaborate rhetorical flourishes are perhaps suggestive of his arguments before the courts, which were used to this style, but his arguments should not be dismissed as insincere. Throughout his life, Bibb struggled to balance the democratic impulses of a man whose wealth depended on his merit as an attorney, not on inherited riches, with the fear of populist despotism. The first impulse caused him to later align himself with Andrew Jackson in the election of 1828; the latter fear caused him to break with Jackson over his authoritarian attitudes as president. Throughout these turbulent political seas, Bibb attempted to hold onto the rock of the law as his philosophical foundation. He could imagine no other. He saw the creation of a native, republican body of common law as reconciling the conflict between democracy and the protection of individual liberty.

Bibb's tenure as reporter was quite successful. In a short time he closed the gap in decisions from 1808, and by the time he resigned the office in 1817, Kentucky's decisions were reasonably caught up. Bibb's reports were critically acclaimed, and unlike those of his predecessors, there is no evidence they lost money. He had met the legislature's requirements for the office, and he had apparently educated the lawmakers to its vital importance. His successors would inherit an institution, not an idea, and there would be no further gap in law reporting.

Following his stint as reporter, Bibb established himself as one of the leading members of the Kentucky appellate bar. Between 1817 and 1826 he argued a staggering 516 reported cases before the Court of Appeals. His service in the state legislature in 1817 may have reduced the number of cases he took that year, but during his peak (1818–1821), he was counsel in about 70 cases a year.[30] In late 1821 he was chosen, along with his friend Henry Clay, to go to Virginia to work out a dispute with that state over whether Kentucky's laws regarding occupying claimants (an elegant term for squatters) violated the separation compact that preceded Kentucky statehood. The two men traveled to Richmond and were "honored and toasted" at a dinner at their hotel.[31] Clay spoke movingly to the Virginia House of Delegates, but despite his charm and oratorical skills and Bibb's common-law arguments, Virginia would not budge. The issue was ultimately decided in 1823 by the US Supreme Court in the case of *Green v. Biddle*.[32] Clay and John Rowan had argued Kentucky's case, but the Court ruled in Virginia's favor, finding that Kentucky's law violated not only the separation pact but also the contract clause of the US Constitution.

While Bibb was toiling away at the Court of Appeals, a storm was gathering that would bankrupt hundreds of Kentuckians and end the state's placid personality-based politics, dividing the dominant Democratic-Republicans into bitter factions and eventually creating two new parties, the Democrats and the Whigs. In the decade after the War of 1812, Kentuckians had engaged in a frenzy of bank building. The Second Bank of the United States had been created in 1816 as part of Clay's "American system" to rebuild the nation's finances and spur economic development. The Bank of the United States had branches in Louisville and Lexington, but its tight credit policies and suspicions of its federal charter led the legislature to expand its own financial institution, the Bank of Kentucky, eventually creating thirteen regional branches.[33] The Bank of Kentucky's charter tied it closely to the state assembly, which elected the bank's directors and president. Bibb was elected a member of the board of directors in 1819 (serving with Sneed). Bibb's father and his brother Richard Jr. both served, in succession, as presidents of the Russellville branch.[34] Nonetheless, Kentucky farmers were still clamoring for inexpensive loans, so in 1818 the legislature chartered forty independent banks, known as the "Forty Thieves" (six more would be added later). These banks were poorly capitalized but thrived amidst the western land speculation that marked the start of the nineteenth century. Without a national paper currency, and with hard money hard to find in a region where gold bullion had to be transported over rough roads and by river raft through a wilderness inhabited by outlaws and hostile natives, all of Kentucky's financial institutions issued banknotes to facilitate trade, in many cases with little attention to the value of the assets backing them.

This was the state of the commonwealth's finances when the national crisis known as the Panic of 1819 started. The panic was partially due to global economic adjustments after the Napoleonic Wars, but land speculation and the overexpansion of the money supply through the issuance of insufficiently backed banknotes were the major causes of the crisis. Unburdened by modern economic theory, the Bank of the United States reacted defensively by calling in loans and hoarding hard currency, which in turn affected state banks. The Bank of Kentucky suspended specie payments and desperately tried to recover on outstanding loans, but it teetered on the edge of bankruptcy. Under pressure to pay notes from the national and state banks, the undercapitalized independent banks quickly collapsed, and the banknotes they had issued became worthless. Since the cosigning of loans for friends (and political allies) was widespread among all classes in Kentucky, no one was untouched. The vicious deflationary cycle set off by these measures was not confined to finance—land values and commodity prices also dropped precipitously.[35]

In the August 1819 legislative elections, voters supported candidates who promised to give them relief from the debts that could not only bankrupt them but also send them to prison. The new pro-relief legislators started cautiously, passing legislation in December that suspended execution sales on the property of debtors for sixty days. In early 1820 they exempted women from debtors' prison. As the depression deepened, pro-relief margins in the legislature increased, and more radical measures were advanced. In December 1821 an overwhelming majority of legislators voted to abolish the imprisonment of debtors altogether. This was a somewhat revolutionary act, but one that was universally supported—even by avowed Federalists such as future law reporter John J. Marshall.[36]

In 1820 the pro-relief supporters elected a sympathetic governor, John Adair, and swelled both houses of the General Assembly. The pro-relief legislature passed two radical laws that, working together, gave debtors comprehensive relief while largely extinguishing creditors' hopes that they would ever be paid. In late November 1820 a new Bank of the Commonwealth was chartered and empowered to print banknotes, which the legislators mandated be accepted for many transactions. In December the legislature passed the Replevin Act, which mandated a two-year moratorium before a creditor could execute on a debt, unless the creditor agreed to be paid in the nearly valueless notes of the Bank of the Commonwealth. (Replevin is a legal action for the return of property; it was often used to attach property securing a loan.)

The leading historian of the relief crisis suggests that Bibb was likely the author of the replevin law, and its framing as an alteration of the procedures of debt execution, rather than substantive debt relief, was an ingenious attempt to evade constitutional scrutiny.[37] Creditors would try to claim that retrospective application of the law violated constitutional protections against ex post facto laws impairing the right to contract, but drafters of the replevin law attempted to avoid that issue by focusing not on the debt obligation (which they admitted was constitutionally protected) but on the governmental procedures a creditor had to resort to in order to recover on that debt. The argument had some merit, at least in theory, because governments regularly tinker with execution laws, but given the excessive length of the moratorium—two years is a lifetime in a financial crisis—and the fact that the commercial paper of the Bank of the Commonwealth was widely considered worthless, creditors had reason to believe the two laws were a legal device to effectively wipe debts from the books. Nonetheless, while historians of the nineteenth and early twentieth centuries have universally condemned these measures, since then, more modest moratoriums on the collection of debts have been enacted by states during the Great Depression and were even considered by some state legislatures in the wake of the 2008 subprime mortgage crisis.[38]

In 1822 the replevin law was first subjected to judicial scrutiny when it was challenged in the Bourbon County circuit court. In the case of *Blair v. Williams,*

Judge James Clark ruled that the law, applied retrospectively, violated the contract clauses of both the Kentucky and the US constitutions.[39] Pro-relief forces were outraged and soon began calling for Judge Clark's head. At the time, Kentucky judges were appointed for life. In addition to impeachment for crimes and misdemeanors, the 1799 Kentucky constitution allowed the removal of judges by a procedure called address. If the governor found "reasonable cause" for a judge's removal that was short of an impeachable offense, he could take this concern to the legislature, which would investigate and, by a vote of two-thirds of each house, could remove the judge. Governor Adair addressed the matter of Judge Clark to the assembly. The judge was brought to Frankfort, where he ably defended himself, and the legislature fell short of the supermajority required to remove him. (The controversy had no lasting effect on Clark, who was elected governor in 1836.)[40]

The Clark removal vote began to firm up the allegiances of the pro-relief and anti-relief factions, and both groups awaited the appeal of the decision to Kentucky's high court. George Bibb defended the replevin law; John Rowan, William T. Barry, and James Haggin did so in a related case, *Lapsley v. Brashear.*[41] In October 1823 opinions were handed down by the Kentucky Court of Appeals in both *Blair* and *Lapsley*, ruling by a 2–1 vote that the replevin act was an unconstitutional impairment of the right of contract under both the state and federal charters.

Bibb petitioned for rehearing of the cases, filing a scholarly brief that was later published as a pamphlet. A fire at the capitol in 1865 destroyed the original pleadings, but this document gives an idea of the arguments made by Bibb and his fellow attorneys in the original case (and adds to the suspicion that Bibb played a role in drafting the replevin law).[42] Bibb argued forcefully that the law was merely an adjustment of debt execution procedures and that similar laws had been passed earlier in Kentucky's history; however, the court was not sympathetic and rejected the rehearing petition. These decisions of the Court of Appeals infuriated the pro-relief forces. In the August 1824 elections, Joseph Desha was elected governor as a pro-relief candidate. Governor Desha asked the legislature to remove Chief Justice John Boyle and Justice William Owsley using the address procedure. Boyle had written the majority opinion in *Blair*, and Owsley had authored the *Lapsley* decision. (Benjamin Mills had dissented in both cases.) Swelled with new pro-relief members, the annually elected state house of representatives voted to remove the two men, but the senate, which had elected only one-third of its members in 1824, failed to reach a two-thirds majority in a close 23–12 vote.

Having failed to remove Boyle and Owsley by address, the relief party proposed a more radical solution: abolish Kentucky's Court of Appeals and create a new high court, with new judges to be appointed by Governor Desha. At this juncture, John Rowan was clearly the public leader of the relief faction, but he was "ably assisted and advised by George Bibb."[43] Rowan and Bibb were old friends; in 1801 a young Bibb had acted as second in Rowan's duel with Dr. John Chambers. (The duel, which ended in Chambers's death, famously arose after a drunken squabble over which of the two men was the more proficient scholar of classical Greek and Latin.)[44] Rowan, with Bibb's assistance, crafted a court reorganization bill that repealed the act establishing the Court of Appeals and then established a new high court with four justices in its place.

In a long speech, Rowan made the legal case in the General Assembly for the reorganization bill. Examining the judicial clause of the Kentucky constitution, he argued that it delegated to the legislature the power to establish courts, mandating only that there be one appellate court and some inferior courts. Having established (to his own satisfaction) that the legislature had the power to reorganize the courts, Rowan argued that once the legislative authority for a court was removed, the judges of that court ceased to have any judicial authority. This attempted to deal with one of the chief textual arguments against the law: that the constitution specifically authorized two methods for the removal of judges—address and impeachment. The opponents of the bill argued that the Court of Appeals had been created by the express language of the constitution, not by the legislature, and that the reorganization law was only a crude stratagem by relief supporters to remove judges they had insufficient votes to remove constitutionally by address (and no grounds to remove by impeachment).

It is interesting to contemplate the kinds of objections that would have been raised if the relief party had merely packed the court with enough new judges to negate the prior court's decision. The Kentucky constitution set no specific number of judges, and in 1813 the legislature had added and then removed a fourth judicial seat (after the fourth judge's resignation). However, this solution might not have satisfied the rabid adherents of relief, who wanted the Court of Appeals judges to be punished. Rowan's arguments were "ingenious and subtle"—perhaps showing Bibb's craftsmanship—but ultimately the New Court was established by raw politics. On December 9, 1824, the senate voted for the court reorganization bill. The measure came to the house floor on December 23. Breaking tradition,

Governor Desha actively lobbied legislators; the bill passed the lower house by a vote of 54–43.[45]

Despite his efforts on behalf of pro-relief forces in drafting and defending the replevin law, and perhaps in drafting the reorganization bill, Bibb played little part in the court controversy after the 1824 legislative session. He was not mentioned as a candidate for one of the four new judgeships, although he probably could have demanded an appointment for his services. He stayed out of the public eye during the political battles in the press in 1825 and 1826. Instead, he continued his lucrative legal work, appearing before both the New Court and the Old Court when it resumed business. The court disruption had reduced his caseload, but less than that of other lawyers. In 1823 Bibb is listed as counsel in forty-seven reported cases; in 1824 he argued fifty-four cases before the Court of Appeals; and in 1825 he brought thirty-eight cases to the two high courts.[46] Somewhat surprisingly, only a year after the Old Court was restored, Governor Desha nominated Bibb to fill a vacancy as chief justice of the court, and Bibb secured enough votes in the senate to be confirmed.

After the triumph of the Old Court party in 1826, Bibb's political allies shifted their attention to the 1828 presidential election. Former New Court judge William T. Barry, door-busting court clerk Francis P. Blair, and Amos Kendall, the fiery editor of the pro-relief *Frankfort Western Argus,* were all early supporters of Andrew Jackson and, by implication, opponents of President John Q. Adams and Secretary of State Henry Clay, who was heading Adams's campaign in Kentucky. Jackson's supporters despised Clay for the "corrupt bargain" that had denied the general the presidency in 1824. In a four-person race, Jackson had received the most electoral and popular votes but not nearly enough to win, which meant that the contest would be decided by the US House of Representatives. There, Clay decided to support Adams, which shifted enough votes to give him the presidency. When Adams later appointed Clay secretary of state, Jackson's adherents accused Clay of buying the office with his votes—a claim both men denied to their deaths.

During the relief controversy, Clay had avoided taking sides publicly, but privately he made it clear that he was opposed to the replevin and court bills.[47] This led to strained relations between Bibb and Clay, but when Bibb came out for Jackson, any remaining ties were cut. More painful was the estrangement between close friends Bibb and John J. Crittenden, Clay's close ally and cofounder of Kentucky's Whig Party. Crittenden, who had read law with Bibb, had named his first son George Bibb Crittenden, and Bibb had named one of his sons John Jordan

Bibb. Although Crittenden would stick with Clay and the Whig Party throughout his career, his basic decency and good nature allowed him to revive his friendship with Bibb in later years.

In the August 1828 elections, candidates sympathetic to Jackson and the old relief party garnered majorities in both houses of the state legislature, which voted 80–53 to send Bibb to the US Senate over Burr Harrison, an obscure legislator from Nelson County. Later that year in the presidential election, Jackson beat Adams decisively in Kentucky on his way to winning the national canvas. Barry (who had narrowly lost Kentucky's gubernatorial election) packed up to join the Jackson administration as US postmaster general, and Blair and Kendall prepared to create a pro-Jackson national newspaper, the *Washington Globe* (as well as to form the original Kitchen Cabinet of unofficial presidential advisers).

Meanwhile, Bibb readied himself for the long trip to Washington and a return to the US Senate. His great-granddaughter Pattie Burnley later shared some family memories with Sallie Marshall Hardy (the great-granddaughter of Chief Justice John Marshall): "He always started on the first of November. The whole family would assemble on the front porch to see him mount his horse, with a negro servant on another horse, leading a third in case of an accident. [The family] would all weep bitterly as he rode off, knowing it would be two months before there could be any tidings of him."[48]

Bibb went to Washington as a Democrat and returned as a Democrat. However, former allies Blair and Kendall, who expected Bibb to be a safe vote for Jackson, would be disappointed. Blair in particular characterized Bibb as a weak opportunist and a tool of stronger men such as Clay and Calhoun. "Bibb was one of those extravagant poor creatures who (always in dependence and laboring to be important) was ever the tool of superiors to whom he looked for support or elevation," Blair wrote in an 1859 letter to Martin Van Buren on the occasion of Bibb's death. "Being elected senator for his Jackson devotion, he no sooner reached Washington than he joined Calhoun . . . then fell with him into Clay's hands again." It should be noted that at the time of this letter, the politically limber Blair had long ago left the Democratic Party, had supported Van Buren's 1848 presidential campaign as the candidate of the short-lived Free-Soil Party, and had helped found the Republican Party in 1856.

It is true that Bibb had never been a party leader; even during the relief battles, he had been happy to provide legal arguments and let more charismatic men like

Rowan lead the fight. But Blair, like many political operatives, defined consistency as loyalty to one's faction through all its turns and twists. Bibb, a jurist at heart, valued adherence to a set of constitutional principles—principles that he believed were endangered by the autocratic Jackson and his fiercely loyal supporters. The tariff issue serves as an example of the conflict. Jackson's 1828 campaign was helped in the South by the general's opposition to the 1824 protective tariff, which was abhorrent to the region because it represented federal intervention in the economy and because it protected nascent industries in the North with import duties that made manufactured goods sold in the South more expensive. Bibb, perhaps because of his connection to rural Logan County, was philosophically opposed to tariffs, even though most Kentuckians were not. As president, Jackson was willing to compromise on the tariff. Bibb was not. On this issue he stood almost alone in Kentucky; he followed neither Clay nor Calhoun in this stance and derived no political benefit from it. Jackson had shifted ground, and he and his loyalists expected all Democrats to follow. Because Bibb adhered to his own principles, Blair deemed him disloyal to the party.

Confounding Blair even more was that Bibb did not fit into Clay's party either. Bibb's strong views on states' rights and the role of the federal government were more in line with those of southern senators than with the Kentuckians and westerners who supported Clay. Whatever cordial relations he maintained with Clay and Crittenden, Bibb could never be a Whig. He was closer to his other War Mess mate Calhoun, but not to the point of supporting his extreme views on nullification, and he was closest to his friend John Tyler (who would later become a very lukewarm Whig). What he did share with Clay and Calhoun, however, was a profound suspicion of the Jacksonians' efforts to use the machinery of the federal government to concentrate power in the federal executive. Because of this, he cooperated with them and the emerging Whig Party but remained a Democrat. When Bibb's term expired in 1835, in the midst of Kentucky's Whig ascendancy, his political career appeared to be finished.

This was all in the future, however. When Jackson was inaugurated in 1829, Bibb joined thousands of fellow Democrats on the south side of the Capitol to celebrate the new administration. History does not record whether Bibb joined the mass of supporters of all social classes who went to the White House, which was opened to all for a postinaugural reception. Supreme Court justice Joseph Story later noted that visitors from the "highest and most polished down to the most vulgar and gross in the nation" clambered into the presidential mansion. "I never saw such a mixture. The reign of KING MOB seemed triumphant." The crowd became so unruly that Jackson had to climb out a window to escape being trampled by well-wishers.[49] A new day had clearly dawned.

Bibb began his term in the Senate as a conventional Jacksonian Democrat. In 1830 he voted against a federal improvements bill that included funding for a road in Kentucky from the port at Maysville to Lexington. The bill, which was promoted by Clay, passed but was later vetoed. Kentuckians were outraged, but the veto was based on a principle Bibb endorsed: that it was unconstitutional for the federal government to fund projects built entirely in one state. In May of that year Bibb voted for Jackson's Indian Removal Act, an odious measure that uprooted Cherokee, Creek, Seminole, and Choctaw from their homes and led to the death of thousands of Native Americans on a forced march to strange lands west of the Mississippi.

Bibb's adherence to Jackson loosened as he saw the president (and Bibb's former allies Barry, Blair, and Kendall) strengthening the power of the federal executive. The Jacksonians used federal patronage not just to expel hostile Federalists but to create a machine loyal to Jackson alone. Federal contracts and postal favors were granted to newspapers that were faithful not to the Democratic Party in general but to Jackson in particular. As this trend became more apparent, Bibb and other Democrats saw it as an offense to Jeffersonian principles. Nonetheless, Bibb was happy to vote against the recharter of the Bank of the United States in 1832, at least after his amendment to allow Congress to set its rates failed. When Jackson vetoed the final bill, Bibb evinced little chagrin.

By the end of 1832, Bibb could no longer be counted as a Jackson loyalist. Early that year he played a small role in a great drama that would shape politics for the next three decades and end Bibb's career in electoral politics. The backstory to this episode started in 1818, when Calhoun was Monroe's secretary of war and Jackson was in command of American troops fighting in the First Seminole War.[50] Calhoun, like many cabinet members, was shocked when Jackson exceeded his orders by invading Spanish Florida, deposing the governor, and executing two British subjects for assisting the Seminoles. He recommended that Jackson be withdrawn and censured, but President Monroe, sensing the general's overall popularity and the opportunity for expansion, decided to use the incident to force Spain to cede the territory to the United States. Calhoun failed to inform Jackson of this incident when he became the general's running mate in the 1828. By the time Jackson discovered the secret in 1830, he had already cooled toward Calhoun. The secretary's wife, the very aristocratic Floride Bonneau Calhoun, had refused to meet socially with Secretary of War John Eaton and his wife, Margaret. (The Calhouns believed Margaret had been having an affair with Eaton while she was still married to her first husband, a naval officer who committed suicide.) The socially respected Floride's snub set off a society row known as the "Petticoat Affair," which crippled Jackson's cabinet (their wives mostly followed Mrs. Calhoun's lead) and infuriated the president. Finding out that Calhoun had called for his removal in 1818 and hidden it from him in 1828 was the last straw. Fearing that Jackson's allies—especially Secretary of State Martin Van Buren—would release state papers related to the matter, Calhoun struck first, publishing them in a sympathetic newspaper in 1831, a move that would lead to the final break.

By 1832, it was clear that Vice President Calhoun would be replaced by Van Buren, who had recently devised a mass resignation to allow Jackson to purge the cabinet of those not suitably loyal to the president (and those considered too close to Calhoun). The president had appointed Van Buren as ambassador to Britain, and he had departed in September 1831 with the nomination still awaiting ratification by the Senate. The stage was set for the kind of political drama Washington relished. Jackson's enemy Clay immediately saw an opportunity to embarrass the president and to cement an alliance between Clay and Daniel Webster's emerging Whigs and the group of southern Democrats loyal to Calhoun. The Van Buren nomination simply lacked sufficient votes, and Clay wanted to feed Calhoun's desire for revenge by giving him a chance to cast the deciding vote against his enemy. Bibb and one other senator were reportedly asked to be elsewhere when the vote occurred, and Bibb obliged by taking care of some business at the US Supreme Court at the time of the vote. This created a tie, which Calhoun, as vice president, was called to break, and he did so with great relish. The pro-Jackson press, especially Blair's *Globe*, assailed Bibb for his bit part in this political theater. It also claimed that Bibb had promised his vote to Van Buren, but the Kentuckian released a letter affirming that he had always planned to vote against Van Buren.[51] Nonetheless, Bibb was now marked as a traitor to Jackson's increasingly insular camp.

In April Bibb pushed forcefully for a bill to exempt newspapers from postage. As a member of the Senate Committee on the Post Office, he was disturbed by the appointment of loyal Jackson men as postmasters around the country. These loyalists were then encouraged to give pro-Jackson newspapers free postage. While prior administrations had propped up favored Washington, DC, newspapers with printing contracts, the systematic and nationwide nature of this effort and its focus on fidelity to the executive branch alarmed Bibb—especially after he himself became the object of attacks in the press. When "a minister [is] rejected by the Senate for humbling the nation at the foot of the throne, the President's corps editorial starts simultaneously," he suggested, pointedly alluding to Van Buren's rejection as ambassador.[52] Bibb's bill would have leveled the playing field and helped friendly independent Democratic papers, like his friend Duff Green's *Washington Telegraph.* The bill failed, but Bibb continued to raise the issue in committee.[53]

In May 1832 Bibb, who had been a widower since the death of his wife, Martha, in 1829, married a "beautiful young widow of the city." The wedding, which took place in Washington, was attended by many of the nation's political class. Clay and Calhoun served as groomsmen. While Bibb was "occupied with his laughing rosy cheeked bride," news arrived that the Democratic convention, meeting in Baltimore, had chosen Van Buren as the party's vice presidential candidate. The vote finalized the factional split in the Democratic Party (as well as opportunities for Clay's newly formed Whig Party), and the guests acted accordingly. One of them, John Campbell, wrote, "News of Van's nomination came in the midst of our hymeneal amusements and congratulations. Calhoun looked sour, lean & lank. Clay went off. Webster also absconded." However, Jackson loyalist "Barry was in high spirits."[54]

Disengaged from the Jackson loyalists, Bibb was more comfortable with the oppositional southern Democrats than with the emerging Whigs. Though loosely associated with Calhoun, who remained a friend, he was uneasy with the South Carolinian's extreme views on the right of nullification; instead, he was most compatible with Virginian John Tyler, whose independence also left him uncomfortably between parties. The nullification crisis of late 1832 and early 1833 found Bibb torn between these two impulses. Bibb—more than any Kentuckian—opposed protective tariffs and was dismayed to find that Jackson was ready to renew them, with only moderate adjustments. In 1832 Congress passed a protective tariff not much different from the tariff of 1828, passed during the Adams administration; Bibb joined Tyler and other southern Democrats in opposition.[55] Jackson signed the tariff into law. In November 1832 South Carolina—with Calhoun's leadership—ruled both the 1828 and 1832 federal tariffs unconstitutional and nullified them. Outraged, Jackson quickly issued a proclamation that December disavowing the doctrine of nullification and declaring that secession was illegal. Jackson also called for a "force bill" that would allow him, as president, to collect the tariff by military coercion. Clay forged a compromise, and Congress eventually passed the less protective "compromise tariff" and Jackson's force bill. Bibb supported the compromise tariff "as a peace offering" but made a long speech opposing the force bill.[56] He carefully laid out the "compact theory" of the Constitution, which held that rather than drawing its power from the people of the union as a whole, the Constitution was a contract between the states. Though Bibb professed his love for the union, he granted the states the power to leave it.[57] (Both Bibb and Calhoun missed the late-night session in which the force bill was passed, leaving Tyler in the "proud position" of being the only senator to vote against it.)[58]

Bibb's concern over Jackson's expansion of executive power—which led critics to depict him in speeches and political cartoons as "King Andrew"—was heightened by the president's decision to withdraw federal deposits from the Bank of the United States and place them in "pet banks"—independent banks run by friends of Jackson. Bibb, no friend of the federal bank, was nonetheless outraged by this brazen use of the treasury and voted for Clay and Calhoun's resolution censuring Jackson for the action. In his last year in the Senate, Bibb also served on a committee examining executive patronage. The committee report, which Bibb helped draft, criticized executive removals and called for measures to discourage the president from removing federal employees without good cause. A resulting bill passed the Senate but died in the House.

Throughout his tenure as a senator, Bibb took advantage of his time in Washington to practice before the local and federal courts (while still practicing in Kentucky during the long congressional recesses). He frequently handled matters in the District of Columbia courts and argued before the US Supreme Court in a dozen cases. He had already appeared in several Supreme Court cases before his 1828 election, but his role as senator certainly enhanced his standing with clients.[59]

Bibb ended his term in 1835 with little hope of reelection. Whigs now controlled the Kentucky legislature, and many still held grudges over the New Court battles. (With Clay's assistance, Bibb had resumed his friendship with Crittenden.) Nationally, Jackson loyalist Blair's anger at Bibb's betrayal would remain raw until Bibb's death in 1859. Even then, showing no reluctance to speak ill of the dead, Blair let loose a stream of malign gossip. However, it is clear Bibb never benefited politically from his break with Jackson. And although he worked with Clay on various issues in the Senate, he refused to join Clay's Whigs. He remained an independent

Democrat in an era of increasing partisanship, which ensured that he would never be reelected as Kentucky's senator.

Bibb returned to the state expecting to practice law, but Governor James T. Morehead appointed him judge of the Court of Chancery in Louisville in 1835. Morehead was a Whig stalwart but had practiced law in Russellville with Bibb. (Blair later accused Crittenden of arranging the appointment as partial payment for betraying Van Buren.)[60] It has been suggested that Bibb took the position of chancellor because he was in financial straits at the time. This theory is based on an 1839 letter to his brother John in which he complained that "the deleterious effects of the banking system, operating upon my own confiding temper, had . . . at one fell swoop, stript me of my own acquisitions."[61] However, it is likely that Bibb's financial losses occurred two years after his appointment to the court, in the Panic of 1837. Though not highly paid, the position of chancellor was very prestigious—only the growing commercial city of Louisville ranked a separate equity court—and antebellum politicians did not view it as demeaning for a former US senator to take a state judicial office. Moreover, whatever Morehead's reasons for appointing him, Bibb was eminently qualified for the job.

When Bibb first arrived in Lexington in the 1790s, that city was the jewel of Kentucky, the "Athens of the West." Louisville, in contrast, was a marshy backwater town of only 350 residents.[62] By 1835, Louisville's coffers and population had swelled, thanks to its key river location and the growth of steamboat transportation. It had two handsome hotels, the Louisville Hotel and the Galt House; a large and well-regarded high school; and myriad impressive churches ministering to a diverse group of Unitarians, Roman Catholics, Baptists, Episcopalians, Presbyterians, and Methodists. Famed architect Gideon Shryock, fresh from designing Transylvania's Morison Hall and the statehouse in Frankfort, was applying his Greek Revival style to the new Bank of Louisville and a magnificent Jefferson County courthouse. Bibb eventually purchased a home on Chestnut Street near Eighth Street, in the residential area just a few blocks south of the Jefferson County courthouse.[63] It was right across from the lot where, in 1838, he would preside over the laying of the cornerstone of the Louisville Medical College.[64] Bibb soon settled into the fabric of Louisville, helping to found the Kentucky Historical Society (with his friend John Rowan) and hosting a civic reception for Daniel Webster when he visited the city in 1837.[65]

An interesting incident occurred while Bibb was chancellor that reflected both his character and the complexity of the slavery issue in Kentucky. When Bibb's father, Richard, died in 1839, he emancipated all fifty-four of his slaves by way of his will, which also established a trust for their care or to pay for their passage to a colony in Liberia if that is what they wished. Bibb's brothers, John and Richard Jr., were named trustees, and John asked George for advice on managing the trust. Based on his response, it is apparent that Bibb disapproved of his father's decision but strongly believed that the intent of the will should be honored. Bibb stated that he had been done a "great injustice" by someone who had "suggested an intention on my part to oppose the will." He explained that, "Poor as I am, struggling at my time of life, by the most intense application to the duties which does not afford any surplus at the years end above the expenses of my family, yet I would not, for the property bequeathed by the will, for all the negroes, nor the value ten times told, insult the memory of our father by an attempt to set aside the writing he has published as his last will and testament."

While the will provided $5,000 to the freed slaves "to be divided out amongst them . . . and paid out to them, from time to time, according to the discretion of my executors," it is important to note that the Reverend Bibb's trust did more than embody his paternal (and paternalistic) concern for his former slaves' welfare. Kentucky law required that freed slaves be provided for financially. Bibb reminded John that the Kentucky statute allowing the emancipation of slaves authorized the county court that authenticated the certificates of emancipation "to demand bond and sufficient security" of the emancipator's executors "for the maintenance of any slave or slaves, that may be aged or infirm, either of body or mind, to prevent him, her, or them, from becoming chargeable to the county."

One interesting side comment by Bibb opens a small window into his feelings about women. In a discussion of how to interpret the language of the will, Bibb urged John to "ask your wife, who is a woman of vigourous intellect and sound sense, her interpretation. Let brother Richard ask his wife her interpretation. I have more than once, when interpreting wills under responsibility of judicial office, read clauses to my wife, to hear her commentaries & profited from her suggestions & as judge of the Court of Appeals felt a confidence of right, because her judgment coincided with my own." Remarkably, just after dispensing legal advice about his late father's emancipated slaves, Bibb conveys some news about a mutual friend who had just purchased sixty-five slaves to be taken from their homes in Virginia to his new plantation in Texas—without any sense of irony.[66]

In 1844 Bibb appeared to be content as chancellor, ably applying his keen legal mind to knotty issues of equity. However, an old friend from the Senate, John Tyler, was not sitting so comfortably and would soon call Bibb back to Washington, this time for good. The 1840 election had finally rewarded the Whigs with the presidency. After two losses, Henry Clay had decided not to run and had instead supported General William Henry Harrison as the Whig candidate. With the aging hero of the War of 1812 in the White House, Clay was confident that he would be able to rule from the Senate, but he had not counted on Harrison dying a mere month after his inauguration. Despite Harrison's age, the Whigs had almost absentmindedly slated John Tyler as Harrison's running mate—a colossal mistake. Clay had served with Tyler in the Senate and surely knew that he was a states' rights Democrat who had drifted into the Whig Party only because his break with Jackson and Van Buren left him no place to go in Virginia politics. (Bibb, in the same position, had retreated into the judiciary.) Tyler, rejecting the notion that he was merely "acting president," took control of his office and immediately fell out with Clay and his fellow congressional Whigs over reviving the National Bank and the tariff. In late 1841 the entire cabinet, save Secretary of State Daniel Webster, resigned. Tyler was expelled from the Whigs and was forced to build his cabinet with independents. In the summer of 1844 he asked Bibb to serve as his fourth secretary of the treasury.

Although he spent only eight months in office, Bibb applied his usual diligence to his duties. As part of his *Annual Report on the State of the Finances* for 1844, he prepared an impressive compilation of statistics that described in detail the nation's financial history since 1789. The report was part of Bibb's unsuccessful effort to promote a "sinking fund" that could be used to pay down the national debt. The fund would be built up by accumulating surplus revenue from customs and internal revenue collections. Although there was a precedent for such a fund, Whigs knew that paying off the debt would reduce the need for customs revenue, removing a key justification for protective tariffs. Bibb's term as secretary was generally praised. However, in 1845 former president Jackson wrote a private letter to then president James K. Polk, urging him to investigate a rumor that Bibb had stolen $90,000 through an "arrangement" with New York banks. There is no evidence that anything came of the inquiry. Perhaps it was just a bit of gossip passed on by an old man who had never forgiven Bibb for turning against him.[67]

After Polk's inauguration in 1845, Bibb remained in Washington, where he would spend the rest of his life. He bought a house in Georgetown on the corner of Second and Fayette Streets and resumed the practice of law in the federal and DC courts.[68] In his later years, Bibb was a senior and much respected member of the US Supreme Court bar. From his first appearance in 1824 until the year before his death, he appeared in fifty-four reported cases before the Court. The Supreme Court bar, composed largely of former congressmen, senators, and cabinet officials, was a very tight-knit group and was socially close to members of the Supreme Court. "Integrated and cohesive, the Supreme Court bar—the inner republic of bench and bar—flourished" in the antebellum area. "In contrast to the modern bar," it was "an official organization, and meetings of its membership were common."[69] As early as 1817, the group had banded together to commemorate the deaths of its members. In 1845 Bibb was secretary of a meeting of the "bar and officers" of the Supreme Court organized to mourn the death of Justice Joseph Story.[70] Lawyers and justices frequently shared the same boardinghouses and often dined together. Those advocates like Bibb who had served in both Congress and the cabinet crossed paths many times.

Bibb also took many cases before the federal district and appeals courts in the DC area.[71] One celebrated case in the Third Circuit was known as the "Pea Patch" case. It involved title to an island in Delaware that had been in contention for almost half a century. Bibb argued the appeal in Philadelphia in late 1847. "The distinguished ex-Chancellor spoke about five hours, rising at times where the subject allowed it, to a strain of eloquence which produced a sensation throughout the assemblage," one Philadelphia journalist recounted. As Bibb reviewed the long controversy, he "related a number of stirring incidents connected with the early history of the country—of the settlement of Kentucky, and the war of the Revolution, which went far to relieve the subject of its natural barrenness." The reporter described Bibb as a "fine old gentleman" who "possessed a keen black eye, which age had not robbed of its lustre." As was his lifelong habit, Bibb was dressed in the "old style . . . worn by the great men who assembled in the Hall of Independence on former and memorable occasions."[72]

His finances had improved, but Bibb still needed to work, so when his friend John J. Crittenden was appointed US attorney general in 1850, Bibb happily accepted a position as "copy clerk." The title was a bit deceptive; the salary of $2,000 equaled that of his position as chancellor in Louisville, and as part of his duties, Bibb represented the government in the federal appellate courts—including the Supreme Court.[73] Bibb resigned in 1853 to take up the case of general and politician John C. Frémont. During the California gold rush, Frémont had acquired considerable wealth and landholdings, but he was soon faced with a number of land-title lawsuits. In the most celebrated case, Frémont had purchased a large tract of land derived from a grant made under the prior Mexican government. A US board of commissioners set up by the treaty ending the Mexican-American War had decided in Frémont's favor, but that ruling was overturned by the US District Court for the Northern District of California. Bibb and Crittenden were hired by Frémont and his wife, Jessie, to reinstate the commissioners' decision in the US Supreme Court. Although Bibb ended up winning the case, his clients sometimes doubted his work. In one letter Jessie complained, "Mr. Crittenden is lazy, . . . and Judge Bibb is in his dotage."[74] Clients are perhaps the harshest critics; a Buffalo newspaper covering the case described Bibb as "eighty years of age, well-preserved, full of law, and as eloquent and powerful as when young," clearly "one of the very ablest of lawyers in the United States." In addition to winning the case, Bibb and Crittenden likely made a lot of money.[75]

In his later years Bibb achieved odd fame as an angler. The rural pastime had taken on the airs of a dignified sport with George W. Bethume's publication of the American edition of Izaak Walton's *Compleat Angler*. Anecdotes of Bibb's fishing along the Potomac were endlessly repeated in the literature of American recreational fishing. The old man also drew notice for his old-fashioned dress, still sporting the "smalls" or knee breeches with stockings that recalled a now distant era and made the genial Bibb a cherished relict as he walked the District.

However, mortality was catching up to Bibb. His friends from the War Mess were gone. The war-whooping Calhoun had died in 1850; Clay had drawn his last card and his last breath in 1852; Jackson had died in 1845, shortly after his poison-pen attack on Bibb. The times had changed so much that his old adversaries Blair and Van Buren had crossed from the Democrats to the emerging Free Soil–Republican side of the spectrum. On April 14, 1859, Bibb died of pneumonia at his home in Georgetown. A joint meeting of the Supreme Court and district bar associations voted to attend Bibb's funeral en masse and to wear crepe in his honor for thirty days.[76] In addition to fellow lawyers, his funeral "was attended by the Cabinet and numerous friends."[77] He was buried in Washington's Congressional Cemetery, where he was honored with a cenotaph. Bibb's remains were later moved to Kentucky, where he is thought to be buried in the Frankfort Cemetery.[78]

5

THE BROTHER

Alexander K. Marshall (1770–1825)

Alexander K. Marshall, *Decisions of the Court of Appeals of Kentucky, Commencing with the Fall Term, 1817, and . . . Ending in the Fall Term, 1823,* 3 vols. (Washington, KY: Printed by Rannells & Collins for the author, 1819–1823).

Bibb's four solid volumes ensured that case reporting would endure, and they set a high standard that his successors would struggle to meet. On Bibb's resignation in 1817, Governor Gabriel Slaughter appointed another member of the regular appellate bar, Alexander K. Marshall, as reporter of the Court of Appeals. Marshall was a Federalist, and Slaughter's earlier appointment of two other conservatives, Secretary of State John Pope and US Senator Martin D. Hardin, had been unpopular. Nevertheless, Marshall was confirmed by the Kentucky senate on December 19, 1817.[1] The next-to-youngest brother of US Supreme Court chief justice John Marshall, Alexander was a gentleman farmer whose law practice was more of a passion than a profession. Despite a workmanlike career, he would leave a slender legal legacy. However, his fertile fields in Mason County are still tilled, and the mailbox outside the entrance still bears the Marshall name.

Marshall's lineage can be traced back to the founding of Virginia, and his family's mythic past stretches back to William the Conqueror's lieutenant William le Mareschal of Normandy. His father, Thomas Marshall, fought alongside George Washington as a colonel in the Continental Army and amassed huge landholdings in Virginia and Kentucky as a reward for his service. Alexander Keith Marshall was born in 1770 in Fauquier County, Virginia, at Oak Hill, the Marshall ancestral home. Although the Marshalls claimed descent from Norman nobility, the earliest historical figure that can be attested to with any certainty is Thomas's great-great-grandfather John, a refugee from Oliver Cromwell's Commonwealth who settled in Virginia in 1650. John fought as a captain in Charles I's cavalry until the monarch's imprisonment; he and his American descendants were active in the Virginia militia and were zealous defenders of the Anglican Church. Thomas Marshall was educated at the Reverend Archibald Campbell's academy along with his friend George Washington, and like the future president, he learned land surveying. He may have accompanied Washington on survey missions, and both men fought in the French and Indian War. On the land he received for his military service, Thomas Marshall built an impressive estate at Oak Hill. He participated in Virginia politics, serving in the House of Burgesses and as a delegate to the convention that declared Virginia's independence. He raised the "Culpepper minute men" as a patriot militia and joined Washington's Continental Army when the Revolutionary War began. He, along with his son John, fought at Valley Forge, and he rose to the rank of colonel. At Brandywine he kept fighting despite having his horse shot out from under him, and he was awarded a sword in recognition of his valor.[2]

The family of Alexander's mother, Mary, also had a distinguished and romantic history. Her father, James Keith, was born in Aberdeenshire, Scotland, where the family had lived for centuries. The family claimed descent from a branch of the Keiths ennobled as Earls Marishal in a past "so exceedingly remote that it is not now, by any human ingenuity, in any way traceable."[3] James's history is on firmer ground. He attended Marischal College in Aberdeen but in 1715 "abandoned his studies to take up arms for the Old Pretender," Prince James Francis Edward Stuart, in his ill-fated rebellion against the Hanoverian monarchy established by the prince's sister, Mary, and her husband, William of Orange. James Keith fought at the Battle of Sherriffmuir, the campaign's high point, but after the collapse of the Jacobite revolt, he remained a fugitive in the Scottish Highlands. In 1719 he was attainted for his activities and, like many disgruntled Highlanders, decided to emigrate to the American colonies. Settling in Virginia, he took orders as an Episcopal priest and married into a prominent family, taking Mary Isham Randolph as his wife. He was a successful planter and raised a strong family. His daughter, Mary Randolph Keith, was remembered fondly by her sons, as much for her common sense and strength as for her love. A biographer of John Marshall writes:

Not only was John Marshall's mother uncommonly well born, but she was more carefully educated than most Virginia women of that period. Her father received in Aberdeen the precise and methodical training of a Scottish college; and, as all parsons in the Virginia of that time were teachers, it is certain that he carefully instructed his daughter. He was a deeply religious man, especially in his latter years,—so much so, indeed, that there was in him a touch of mysticism; and the two marked qualities of his daughter, Mary, were deep piety and strong intellectuality. She had, too, all the physical hardiness of her Scottish ancestry, fortified by the active and useful labor which all Virginia women of her class at that time performed.[4]

Mary married Thomas Marshall in 1754 and eventually accompanied him to Kentucky. When she died in 1809, her grave was marked by a huge gravestone with a wry epitaph: "SHE WAS GOOD BUT NOT BRILLIANT. USEFUL BUT NOT GREAT." A stern portrait of her captures her stoic manner.[5]

After the war, Colonel Thomas Marshall and his older sons were rewarded for their service with land warrants. The colonel served in 1780 as surveyor general of Virginia's Kentucky Territory and took advantage of the opportunity to acquire particularly attractive properties in the fertile areas of Woodford and Mason Counties. In 1785 he moved to Kentucky with fifteen-year-old Alexander and several younger children in tow (John, the eldest, remained in Virginia). The Marshall family settled first in the Bluegrass, near the territorial capital of Danville, where the colonel involved himself in the drive for Kentucky statehood and in land speculation, later establishing his estate Buckpond in Woodford County.

Alexander was educated in the classics and English literature by Scottish tutors employed by his father, but he received a political education in Danville, the site of ten conventions where Kentuckians discussed separating from Virginia and forming a government for the new state. His uncle Humphrey was a towering figure in local Federalist circles and a regular visitor to the Marshall home. Alexander was mentioned frequently in his older brother John's account books for 1788–1791, and he may have traveled to Virginia to read law at Oak Hill. At least one entry detailed his travels to Virginia; another had him couriering money to his father in Kentucky, perhaps as part of the family's many land transactions.

Although the record is silent about his legal education, the start of Alexander's legal career in Danville is better documented. An advertisement in the July 19,

1790, edition of the *Kentucky Gazette* notified clients of the late James Overton that Alexander K. Marshall would be taking over their cases. Over the next few years, the newspaper also reported his participation in cases in the nearby Bluegrass counties of Woodford and Bourbon. Some biographical sketches list "clerk of the Court of Appeals" as one of Marshall's offices, which is puzzling because he does not appear on the short but certain list of the court's antebellum clerks. However, it is possible that he served as an assistant clerk or tipstaff for one of the court's first clerks, Christopher Greenup (1792–1796) or Thomas Todd (1796–1801), both of whom lived in Danville and served as clerks of one or more Kentucky statehood conventions. Marshall may have seen service on the court as both an interesting diversion and an entrée to appellate practice.

In 1794 Marshall married Mary McDowell, the youngest daughter of Judge Samuel McDowell, a prominent and wealthy pioneer.[6] Before settling in Kentucky and becoming one of its first judges, McDowell's legendary military career included serving as a captain under George Washington in the French and Indian War, as an aide-de-camp to Isaac Shelby in Lord Dunmore's War, and as a colonel in Nathanael Greene's campaign in the Revolutionary War, where he witnessed Cornwallis's surrender at Yorktown. The couple received a marriage gift of 10,000 acres in Mason County from Thomas Marshall. Alexander's siblings received similar gifts, including his older brother Captain Thomas Marshall, who had served with his father (and with oldest brother John) in Washington's Continental Army during the Revolutionary War. (Thomas apparently never used the appellation "junior" during his lifetime, so he is generally distinguished from his father, the "Colonel," by his rank.) The younger Thomas Marshall built Federal Hill, a nationally recognized historic landmark that still overlooks the town of Washington, Kentucky; it contains the old Marshall cemetery and the mortal remains of the family patriarch and matriarch.[7] The Marshall brothers and their descendants would form the core of Mason County's leading families for much of the nineteenth century.

Washington was a small but thriving town a few miles south of the Maysville river landing, an area with rich soil suitable for agriculture. Early settlers preferred to avoid the actual riverfront, which could be easily attacked by Native Americans, so they established their homes in Washington. The early houses—like that of George Mefford, which still stands—were "built of boards from the flatboat" on which the early settlers had floated down the Ohio River.[8] Washington stood near the road between Maysville and Lexington and was a way station between Kentucky and

Philadelphia and beyond. At the inception of the new commonwealth, Washington was the "second largest town in the state after Lexington. Washington had 119 log houses, 462 people, 22 wells, several private schools and, in 1798, the first post office west of the Alleghenies."[9] As Kentucky grew, Maysville gradually supplanted Washington; after the county seat was moved there in 1848, Washington almost disappeared as a city. The rich land around it, however, became a powerhouse of farming and livestock raising, and even today, the Marshall lands are working farms.

Alexander and Mary built "a quaint brick house" in a grove of walnut and locust trees a few miles from the town of Washington.[10] Marshall's great-granddaughter, Lucy Marshall Bentley, lived there as a child in the 1850s and described it as a "large old colonial house" with long halls and high ceilings. "The living rooms were partially heated by the large open fireplaces, very beautiful with their brightly burning logs and highly polished andirons, presenting a vision of comfort," Bentley recalled. However, that comfort "was highly deceptive as the large rooms were rarely ever warm." A "thirty-acre grove of walnuts had been set out under Marshall's direction to form a park through which to approach the house"—hence the estate's name, Walnut Grove.[11] Like many country lawyers, Alexander Marshall built a small detached outbuilding to serve as a law office. One can imagine that it resembled the law office of John Rowan, which has been restored outside Federal Hill in Bardstown, the famed "Old Kentucky Home" that inspired the Stephen Foster song of that name.[12]

At Walnut Grove, Marshall lived a life of secure wealth. He made his money mostly by renting land to others who farmed it, but he also speculated in land and acquired other properties. The 1810 census lists him as the owner of 20 slaves (the number dropped to 14 in 1820), suggesting that he farmed only a small portion of his lands.[13] As a comparison, Thomas Jefferson's Monticello was about half the size of Marshall's estate, but between 1774 and 1827, Jefferson owned between 117 and 223 slaves.[14] Walnut Grove was later utilized extensively for sheep and cattle raising, and it is possible that this less labor-intensive use began with Alexander. By all accounts, his passion was not farming but the law, which he practiced "for the excitement and employment it afforded [rather] than the income derived" from it.[15] From his small brick office a short distance from the main house, he built a reputation as "one of the very ablest lawyers of his day."[16]

In 1797 Marshall was elected to represent Mason County in the Kentucky house of representatives—the first of four consecutive one-year terms lasting through 1800.[17] He was an active legislator and secured a charter for the Franklin Academy and for the city of Lewisburg.[18] Like all members of the Marshall family during this era, he was a fervent Federalist in a predominantly Jeffersonian state. This would have limited his political options, but there is little evidence that he desired such a career. His uncle Humphrey Marshall—the undisputed head of the Federalists in Kentucky—approached politics with a fearless and unmerciful fervor. He was twice the victim of mobs provoked by his "blistering tongue and cutting pen" and fought a number of duels. Once he was dragged to the Kentucky River and escaped being ducked (or worse) only by a stratagem; later he was "actually stoned out of Frankfort."[19] Having been tutored in the home of his brother, Colonel Thomas Marshall, Humphrey was close to his nephews. Alexander's older brother James Markham Marshall was close in age to his uncle and a key ally; Alexander and his next younger brother, Louis, were solid foot soldiers.[20] During Humphrey Marshall's 1806 attack on leading political figures for their real (and imagined) participation in the so-called Spanish conspiracy, Alexander and Louis provided moral support and reportedly some muscle.[21] A letter to Henry Clay mentions the two protecting Joseph M. Street, editor of the *Western World,* which served as the "mouth piece of Humphrey Marshall."[22]

While resident in Frankfort, Alexander likely tended to legal matters in the nearby circuit courts and attended sessions of the Court of Appeals. In later years, Marshall argued a number of cases before the court.[23] Having participated in the excitement of political life, it appears that Alexander preferred the life of a lawyer-planter—especially as the Federalist Party continued its slide into irrelevance on the frontier.

In 1818 Marshall took over as reporter of the Court of Appeals from the venerable Bibb, who had set a high bar. He would edit three volumes covering the years 1817–1821. Tradition would mark them as less than impressive, but to a large extent, that was the opinion of one critic, George Robertson, chief justice of the Court of Appeals from 1829 to 1843 (and again in 1870–1871). Robertson wrote about the court for Lewis Collins's history of the state and briefly assessed Kentucky's law reports. Of Marshall's reports he said, "They are signally incorrect and deficient in execution."[24] It is important to note that Robertson might have been somewhat partial to reports that contained opinions he had written (such as Dana's). Nonetheless, he served on the bench at a time when Marshall's reports were regularly cited, so he would have been well acquainted with their flaws. Therefore, it is possible that the reports of the gentleman lawyer Marshall were less well executed than those of the workaholic George Bibb, the fastidious William Littell, and the experienced newspaperman James G. Dana.

We know that Marshall did some work from his home in Mason County. In July 1823 he was working on his third volume when he wrote to his Lexington printer, William W. Worsley, from his Washington, Kentucky, address. Worsley had founded the *Kentucky Reporter,* a Lexington newspaper, in 1807.[25] It is clear that Marshall was running close to his deadline and having problems with some of the contractors he had hired to fulfill the statutory requirements of his office:

> 23th July 1823
> Washington Ky.
>
> Dear Sir,
> After some considerable trouble, I have succeeded in procuring a wagon to take the remaining package of the 3rd vol. which is now sent. The index will be ready in about a week when it shall be sent and in the meantime I hope you will [have] the young gentleman of whom you have spoken engaged in folding.
> The volume must be delivered by the first of Sept. in the secretary's office. If you cannot *certainly* have 250 vol. ready for delivery by the 20th August, I entreat you to divide the work, retaining such part as my friend can execute by the 20th of August and giving the remainder to such other binder as can be relied on both for [punctuality] and neatness.
> I regret that I have the perspicacity to trouble you with business, but rely with some confidence that you will excuse this when you recollect that my binder has not apprised me of his inability to perform the work til less than a week before I write you.
> > Respectfully,
> > A. K. Marshall[26]

Maybe it was during this time, while scrambling for substitute binders and trying to find wagon transportation on the treacherous road from Maysville to Frankfort, that Marshall decided to call it quits.

Alexander K. Marshall's greatest legacy might in fact be his descendants, one of whom became the Marshall family historian. Marshall had five children: daughters

Maria, Lucy, and Jane, and sons Charles and James. Charles, known as "Black Dan" to distinguish him from another Charles in the Marshall clan, became a prominent farmer in Lewisburg. James relocated to Lexington. The youngest daughter, Jane, married William S. Sullivant and moved to his home in Columbus, Ohio. The middle daughter, Lucy, married a cousin, John Marshall, a son of Captain Thomas Marshall. Their son, Dr. Alexander K. Marshall, was a prominent Nicholasville physician and member of Congress.[27]

The oldest daughter, Maria, married James A. Paxton, a Mason County attorney who also maintained an inn on Washington's Main Street. It, along with the Paxton home, is still standing. Paxton's Inn, renovated during the 1960s, currently serves as the chapter house for the Daughters of the American Revolution.[28] One of James and Maria's sons, William McClung Paxton, moved to Missouri to practice law, but he was also a poet and historian. Based on both meticulous research and oral history from his far-flung family, Paxton preserved the history, legend, and lore of the Marshalls in the 415-page *Marshall Family*. James and Maria's daughter Phoebe married Charles A. Marshall, a grandson of Captain Thomas Marshall. Whether by inheritance or purchase, Charles reclaimed his mother-in-law's birthplace, Walnut Grove. Unfairly described by one writer as "an unambitious but sensible man," he was in fact an innovative agriculturalist, championing new strains of hemp and breeds of cattle while playing a leading role in agricultural societies.[29]

On February 7, 1825, only a few years after resigning as reporter, Alexander K. Marshall died at Walnut Grove and was buried there. He was mourned by the Kentucky bar, but his great landholdings and numerous relatives kept its members employed for many years; no fewer than seven cases reported by his predecessors derived from controversies over his estate. As for his relatives, the estate served them well, too. The old homestead is still a productive farm owned by his descendants. And just a few miles away is Federal Hill. It is owned by the estate of a Lexington lawyer who took seriously the responsibility of tending the private graveyard where the parents of Justice John Marshall rest.[30]

6

THE POET

William Littell (1768–1824)

William Littell, *Reports of Cases at Common Law and in Chancery, Decided by the Court of Appeals of the Commonwealth of Kentucky*, 5 vols. (Frankfort: Amos Kendall & Co., 1823–1824).

William Littell, *Cases Selected from the Decisions of the Court of Appeals of Kentucky Not Heretofore Reported [1795–1821]* (Frankfort: Amos Kendall & Co., 1824).

The selection of William Littell as the official law reporter brought great scholarship, literary competence, and publishing experience to the position. By the time of the appointment, nearly a dozen imprints bearing Littell's name had been published, including seven volumes of Kentucky statutes that were the state's de facto code, Kentucky's first historical monograph, and its first book of satire. However, the appointment was also a brave one; it took a confident panel of judges to choose someone as accomplished, intellectually self-confident, and opinionated as Littell.

Littell is a curious figure in Kentucky legal history, scholarship, and literature. He almost single-handedly created the infrastructure of legal research in the state, compiling the first comprehensive collection of statutes, the first digest of cases, and six volumes of case law. All his works were comprehensive, accurate, and annotated with a critical eye. Outside of the law, he wrote poetry, political satire, and history and was learned in theology and medicine. But Littell was a solitary, eccentric figure who was disliked by many and politically and socially neutralized by his uncompromising pen. He was one of those unfortunate people shunned in most eras—someone who tells the truth as he sees it.

Perhaps because of his unconventional nature and the fact that he spent his first thirty years outside of Kentucky, Littell's contemporaries knew little of his life before he moved to Frankfort. Early biographies give widely divergent accounts of his birth and migration to Kentucky, some even suggesting that he was British.[1] Thanks to the work of family historians and greater access to court records, we can do somewhat better. Littell was born in 1768 (or 1767) in New Jersey, likely near South Amboy, where his parents Job and Elizabeth were married.[2] He had one known brother, Samuel Lucius Alonzo Littell, whose son, Alonzo Lucius Littell, later chronicled the family history.[3] Job moved his family to Fayette County, Pennsylvania, in 1783 when William was in his teens. He was "given some of [the] schooling available at that time." Littell's later efforts in theology, medicine, and law indicate some higher education, but other than a vague report that he attended college in Philadelphia, we do not know where.[4] Kentucky pioneer William Sudduth told researcher John D. Shane that Littell was "first educated as a clergyman but didn't like it."[5] Littell himself alludes to a well-educated youth:

I've wander'd in the thorny maze
Of science, from my infant days.
And, through ambition to be wise,
I have almost read out my eyes.[6]

When Littell first emerges into the light of history, it is as an educator. James Veech's sketch of early Fayette County, Pennsylvania, notes one of his first recorded professional endeavors:

We have before us a newspaper of 1794, wherein is an advertisement by Rev. James Dunlap, then the Presbyterian Pastor of Laurel Hill and Dunlap's Creek, afterwards President of Jefferson College, Pa., and William Littell, Esq., afterwards a lawyer and author of eminence in Kentucky, setting forth that they had opened a school in Franklin township, where they teach "Elocution and the English language grammatically, together with the Latin, Greek and Hebrew languages, Geometry and Trigonometry, with their application to Measuration, Surveying, Gauging, &c., likewise

Geography and Civil History, Natural and Moral Philosophy, Logic and Rhetoric," and where "boarding, washing, &c., may be had at reputable houses in the neighborhood, at the low rate of ten pounds ($26.67) per annum."[7]

Sometime in the late 1790s Littell moved to Kentucky. Although early biographers were confused about the timing of this migration, settling on somewhere between 1801 and 1805, historian Robert S. Cotterill mined early court records to provide concrete evidence of an earlier date.[8] He found a record of Littell's early 1799 appearance as an attorney, where he "produced a license to practice law in the commonwealth" to the Fleming County Court of Quarter-Sessions and was sworn in to the county bar. This means that his legal training likely occurred in Pennsylvania—although an examination by the judges of the Court of Appeals in Frankfort would have been required to obtain a license to practice law in Kentucky.[9] The city of Flemingsburg was still only three years old when Littell settled there, along with many other migrants from western Pennsylvania. He resided there for nearly four years, building a law practice and briefly serving on the county court in 1801; he also made appearances in the Mason and Clark County circuit courts. In late 1802 Littell relocated to Mt. Sterling in Montgomery County, where he reportedly dabbled in medicine. However, he still attended the Fleming County courts, defending a young woman in 1804 for "concealing the birth of a bastard child."[10]

In January 1805 Kentucky newspapers carried an appeal to "the Citizens of Kentucky and particularly the Professors of Law," proposing to publish "a complete edition of the statute law of Kentucky." Although the notice was signed "Justinian," William Littell of Mt. Sterling was listed as the project's proponent. The plan was an ambitious one: in addition to publishing "all acts of a public nature which have been enacted in this state," Littell proposed to include any Virginia acts that "have any force" in Kentucky, a "historical view of the laws of this country from the first settlement of Virginia to the present time," and any "alterations in the common law of Great Britain." The work would also include references to cases from the Kentucky and federal courts related to the statutes. Littell set out his egalitarian political justification for such a publication, noting that "there is no principle more truly republican than that the people who are amenable to the laws should know their import." The idea that the law should be public and readily accessible to those under its rule occurs often in his writings.

Subscriptions were sought for the project, but Littell would later seek a subsidy from the Kentucky legislature, only to be rebuffed (after a hearing that Littell would later parody in print). Littell was entering a field that had some competition. Some (but not many) copies of the "session laws" issued at the end of each meeting of the General Assembly were available, and the first public printer, John Bradford, had published *Laws of Kentucky*, a collection of early public acts, in 1799; he would add a second volume in 1807.[11] But whereas Bradford's *Laws* were augmented by nothing but an index and a list of private laws, Littell planned to create a full-featured statutory tool for lawyers that placed the statutes in the full context of Kentucky law. He created editorial enhancements (using footnotes, marginal notes, and tables) that clarified which laws were in force, which ones had been amended, and (for the first time) which ones had changed the laws inherited from Virginia. In volumes 1 and 2, Littell appended the state and federal constitutions, the Proclamation of 1763, the compact of separation from Virginia, a table of cases from the Court of Appeals (this table would be supplemented in each succeeding volume), and extracts from "Laws of Virginia and Acts of Parliament in Force in This Commonwealth." In volume 3, a large appendix republished all Virginia acts "establishing and regulating towns, academies, ferries and inspections" in Kentucky. In the 1814 update, Littell added several more appendices, each serving as a mini-treatise. The first appendix surveyed the Kentucky law on real estate, wills, promissory notes, and bonds. It was followed by a manual for justices of the peace and sheriffs and a short guide to chancery practice. In the volumes of *Statute Law of Kentucky*, Littell provided lawyers with a library of useful materials—covering subject matter that easily could have filled several monographs—and the apparatus to thoroughly research the statute law.[12]

With some encouragement in the form of subscriptions, Littell moved to Frankfort in 1805 to begin work on his statute law project. However, he was immediately drawn into the political turmoil of the new commonwealth. He was hired by federal district court judge Harry Innes to defend him and his Democratic-Republican allies (John Brown, Benjamin Sebastian, and Caleb Wallace) against attacks by Humphrey Marshall and his pro-Federalist newspaper the *Western World*. The 1804 prosecution of Aaron Burr for treason had allowed Marshall to revive charges that his Democratic enemies had engaged in pre-statehood contacts with Spain in the 1780s (when all Kentuckians were hedging their bets out of fear that their shipping rights to Spanish New Orleans would be sacrificed for eastern interests). Marshall cleverly recast these dealings as treason against the current

United States. Littell countered these arguments with articles in the sympathetic *Kentucky Gazette* and in a well-written 1806 pamphlet that put the matter in its historical context. The latter, *Political Transactions in and Concerning Kentucky*, was organized as a historical narrative.[13] Littell expertly wove in evidence from dozens of contemporary documents and letters, all which were republished as an appendix.[14] The writing is so calmly persuasive and its polemic purpose so subdued and without rhetorical flourish that the pamphlet reads like a straight work of history. Another measure of Littell's effectiveness is that much of Humphrey Marshall's *History of Kentucky* (1814) was designed to counter Littell's version of events (but without any of the subtlety).

After arguably publishing Kentucky's first political history, Littell published its first long-form version of political satire. In the *Epistles of William Surnamed Littell* (printed first in 1806 and then again in 1814, along with some poetry and other satire, as *Festoons of Fancy*), he lampooned supporters of state and local banking interests, mocked Kentucky's divorce laws, and recounted his efforts to convince the state legislature to support the publication of its statutes.[15] Littell was not the state's first political satirist. As early as 1798, Tom Johnson, the Drunken Poet of Danville, was sending bitter barbs to the commonwealth's political institutions:

> I hate Kentucky, curse the place,
> And all her vile and miscreant race!
> Who make religion's sacred tie
> A mask thro' which they cheat and lie.
> Proteus could not change his shape,
> Nor Jupiter commit a rape
> With half the ease these villains can
> Send prayers to God and cheat their man!
> I hate all Judges here of late,
> And every Lawyer in the State,
> Each quack that is called Physician,
> And all blockheads in Commission—
> Worse than the Baptist roaring rant,
> I hate the Presbyterian cant—
> Their Parsons, Elders, nay, the whole,
> And wish them gone with all my soul.[16]

Littell's *Epistles* offers a clear window into his legal and political views. His wry faux-biblical framework pokes fun at the pompous rhetoric of politicians and makes good use of his religious training. A few early epistles deal with an issue that would bedevil the state for the next three decades: banking. The first part deals with the legislature's effort to repeal the charter of the Bank of Lexington, and it sets the whole work's tone. He recounts that the "wise men and chiefs gathered themselves together in the eleventh month of the year" to open the 1806 session of the Kentucky General Assembly. The repeal effort was led by "Felix [Grundy], a mighty man of words," while the "merchants of the town of Lexington" were defended by "Henry [Clay], an exceedingly wise counselor." Grundy's oratory carried the day, and the charter was repealed. They then "besought Christopher [Greenup], the Prince of the Realm," to give his assent: "Now Christopher had not heard the cunning speeches of Felix; when therefore the wise men and chiefs of the people told him what they had done, he was astonished, and sat himself down and remained silent for the space of ten days." This is likely the most sublime description of a governor's use of a pocket veto in American literature.[17]

The next epistle recounts the follow-up attempt to establish a state bank to "make money out of rags." (The *Kentucky Gazette* regularly published ads by paper mills seeking rags, which they used to make the excellent bond paper on which the books of this era were printed.)[18] However, "there arose a great strife between Felix and Henry about the manner of changing rags into money," specifically, over whether the right to issue commercial paper should be the exclusive privilege of the new state bank in Frankfort or shared with the private bank of the "merchants of Lexington." Ultimately, Governor Greenup threw his weight toward allowing both banks to issue negotiable instruments (sowing the seeds of the hardships of the 1820s). This leads to "The Song of Triumph" of the Lexington merchants, a mock elegiac of biblical celebration leavened by classical hubris.[19]

Another epistle deals with an issue about which Littell was passionate: enactment of a general divorce law. The common law did not allow for divorce. This led to hardship in Kentucky's expanding frontier, where abandoned spouses left alone in the harsh environment could not survive without a functioning nuclear family. The only legal remedies were religious annulment (a nullity in America, which had no established church), a form of legal separation with no chance of remarriage called divorce *mensa et thoro* (bed-and-board divorce), and legislative divorce—a private law voiding the marriage. Legislative divorce required the resources to prepare a case and lobby the General Assembly, and the process was public, unseemly, and often unsuccessful.[20] In 1805 Littell petitioned the Kentucky house of representatives to pass a law that would grant a divorce to a man who could prove abandonment, an act of adultery, or conviction of a felony by his wife, and to a woman who could show abandonment, adultery of such a repeated nature that it constituted abandonment, conviction of a felony, or extreme physical cruelty by her husband. The House Journal for the session illustrates the problem the bill sought to solve. Spread across its pages are dozens of petitions for divorce presented to the legislature and duly referred to the "committee of Religion," which held hearings and reported its findings (usually denials, especially when the petitioner was a woman).[21] Despite the apparent need, Littell's measure failed after surviving two readings and some committee consideration.[22] (The legislature eventually passed a similar measure in 1809.)

Littell's response to the failed divorce bill was a particularly cutting satire. In this epistle, he recasts his petition as a censorious jeremiad. Going immediately for the jugular, he decries that so many of Kentucky's young men "go in unto Ethiopian women, with [which] the land swarmeth, and beget sons and daughters, and these sons and daughters become bond men and bond women." As a result of using slaves as prostitutes, the men become "sorely afflicted," but "nevertheless they marry the fair daughters of the land, and betake themselves to strong drink." Drunk and impotent from disease, these men make poor husbands, and their wives "bewail their calamity." Moreover, Littell asks, how can a wife expect love from a husband who has so "little natural affection" that he can "willfully consign his children to infamy and everlasting bondage?" Coarsened, the "gentle spirit of love hath departed" from these men, who deprive their wives of "food and raiment" to buy strong drink and, worse, "beat their wives with staves and tear their flesh with instruments of iron." Littell urges that the law should reflect the simple principle that marriage is "sacred to love, to tender affection and cordial sympathy" and "ought to have its beginning and end with these."[23]

It is perhaps this one piece of writing that placed Littell permanently outside the pale of polite society. Even mentioning the sexual abuse of slaves by slave owners and the progeny this abuse produced violated a hardening taboo; mocking it in print was scandalous. Littell's abhorrence of slavery is palpable (although there is no hint of sympathy for its direct victims). Moreover, Littell's conception of divorce is decidedly radical. He moves beyond the narrow fault-based system envisioned by the failed divorce bill to suggest a principle close to our modern standard of irreconcilable differences: that is, once love, affection, and mutual sympathy are gone, the marriage has failed. Finally, one is struck by Littell's sympathy to women in this satire. He argues that the legislative divorce process is biased against women. Men who claim adultery are granted "a certain writing called a Bill of Divorce" from the "wise men" of the legislative committees of religion, while women "findth no one to pity or succour" them. At one point he even justifies adultery by women who are shunned by their husbands. And Littell's trenchant comments on the deleterious effects of strong drink on women foreshadow the life mission of another Kentuckian: Garrard County's Carry Nation.

A lighter example of Littell's epistles deals with his attempt to convince the legislature to subscribe to a "certain number" of copies of his planned compilation of statutes for use by the state. As he describes it, "William whose surname is Littell" had perchance to find "the book of Law, which had been lost, and when he found it he rejoiced greatly." He then decided to "speak unto the wise men and chiefs of the people" so that copies could be made and "dispersed throughout the land." His petition was referred to an "assembly of cunning men" (more prosaically called the house committee for courts of justice). The committee reported the bill out unfavorably, but John Allen moved to revive it on the floor. "Thirty and three of the chiefs" agreed to Allen's motion, versus only twenty-one negative votes. However, "it came to pass" that Satan entered the fray, and on December 24 (at the time, the Kentucky legislature met through the Christmas season) the subsidy was killed by a 23–22 vote. Littell "became exceedingly sorrowful," and "he sat himself down and wrote an Epistle to all the Realm."[24]

With notable works of both political history and political satire sitting on the shelves of Kentucky bookstores, Littell turned his attention to his statute laws project over the next several years. The first of three planned volumes came out in 1809, a second in 1810, and the third in 1811. The proof of its utility would be its financial success. It was so successful that it was updated in 1814 and 1819, for a total of five volumes. Even the legislature took notice. It is hard to find an edition of the legislative journals for years afterward in which the purchase of a set of Littell's *Statute Law* is not authorized for some state agency. In 1821 the Kentucky legislature commissioned Littell and his good friend Jacob Swigert, the author of *Kentucky Justice* (1823), to compile a compact digest of Kentucky statutes. Their work, *Digest of the Statute Law*, was completed in two volumes and published in 1822.[25] It was immediately recognized (even by Littell's many critics) to be of the highest quality, and it cemented Littell's reputation as a legal scholar. The legal scholarship of *Statute Law* was recognized when Transylvania University, the leading institution of higher learning in the western frontier, granted Littell an LLD degree.

While preparing his statutory compilation, Littell published *Principles of Law and Equity* in 1808, the first digest of Kentucky case law.[26] The work was likely a spin-off of his efforts to ferret out citations to Kentucky statutes in published judicial decisions. Like any prudent writer, Littell never let good research go unpublished. That publication began a series of case law digests that has assisted Kentucky lawyers up to and beyond the computer age.[27]

Despite his prodigious writing record, Littell was still a working lawyer. From his early career in Flemingsburg, when he rode circuit to Mason and Clark Counties, he was an active attorney with business in many courts. Perhaps because of his difficulties soliciting business personally, Littell was an effective early user of advertising to attract clients over a wide geographic area. In 1807 he placed an advertisement in a Cincinnati newspaper offering to represent clients in the Ohio chancery and appellate courts if they allowed sufficient time to prepare (and, presumably, to commute from Frankfort).[28] Although this line of business did not work out, he began a lucrative practice in Kentucky's growing city of Louisville. In 1814 he began running ads in the *Louisville Correspondent,* announcing his attendance at the Jefferson, Hardin, and Bullitt sittings of the circuit courts, as well as touting his practice before the Court of Appeals. Hezekiah Hawley was named as his agent (apparently adopting the barrister-solicitor model for his out-of-town business).[29] In 1816 Littell moved his permanent residence to Shelbyville, and he advertised his practice before the Shelby and Jefferson circuit courts (noting that "while in Louisville he lodges at Mr. Allen's").[30] A clue to his ability to operate such a far-flung practice appeared in the Louisville papers around this time, when he advertised the sale of a "gig of uncommon strength and elegance with Plated Harness." He airily explained that his "only motive for parting with it is that I have more carriages than I have use for," and he warned that the price was firm because he would prefer to "present it as a gift" if he could not sell it on his terms.[31]

Littell decided to return to Frankfort in 1819 and confine his business to courts in the capital city. He announced this in a number of newspapers, noting that he would continue to attend the Jefferson and Shelby courts until his business there was complete.[32] Nonetheless, this did not end his attempt to find new clients—especially after the 1819 panic depressed the state's economy. In 1824 he announced a partnership with Uriel B. Chambers of Scott County. Chambers would attend the local courts of the county, while Littell would handle cases before the Court of Appeals and matters before the "special chancery term" of the Scott circuit court.[33]

While living in Frankfort, Littell developed a successful practice arguing cases before the Court of Appeals. He is named as counsel in ninety-four reported cases, a number that surely underplays his role. The peak of his career occurred during a time when the names of counsel were imperfectly recorded in *Sneed's Decisions* and omitted by choice in the four volumes of reports by Bibb (a period covering mid-1808 to mid-1817). Based on existing records, he appeared in an average of a dozen cases a year from 1808 through 1822, when his own decision to omit lawyers' names from his first two volumes obscured the record.[34] His effectiveness as an appellate lawyer was his erudition, not his oratory. Fellow law reporter Ben Monroe related a story he had heard from George Robertson, chief justice of the Court of Appeals: Littell had appeared before the court and made a "very sensible and pertinent" argument, "but when he had gotten apparently about two-thirds through," he stopped, "closed his manuscript," and told the court "the rest was declamation."[35]

When Alexander K. Marshall vacated the position in late 1822, the legislature decided it wanted to go in a different direction. Before Governor Adair appointed a new law reporter, the General Assembly repealed the 1815 law under which Marshall had operated and enacted a law directly appointing Littell as reporter in January 1823. This reflected the body's appreciation of his statutory compilations (it had just received *Digest of the Statute Law* commissioned from him and Swigert) and perhaps some dissatisfaction with the quality and promptness of Marshall's reports. The law provided for a subscription of 250 copies "at the rate of one dollar for every hundred pages," including tables and indexes (a slightly better rate than that offered by the 1815 law). However, the legislature required that "the letter and paper be of the same size as Littell's edition of the laws of Kentucky," that "no argument of counsel be printed," and that the Court of Appeals certify its approval of each volume.[36] Another law passed in December 1823 determined that the Court of Appeals did not need to deliver written opinions in cases involving "matters of fact only" or that applied only "principles of law previously settled," which culled the number of cases Littell needed to publish.[37]

As he started, Littell realized that the collection of decisions in the clerk's office had been left in some disarray. In the preface to his first volume, Littell complained of the severe "inconvenience resulting from the Reporter's not having been supplied with the original Opinions," but noted that he had been "partially furnished with them at last." The problem forced him to publish the first two volumes in reverse order, leading to this notice in the preface of the second volume: "It will naturally be asked, 'why is the second volume published before the first?'" Nonetheless, he was able to catch up with the 1822 backlog in the first two volumes, which were published in March and June 1823, and he got back on track with volume 3 (1823 spring term), published in August 1823.[38] Littell signaled his political sensibilities by dedicating two of his volumes to New Court leading lights William T. Barry (volume 1) and John Rowan (volume 2). Apparently, he took some heat from colleagues for reverting to Bibb's policy of not naming the lawyers arguing cases. In the preface to the first volume (but the second to be published) he informed readers that, in the future (starting with volume 3), "the Reporter, yielding with deference and pleasure to what he now believes to be the general wish, will, in every subsequent volume, mention the court from which each case was brought, and the counsel employed in the appellate court."

Littell's work took place in an economy that was still sorting through the rubble of the 1819 panic and the collapse of the Kentucky banking industry in the early 1820s. Without short-term lenders, Littell apparently had difficulty buying paper for his later volumes. In 1824 the legislature agreed to pay him in advance for those volumes. However, since the legislature was also in austerity mode, it ordered the law reporter to make a few changes to reduce costs. He was directed to place abstracts of the cases in the margins rather than in text, and he was instructed to drop any "tables of statutes and cases cited." This no doubt referred to the eight-page table of statutes cited he had included in volume 2. (Littell complied, but he ended up moving the table to the smaller-type index under the "Statutes" header.) The legislature also dropped the requirement that volumes be delivered to the secretary of state within sixty days of the end of each judicial term. Perhaps the legislators realized that setting the abstracts in small type in the margins would reduce the page count but complicate the typesetters' work, adding time to the process.[39]

After his five volumes of reports were finished, Littell published a volume of selected decisions in May 1824. That project had been initiated by the legislature in its December 1823 law, which directed the law reporter "to report the decisions thereof given previous to the period at which the present reporter commenced, and not reported by his predecessors." Given the gaps in the years covered by the first ten volumes of case reports, the legislature no doubt wanted to publish omitted decisions that were being discussed and cited, making them more accessible to attorneys who did not have the time to page through manuscript files in the clerk's office. However, perhaps after additional consultation with Littell, an 1824 act clarified that, rather than publishing all omitted opinions, "no case shall be published unless it settles some principle of law not settled in any of the decisions of the Court of Appeals heretofore published."[40]

Despite the Kentucky legislature's occasional editorial meddling, the lawmakers had confidence that their publishing workhorse would persevere and that only death could stop him. Littell died on September 26, 1824, "after an illness of near two months." He had been "severely attacked with the prevailing Epidemic about the second week of August" and had nearly recovered, but then he "sunk into the arms of death" after his son William died.[41] The epidemic was an undefined fever that was plaguing North America and had been widely reported in Frankfort the prior year.[42] Situated in a crook of the Kentucky River, Frankfort was swampy and susceptible to various fevers. This particular fever could have been the same bilious fever reported in medical journals and afflicting Louisville a few years earlier.[43] Littell was survived by his second wife, Martha (Irwin) McCracken, and a son Philander (William's half brother). Littell's will (signed before the younger William's death) left his estate to his two sons.[44] He died with significant landholdings but also significant debts. In the depressed economy of 1824, a quick land sale would have barely covered those debts. The legislature Littell had served for so long passed an act in 1825 "for the benefit of the infant heir of William Littell," which set aside the normal rules for the disposal of real property to settle the debts of an estate and allowed the Franklin circuit court to manage the timing of those sales in the best interest of Philander.[45]

In assessing Littell's life and work, there are two widely divergent traditions that color all biographical treatments. The negative tradition appears to issue out of contemporary animus against him, and it has a strong and vicious social cast. The other is more positive and reflects not only the feelings of his friends but also the appreciation of later generations for his work. Both traditions accept the quality of Littell's legal works and his eccentric nature. The positive tradition is best reflected in the obituary that appeared in the *Frankfort Argus;* it was likely written by a friend, perhaps Jacob Swigert. After stressing the parental love that hastened Littell's death, the writer admits that his subject was "somewhat eccentric in his manners and opinions," but he was "a man of great goodness of heart." Littell's hard work and judgment "rescued our code [of statutes] from such a mass of confusion as had no parallel," and for this deed he "was never suitably rewarded." The obituary writer notes that Littell "was excelled by few" in his knowledge of law and learned in "Physic and Divinity." Taken together, his poetic and satirical works were "serious, comic, and sentimental" and "will long be remembered and admired for their genuine humour and faithful delineation of character."[46]

For Littell's enemies, his eccentricity was a window into his immorality, and it was held up to cruel ridicule. Historian Lewis Collins is perhaps the best example of this viewpoint. Collins was twenty-seven when Littell died, old enough to imbibe firsthand this negative tradition. In a short sketch in his *History of Kentucky*, he describes Littell as "a lawyer of no special reputation" with "bad morals." He "was very eccentric; in walking his gait was rapid, his stride long, giving him an undulating motion by which his head bobbed up and down." He criticizes the lawyer's standoffishness, noting that "if he met forty men, unless first addressed he neither looked at or spoke to any of them."[47] While Collins barely mentions Littell's satires, the author of the entry on Littell in the *Dictionary of American Biography* also draws on this negative tradition and reports that rather than being admired, "his *Epistles* was of such a character as to bring him into disrepute and give him a reputation for flippancy and scurrility that he never succeeded in living down." Trying to support Collins's charge of bad morals, the writer observes that Littell's will "hints at domestic unhappiness" (presumably because he left nothing to his second wife). He admits that this is somewhat contradicted by the fact that he "named a clergyman" as guardian of his children in that same will, but he does not point out that the cleric was a leading Episcopal minister and founder of the Kentucky diocese.[48]

Littell's true "moral" transgression was to cast his satiric lamplight into the darkest corners of a new frontier society that was desperately trying to attain respectability. Criticizing slavery, accusing men of drunkenly abusing their wives, and justifying the rebellious act of female adultery insulted the civilized society the elites of Kentucky were trying to project to the world. But these were minor offenses compared with the social effrontery of openly recognizing the features of slave owners on the faces of their slaves. And as the color line hardened in the slave states, a code of silence with regard to the consequences of sexual violence across that line came to be rigorously enforced by society—a code that Littell had blatantly violated and that still needed to be upheld as his writings survived him.

7

THE REBEL

Thomas Bell Monroe (1791–1865)

Thomas B. Monroe, *Reports of Cases at Common Law and in Equity,
Argued and Decided in the Court of Appeals of the Commonwealth of
Kentucky [1824–1828]*, 7 vols. (Frankfort: Amos Kendall & Co., 1825–
1830).

In 1825, in the midst of the Old Court–New Court controversy, pro–debt relief
governor Joseph Desha appointed Thomas B. Monroe as reporter of the Court of
Appeals.[1] The legislature provided no special guidance for this unique situation.
The question of how or even whether to cover the two competing courts would be
his to decide. Clearly, one or the other would eventually prevail, but the outcome
was hard to perceive. At this point in his life, Monroe was just one man caught up
in the great court controversy, but he would go on to become a giant of the bar as
both an influential federal judge and founder of a private law school at his Frankfort
estate. With homes in both Kentucky and Louisiana, his intellectual reach extended
far beyond the Bluegrass. His large extended family and network of friends were
woven into the fabric of the Confederacy. Monroe was one of a handful of federal
jurists who renounced their lifetime appointments and instead gave their allegiance
to the rebel government.

Thomas B. Monroe was born in Albemarle County, Virginia, on October 7,
1791.[2] The Monroes traced their descent from Robert Munro, the chief of the clan
Munro who famously died while fighting English invaders at the Battle of Pinkie
Cleugh in 1547.[3] Thomas's father, Andrew, was a distant relative of President James
Monroe,[4] and his mother, Ann Bell, was the daughter of Scotch-Irish immigrants.

As an adult, Thomas showed his reverence for his Scottish roots by naming his Frankfort estate Montrose, after the royal town where Castle Munro once stood and the last place in Scotland where the "Old Pretender," James Stuart, slept before his long exile in France. The first confirmed member of the Monroe family to step out of the mists of legend and onto the firm ground of America was Thomas's great-great-grandfather, Andrew Munro of Katewell, Scotland (1625–1668).[5] Andrew settled in Westmoreland County, Virginia, sometime in the 1650s. According to some accounts, he was the same Major Andrew Munro who fought with Charles I in the Battle of Preston, where he was taken prisoner and banished to Virginia.[6] The Munros (later spelled Monroe) acquired land and became a leading family in Westmoreland County. Andrew reportedly served as county commissioner; his grandson, William Monroe Jr. (1690–1775), held the rank of colonel in the militia, was a justice of the peace, and represented the county in the Virginia House of Burgesses. William married twice and had a large family; the eighth of his twelve sons decided to try his fortune in the freshly minted state of Kentucky.[7] Around 1792 Andrew Monroe moved his young family, including Thomas and his three-year-old brother Benjamin, to Scott County, Kentucky.[8]

History is silent about these early years, but it is likely that Thomas and his brother were educated by tutors. There were few common schools, and the careers of the brothers betray no educational deficiencies. In 1816 Thomas B. Monroe married Eliza Palmer Adair, the daughter of General John Adair, a Revolutionary War veteran and the leader of Kentucky's militia forces in the War of 1812. Adair had gained fame commanding the state militia during the Battle of New Orleans.[9] The young couple moved to Barren County in western Kentucky, the state's new frontier. Thomas's brother Benjamin had moved to Columbia, in a section of neighboring Green County that would later become Adair County. The brothers involved themselves in the financial development of the region, displaying an interest in the affairs of the Green River branch of the Bank of Kentucky and the Glasgow Independent Bank. In 1816 Thomas represented Barren County in the legislature.[10]

After a "reverse of fortune in 1819," Monroe began to read law, perhaps with the assistance of his colleague in the legislature Judge Joseph R. Underwood.[11] It is suggested that he was admitted to the Kentucky bar at this time.[12] Monroe entered Transylvania University in Lexington in 1821, earning a degree in 1822. In 1820 his father-in-law was elected governor of Kentucky. Adair appointed Monroe secretary of state in September 1823. Monroe remained in office until the end of Adair's term in late 1824. In addition to carrying out the light duties of the secretary of state's office, he made several appearances before the Court of Appeals (a total of thirty-six cases in the 1823 and spring 1824 terms).

In politics, Monroe was a confirmed New Court supporter and even scuffled with the always voluble Old Court partisan Patrick H. Darby. Sometime in early 1826 Darby was indicted for what he called "a little assault and battery" in a politically motivated attempt to cane Monroe—a common way to provoke a duel. Monroe apparently did not take the bait. (The manic Darby has been described as a "noisy, mischief-making demagogue" with "more zeal than brains," and Monroe may have shunned him as a dueling partner, considering him socially inferior.)[13] An editorial in the pro–Old Court weekly *Spirit of '76* called Monroe "one of the most famous relief leaders, who has the credit by his party" of publishing pieces under the pseudonyms "Patrick Henry" and "Jefferson" in various pro-relief papers.[14] The same paper named him (along with Bibb) a leading member of the "Lawyer Faction" behind the relief party.[15] His prominence even inspired the poetic muse of his opponents. A bit of doggerel in the same issue began with this line: "In front was Jo [Desha], George [Bibb], and Monroe," although the author claimed Monroe's name was "introduced but for the purpose of making the rhyme."[16]

The new governor, Joseph Desha, had been elected with the support of pro-relief forces, and Monroe seemed a reliable candidate to replace the late William Littell as reporter of the Court of Appeals. Monroe settled in as reporter just as the New Court was beginning to organize. More of an independent contractor than an employee, the reporter was nonetheless highly dependent on court personnel. When Monroe began his work, he first had to organize some of the 1824 decisions of the ousted Court of Appeals for publication, while preparing to collect the opinions from the upcoming first term of its replacement (the Old Court had adjourned its spring term without hearing cases, hoping to let tempers cool, but it never disbanded). His tasks required contact with both the Old Court clerk, Achilles Sneed, and the New Court clerk, Francis P. Blair—who were at dagger points. Adding to the complexity, once both courts were sitting, he must have known that the political forces backing them were nearly equally divided and that the ultimate outcome was in doubt. His solution was to collect the decisions of both courts, and it is a testament to his skills that, in the end, he was able to document all the decided cases of the era (and to get the secretary of state to pay for the 250 copies of each volume that assured Monroe a profit).

The decisions of the 1824 fall sessions of the Court of Appeals were published in Monroe's first volume, issued in 1825. In his second volume, printed in 1826, he published the seventy-eight decisions of the New Court. These opinions were preceded by a copy of the 1824 law reorganizing the Court of Appeals. As a supporter of the New Court, Monroe came under attack from the Old Court press, especially James G. Dana's *Commentator,* which called Monroe's second volume a "queer little book" of "sayings and doings of the Fungus Court."[17] In 1827 Monroe published his third volume, which contained the handful of decisions from the Old Court's 1825 fall term (when it sat simultaneously with the New Court), as well as the opinions from its 1826 terms (many of them rehearings of cases decided by the now dubious New Court). This volume was preceded by the 1826 act that repealed the reorganization law and declared the acts of the New Court null and void. The cases in Monroe's second volume (later renumbered as 18 *Kentucky Reports*) were thus deemed nonprecedential, which meant they should not be cited as authority in Kentucky courts. However, because this was done by statute, there was some confusion until 1935, when the Court of Appeals confirmed that act in *Smith et al. v. Overstreet's Adm'r.*[18]

Over the next three years (1827–1830), Monroe published four more volumes, for a total of seven volumes. There may have been a brief gap in his service; the 1828 Senate Journal mentions a January 1829 appointment and ratification, so it is possible that Monroe resigned to allow the new Whig governor, Thomas Metcalfe, an opportunity to replace him. In any event, he eventually resigned as reporter when, on December 14, 1830, President Andrew Jackson appointed him US attorney for Kentucky; his appointment was confirmed by the Senate on February 8, 1831.

On February 19, 1834, Jackson nominated Monroe as judge of the US District Court for Kentucky. The appointment was quickly ratified by the Senate on March 6, 1834.[19] Judge Monroe was sworn in at the federal courthouse in Frankfort two days later; he would serve for almost twenty-seven years. At the time, the duties of a federal district court judge were more expansive than they are now. The judge alone presided over the district court, which had jurisdiction over civil cases arising out of federal legislation. However, this was the era of "circuit riding," which meant that the district judge sat also on the circuit court, paired with the US Supreme Court justice assigned to that circuit. The circuit court had appellate jurisdiction over district court cases, but for the most part, it was a trial court for major federal criminal cases and diversity cases (civil cases in which the plaintiff and defendant were from different states). The circuit court system raised the prestige of district court judges, placing them in close contact with justices of the high court. As a practical matter, Supreme Court justices (who were assigned three to five states) could not visit all their far-flung circuit courts. Thus, the practice arose that if the justice was absent, the district court judge would hold court alone. From Monroe's appointment in 1834 until 1837, Kentucky was in the Seventh Circuit, made up of Kentucky, Tennessee, and Ohio, and Monroe was paired with Justice John McLean. From 1837 on, he was paired with Justice John Catron in the Eighth Circuit, which included Kentucky, Tennessee, and Missouri. Monroe occasionally sat with Justice John McKinley, who was assigned to the Fifth Circuit and later the Ninth Circuit, centered in the Deep South. McKinley lived in Louisville and occasionally swapped circuits with McLean or Catron when his ill health forced him to remain close to home.[20] (Federal judges had no defined pensions until the Federal Judiciary Act of 1869, which meant that, despite debilitating health issues, antebellum Supreme Court justices seldom retired. Their colleagues simply made do.)

Perhaps Monroe's most famous case involved determining the validity and scope of Samuel Morse's 1840 patent to the telegraph. That case placed Monroe in the same courtroom as his brother Benjamin, who handled some preliminary matters, and Morse's partner Amos Kendall, an old friend and ally from the court controversy and Democratic politics in Kentucky. The case involved a rivalry between Morse and Henry O'Reilly that was played out in Kentucky. In 1847 Morse convinced the General Assembly of Kentucky to pass an act for the construction and protection of Morse telegraph lines from Maysville, Kentucky, to Nashville, Tennessee, connecting Louisville, Frankfort, Lexington, Bardstown, and Bowling Green. The Morse Company finished its line from Louisville to Frankfort in February 1848, and in March the line to Lexington was completed. Meanwhile, Henry O'Reilly's rival People's Line had succeeded in running a line from Louisville to Nashville, beating Morse. Morse filed suit in the federal district court for Kentucky. The trial began in Louisville on August 24, 1848, with Judge Thomas Monroe presiding. On Saturday, September 9, the sixteenth day of the trial, Judge Monroe delivered his opinion, ruling that O'Reilly's telegraph was an infringement on Morse's patent and granting an injunction on the People's Line. The case was appealed to the US Supreme Court, which upheld Monroe's decision confirming Morse's patent on "combining two or more electric or galvanic circuits, with independent batteries for the purpose of overcoming the diminished force of electromagnetism in long circuits."[21] However, it denied as too abstract the claim to an "exclusive right to every improvement where the motive power is the electric or galvanic current, and the result is the marking or printing of intelligible characters, signs, or letters at a distance."[22] (Interestingly, this is the most cited part of the Court's decision, but it played little role in the arguments before Monroe's court.)

His judicial duties did not keep Monroe from engaging in his greatest passion: the education of young men. Each summer he ran a prestigious proprietary law school at his estate at Montrose, where he trained lawyers from all over the United States.[23] Among his students were future Confederate general J. Patton Anderson of Tennessee,[24] Senator George Graham Vest of Missouri, Louisiana chief justice Edward E. Bermudez, and Henry J. Leovy of New Orleans (who later married Monroe's daughter).[25] Monroe also served on the faculty of the Law Department of Transylvania University, and for three years he taught at the University of Louisiana (a predecessor of Tulane) from his winter home in New Orleans.[26] (Thanks to the railroads, Monroe and his family became a thoroughly blended Kentucky-Louisiana clan.) For a time in the 1850s, Monroe also taught "International, Military and Constitutional Law" at the Western Military Institute at Drennon Springs.[27] Until the mid-1840s, he still appeared before the Kentucky Court of Appeals (which, in this era, was not considered a conflict with his federal judicial activities).[28]

Monroe, a Democrat with strong ties to the South, watched with apprehension as one state after another left the Union after the election of President Abraham Lincoln. Louisiana, Monroe's winter home, seceded on January 26, 1861, and the people of Virginia, his birth state, opened a convention on secession on February 3 (its secession articles were ratified by popular vote on May 23). On April 12, three weeks before Lincoln's inauguration, South Carolina rebel batteries fired on Fort Sumter—the first shots of the Civil War. Kentucky governor Beriah Magoffin sought and received resolutions of neutrality from both houses of the General Assembly, which he formally declared on May 20. However, the people of Kentucky were choosing sides, and both armies were recruiting units from the state. Pro-Southern forces were dealt a blow in the August elections when Unionist candidates ran up large majorities in both houses. Meanwhile, responding to the buildup of Confederate forces in the region that included western Kentucky, General Ulysses S. Grant took Paducah on September 6. Magoffin urged the Kentucky General Assembly to condemn the violation of its neutrality by both sides, but the legislature passed a measure ordering only the Confederate army out of the state. When both chambers overrode Magoffin's veto on September 13, the state's neutrality was effectively over.[29]

With his ties to Louisiana, and with both a son and a favorite brother-in-law editing fire-eating rebel newspapers, Monroe's loyalty came into question. An early August debate of a judicial bill in the US Senate sparked a "long discussion" regarding the Kentucky district court judge's allegiance to the Union. On September 18 Monroe finished his work and rode to the Confederate lines, along with several family members. Passing through Bowling Green on September 28, he posted his resignation as a federal judge.[30] The clerk of the court penned a brief entry in the court's minute book: "Went south to join Confederate forces. This court has no judge."[31] (This would have been a new clerk. Monroe's son, John A. Monroe, resigned as the clerk of the federal district court for Kentucky around the same time as his father.) According to Ed Porter Thompson, a family friend, Monroe had been tipped off that he was about to be arrested.[32] Monroe went to Nashville, where he swore in the Confederate States District Court for the Middle Division of Tennessee: "I, Thomas B. Monroe, hereby declare that, having renounced my citizenship of the United States, I hereby adopt myself a citizen of the 'Confederate States of America,' and solemnly swear that I will support their Constitution and will true allegiance bear to its Government so long as I am a citizen thereof."[33] He passed through Canton, Mississippi, and Marietta, Georgia, before settling in Richmond in October 1861, where he took up residence in the tony Spotswood Hotel.[34]

Monroe was immediately selected as a delegate from Kentucky in the provisional Confederate Congress sitting in Richmond. He served until February 17, 1862, when that congress gave way to the body envisioned by the Confederate constitution of 1862.[35] He practiced law in the Virginia and Confederate courts and also contributed an occasional article to the Richmond press. In December 1861 the *Charleston Mercury* praised a "long article in yesterday's Enquirer on the seizure of MASON and SLIDELL, in which the international law points involved are so indefatigably discussed, [it] is attributed to Judge MONROE."[36] This is a reference to the international incident that occurred when a US warship stopped a British mail ship, the *Trent,* and captured two Confederate diplomats, James Mason and John Slidell, who were on their way to Europe to try to obtain recognition of the Confederacy in Britain and France. Monroe became close to President Jefferson Davis, who had been born in western Kentucky not far from Monroe's former home in Barren County, and he remained a supporter when recriminations grew louder as the war wore on. His wife, Elizabeth, became friends with the first lady, Varina Davis.

The 1861 Confederate constitution provided for a supreme court, and Monroe's name was brought up as an almost certain candidate for a judgeship.[37] Unfortunately, the increasingly dysfunctional rebel congress never passed an enabling act to create the court.[38] This did not stop Monroe from employing his legal skills to the Confederacy's benefit. In 1864 he argued, along with district attorney Patrick Henry Ayett, on behalf of the Confederate government in defense of the constitutionality of an 1864 act authorizing President Davis to suspend the writ of habeas corpus—a very controversial topic in rebel politics. The case came before Judge James Dandridge Halyburton in the Confederate District Court for Eastern Virginia.[39] Halyburton, like Monroe, had served as a federal judge before the war, and he likely would have joined Monroe on the never established Confederate supreme court. Given the lack of a supreme court, decisions of the district courts were final, and the District Court of Eastern Virginia, sitting in the capital of the Confederacy and headed by the respected Judge Halyburton, was a favored venue for constitutional cases.[40] Halyburton was no stranger to habeas corpus cases and had granted the writ (during times it was not suspended) when zealous recruiters had forcibly impressed Virginians who were otherwise exempt from conscription.[41] The attorneys argued the case over several days, and Monroe was ultimately victorious when, "after mature deliberation," Halyburton sustained the constitutionality of the habeas corpus act.[42]

Monroe and his family paid a heavy price in the war, and their fortunes were entwined with those of the Confederacy. Two of his sons fought with the Fourth Kentucky Infantry, part of the legendary "Orphan's Brigade." Twenty-eight-year-old Thomas Jr. and his brother Ben, age twenty-five, both died from injuries they received at the Battle of Shiloh.[43] Thomas expired in a battlefield hospital shortly after seeing his wounded brother carried off the field. Ben died weeks later in Corinth, Mississippi, surrounded by family, including Judge Monroe, who had rushed there from Virginia. Also serving in the Confederate ranks were two sons of Monroe's oldest son Victor (who had died in 1855 while serving as a judge in the Washington Territory). Grandson Winder was nineteen and his brother Frank only seventeen when they enlisted. Frank fought with the "Orphan's Brigade," and Winder served with the First Kentucky Cavalry, "Morgan's Raiders." Winder's active service ended prematurely; in 1861, while scouting for John Hunt Morgan's force in Indiana, he was captured near Corydon and spent most of the war as a prisoner at Camp Douglas in Chicago.[44] Monroe's son-in-law Henry Leovy, the thirty-five-year-old husband of his beloved daughter Elizabeth, participated in a different wartime mission. He used his legal talents to investigate and later try cases of espionage and treason in western Virginia.[45]

The breadth of the Monroe family's participation in the Confederate cause is a vivid reflection of the judge's influence. Sons, grandsons, and son-in-law were all powerfully shaped by him, not only as the family patriarch but as the man who raised many of them, educated them, and fashioned their worldview. Each strongly identified with the South, of which Kentucky was an integral part, as was Louisiana, the family's other home. The violent separation from their beloved Montrose—lost to occupation by Union troops—shattered that world. But the old judge, no matter his residence, remained the beating heart of his clan.

While his family served the rebel cause in uniform, Judge Monroe remained in the midst of political life in the Confederate capital, where he increasingly felt the failing fortunes of the Confederacy. The approach of Grant's troops made Richmond a hard place for an aging couple to live, and sometime in early 1865 the Monroes relocated to Abbeville, South Carolina. It was at Abbeville, in May 1865, that all the various Monroe stories converged and joined with the flickering lights of the fading Confederacy.

Paroled in early April 1865, grandson Winder Monroe and a few friends headed for southwestern Virginia, hoping to find the remnants of their old unit. When Winder heard that his grandfather was in Abbeville, South Carolina, they rode there. "We found the Judge and his family as we expected very hospitable and much pleased to see Winder," his friend later wrote. "They were living on the bare necessities," and the boys added their rations to "their scant larder." Hearing nothing but rumors in the town, they decided to stay put until they knew what was happening.[46] Meanwhile, once Colonel Leovy received news of General Lee's surrender in April, he too headed for Abbeville, hoping to join his wife Elizabeth there. Winder's brother Frank had arrived earlier, and Abbeville became the site of a joyful family reunion. The Monroes' busy home also hosted Confederate first lady Varina Davis, and it soon became a central tableau of the Confederacy's last acts.

Mrs. Davis sent Leovy with a message to President Davis, who was then in Laurens, South Carolina. There Leovy met two members of the rebel cabinet, Secretary of War John C. Breckinridge and an old friend, Secretary of State Judah P. Benjamin. On May 2 the three men tried, unsuccessfully, to convince Davis that the war was lost. Benjamin decided to retreat to Florida and then to Cuba. He burned some sensitive papers in his possession and sent the rest to Leovy's wife, Elizabeth, for safe keeping in Abbeville. Leovy agreed to accompany Benjamin part of the way to Florida; he would then continue on to Pass Christian, Mississippi, where the Leovy family had a summer home.[47] Meanwhile, Varina Davis headed south with a bodyguard of Kentuckians, including Winder Monroe, and met up with her husband a few days later. At dawn on May 9, Davis and his escort were captured by Federal troops. Winder Monroe was sent to prison at Fort Henry in Baltimore, where he would be locked away for two months in solitary confinement because of Secretary of War Edwin M. Stanton's stubborn belief that he had been part of a plan to assassinate Lincoln. Freed in July, Winder would be one of the last Kentucky soldiers to spur his horse home to the Bluegrass.

As the leaders of the crumbling rebel cause retreated southward to refuge, they were escorted by members of the Monroe family, who hoped to provide them with a dignified exit. Meanwhile, the Monroe patriarch's health was failing. Judge Monroe, his wife, and daughter Elizabeth left Abbeville and traveled west to the Leovys' summer home in Pass Christian. Thomas Bell Monroe died there on December 24, 1865, and was buried in the Leovy section of the Trinity Lone Oak Cemetery. There he rested in peace until 2005, when Hurricane Katrina devastated Pass Christian and left the cemetery in ruins.[48]

A

REPORT OF THE CAUSES

DETERMINED BY THE LATE

Supreme Court

FOR THE

DISTRICT OF KENTUCKY,

AND BY THE

Court of Appeals,

IN WHICH THE TITLES TO LAND WERE IN DISPUTE.

By JAMES HUGHES.

LEXINGTON:
PRINTED BY JOHN BRADFORD.

1803.

Title page of *Hughes's Reports.*

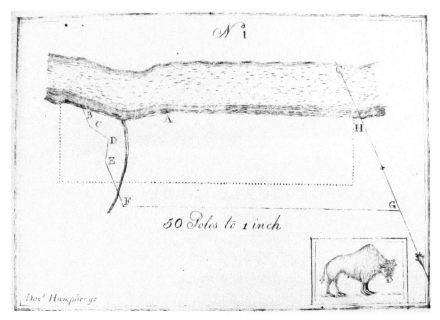

Drawing by David Humphreys for *Hughes's Reports.*

Detail of a fanciful illustration of a bison in *Hughes's Reports.*

Restored legislative chamber at the Old Capitol in Kentucky. It would be the site of debates from 1830 to 1910.

Copy of *J. J. Marshall's Reports* on a desk in the legislative chamber.

Matthew Harris Jouett's portrait of Martin D. Hardin. (Filson Historical Society)

George M. Bibb in his later years, still dressed in the style popular in the founding years of the American republic. (Library of Congress)

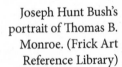

Joseph Hunt Bush's portrait of Thomas B. Monroe. (Frick Art Reference Library)

CHAP. V.

ON THE ORIGIN OF APPLICATIONS FOR DIVORCE, AND THE ATTEMPT TO INTRODUCE A GENERAL DIVORCE LAW.

IN the realm of Kentucky there are many sons of Belial ;

2. And these men in their youth, go in unto the Ethiopian women, with which the land swarmeth, and beget sons and daughters, and these sons and daughters become bond men and bond women.

3. Moreover it oftentimes happeneth that by going in unto the Ethiopian women, these men become sick and sorely afflicted with a rottenness in their reins ;

4. And though they die not, yet fervid love and manly vigour depart from them and return no more.

5. Nevertheless they afterwards marry the fair daughters of the land, and betake themselves to strong drink ;

6. So that whatsoever of virility the Ethiopian women had not destroyed, strong drink consumeth.

7. Thus it cometh to pass that many of the fair daughters of Kentucky find themselves in the noontide of life married to men who have made themselves eunuchs, not verily for the sake of the kingdom of Heaven, but

Page from Littell's *Epistles of William, Surnamed Littell.*

Alvin Duvall. (*Louisville Courier-Journal*)

W. P. D. Bush. (University of Louisville Law Library)

8

THE SCION

John James Marshall (1785–1846)

John J. Marshall, *Reports of Cases at Law and in Equity Argued and Decided in the Court of Appeals of the Commonwealth of Kentucky: Containing the Cases Determined between the 15th January, 1829, . . . and the 5th November, 1832, Inclusive,* 7 vols. (Frankfort: J. H. Holeman, Printer, 1831–1834).

After Thomas B. Monroe resigned in 1830, John J. Marshall was appointed law reporter by Governor Thomas Metcalfe and confirmed by the Kentucky senate. The appointment was somewhat of a consolation prize. In 1828 Marshall had been one of four men appointed to senator-elect George M. Bibb's vacant seat on the Kentucky Court of Appeals and then rejected in quick succession by the narrow majority of former New Court loyalists in the senate. When the August elections gave Metcalfe's conservative National Republican Party a legislative majority, the senate finally agree to send the twice-appointed George Robertson to the Court of Appeals and Marshall to the reporter's office. Like Bibb, with whom he would later share a courthouse, Marshall was a brilliant lawyer and a promising politician whose career would be stunted by inconvenient political views and the grave misfortunes of uncertain economic times. Possessing both a distinguished name and an onerous financial debt, Marshall would bear his burden with an equanimity and grace that allowed him to remain in communion with an abolitionist brother-in-law and his pro-slavery family.

John James Marshall was born on August 4, 1785, in Woodford County, near

Versailles, Kentucky.[1] His father, Humphrey Marshall, was the lion of the Federalist Party and a muscular voice in all the political controversies of Kentucky's early years. Born in 1760 in the cradle of the Marshall family in Fauquier County, Virginia, Humphrey Marshall served in the Continental Army during the Revolutionary War. With the land warrants he received for his service, along with some shrewd purchases, he acquired a substantial estate in Woodford County. A prominent lawyer, he served in the first sessions of the Kentucky legislature and in 1795 was elected to the US Senate, serving until 1801. In 1806 he was a major force in the Spanish conspiracy scandal, writing some fiery editorials. Although Humphrey Marshall was elected to the state house of representatives and served from 1807 through 1809, his Federalist Party fell into steep decline.[2] In 1809 he clashed with Henry Clay, a leader of the Democratic-Republicans, over Clay's populist measure requiring all Kentucky legislators to wear suits made of homespun cloth rather than imported British broadcloth. This clash led to a challenge of honor, resulting in one of many duels in the elder Marshall's life. Both men were slightly wounded in the only known duel in Kentucky fought over fashion.[3] As his politics fell from favor, Humphrey Marshall turned to literature, and in 1824 he wrote the first history of Kentucky, a contentious rehashing of old battles.[4]

His son's early education likely began in the typical Marshall family manner, with tutoring at home followed by "a varied course of instruction at private academies."[5] John's younger brother, Thomas A. Marshall, was enrolled in a private preparatory school maintained by Joshua Fry in Mercer County, which John might have attended as well. He apparently attended Washington and Lee University (then known as Washington Academy) for a time; he is listed as an alumnus of 1800–1803 in the school's register of alumni.[6] However, by all accounts, John's greatest educational accomplishment was graduating with top honors from the University of New Jersey at Princeton in 1806.[7] Like George M. Bibb, it is likely that Marshall participated in the university's spirited debating clubs, the Cliosophic and American Whig Societies, both of which had recently moved into the "Library," later renamed Stanhope Hall (Princeton's third oldest building). Among his fellow 1806 graduates were James Iredell, a future North Carolina governor (1827–1828), state supreme court justice, and US senator (1828–1831); Samuel Spring, the governor of Maryland (1819–1822); and John Williams Walker, Alabama's US senator (1819–1822).[8] Returning to Kentucky, Marshall read law with his uncle Alexander K. Marshall in Mason County and was admitted to the bar.[9]

In 1809 John Marshall married Anna Reed Birney of Danville, Kentucky. Anna's brother, James G. Birney, would later become a national campaigner against slavery, and he was the abolitionist Liberty Party candidate for president of the United States in 1844. Despite their significantly different political views on slavery, Marshall and his brother-in-law remained close.[10] In 1844 Marshall sent an odd letter to an abolitionist newspaper defending Birney's antislavery bona fides. This episode sheds light on the peculiar institution's tangled ties in the border states. Like many Kentuckians, Marshall had an ambiguous relationship with slavery. Census records show that he owned slaves—at least before his financial reverses in the 1820s—and an 1824 newspaper advertisement offering a reward for a runaway slave lists him as the agent for the owner, his uncle Alexander. Yet he also supported the American Colonization Society, which envisioned a gradual end to slavery. In 1839 Marshall's father-in-law died and left twenty-three slaves to Anna and her brother the abolitionist. After much discussion, the Marshalls agreed to "entirely [make] them over to" Birney, and the slaves were emancipated. Marshall later wrote that he would have opposed this deal if he had not thought his wife's share of the slaves would have been attached for debt. Perhaps this was true, but the story raises a few eyebrows. Marshall was a good lawyer, and even before the enactment of laws protecting married women's property, there were ways to shield a wife's inheritance from her husband's creditors. Years later, abolitionist theologian J. Freeman Clark recounted a visit to Marshall's home in Louisville:

> A young man from Boston called upon Dr. Clark in Louisville, and was invited to take a drive with him into the country to visit some of the plantations. The Boston youth was a member of one of the very conservative New England families who opposed abolition as a fanatical movement, and thought the abolitionists endangered the safety of the union. The first place they came to was the home of Judge Jno. J. Marshall, who belonged to one of the old families of Virginia and Kentucky, Mrs. Marshall being the sister of Jno. G. Birney, after wards a candidate for the Presidency on the Free Soil ticket. As the Marshalls owned slaves, and there were a large number of Negro children about the yard, the young man thought it opportune to speak favorably of the institution. "Mrs. Marshall," said he, "I think our people at the North are very much mistaken in attacking slavery as they

do. It seems to me there is nothing so very bad about it." Mrs. Marshall replied: "It will not do sir, to defend slavery in this family. The Marshalls and the Birneys have always been abolitionists."[11]

On the occasion of his marriage, Marshall was given substantial property by his father and established his principal residence in Frankfort. He is listed among the early owners of the fine Federal home on Wilkinson Street known today as the Crittenden-Garrard House, which was built in 1795.[12] He became an active member of the Frankfort bar as a partner in the law firm of Brenham & Marshall.[13] Robert Brenham was prominent among Frankfort Masons and belonged to Hiram Lodge No. 4, but there is no evidence that Marshall joined the order.[14] In 1831 Marshall and two friends gave Franklin County the plot on St. Clair Street to build its courthouse. The building, designed by Gideon Shryock, was dedicated in 1834.[15]

In 1815 and 1816 Marshall represented Franklin County in the Kentucky house of representatives.[16] In 1817, however, he was caught up in the controversy over lieutenant governor Gabriel Slaughter's succession to the governorship after George Madison's untimely death. The appointment of John Pope as secretary of state had revived public anger against the Federalists, who were reviled because of their opposition to the War of 1812. Pope was not a Federalist, but as a US senator he had voted against the war. Capitalizing on the public mood, George M. Bibb ran a successful populist campaign to unseat Marshall, the one genuine Federalist who was pulled into the controversy.[17] The setback for Marshall was minor; in 1820 he was elected to a four-year term in the state senate, having just reached the qualifying age for that office.[18]

The results of the Panic of 1819 were soon felt in the legislature, and although he supported the abolition of debtors' prison, Marshall was a staunch opponent of all other debt-relief measures. This was true even though he was burdened by debt issues of his own. A claim against him by the Bank of the United States is described in the letters of the bank's attorney, Henry Clay, to its president, Nicholas Biddle. The negotiations were legally contentious, but an agreement was reached. On June 11, 1827, Clay reported the resolution of the matter to Biddle: "The arrangement with Mr. Marshall is not finally completed but the execution of it is in process." Clay went on to say that Marshall had conveyed "the Mansion House and other real estate" in Frankfort to the bank, as well as "the dwelling house and its offices adjoining the Mansion."[19]

An unknown obituary writer described Marshall's financial problems in overview, although it is hard to parse the exact timing of the unwinding of his debts:

> Possessed of a magnificent estate, at a period of wild and ruinous speculation, his purse was at the service of his friends, and his name freely attached to whatever paper they presented. His credit was almost as unbounded as his generosity; and his confidence in the integrity of others was based upon the honesty of his own heart. A very brief period brought reverses, and whelmed him in a debt he had not wholly discharged when his life was terminated. In no single instance that can be remembered by the writer wherein he became endorser, did he escape the entire involvement. His powerful energies were at once applied to the adjustment of his difficulties, and his immense estate was devoted, at ruinous sacrifices, to the discharge of the enormous debt devolving upon him. For one firm alone he paid the large amount of two hundred and thirty thousand dollars; and the whole of his liabilities for others, in which he had not the slightest pecuniary interest, have been computed at little short of half a million. For nearly thirty years he has labored without cession to relieve himself from the burden by discharging the uttermost farthing. Even his salary, after his appointment to the bench, was subjected to the payment of obligations incurred to discharge old securities. At times his spirits were cheered with a fond hope that he would soon again be free; but he was baffled in his expectations and endeavors, and death at last was his only release. He submitted to every sacrifice, save of honor and integrity, to meet his engagements, and saw, without acerbity, acre by acre of his broad lands, and block after block of city property, pass away for the debt of others.[20]

A conservative at heart, Marshall fought most strenuously against the court reorganization measure. When his reelection bid to the General Assembly failed, Marshall's rhetorical skills were enlisted as a writer for the *Spirit of '76,* the pro–Old Court newspaper.[21] So while future law reporter James G. Dana was editing the pro–Old Court *Commentator* and Thomas B. Monroe was contributing to New Court papers, and past reporters Achilles Sneed and George M. Bibb were penning pamphlets and legal briefs, Marshall added a fifth quill to the battle of law reporters past, present, and future.

After the restoration of the Old Court, Marshall practiced law and tried to settle his debts. He was elected president of the Commonwealth Bank by the state senate in 1825, and in late 1826 Marshall briefly relocated to Cincinnati. The completion of the Miami and Erie Canal in 1827 had caused a boom in the Queen City, resulting in lots of business for lawyers. It was from there in 1827 that he suggested Clay seek the appointment of John J. Crittenden as US attorney to replace Bibb, who had just been appointed chief justice of the Kentucky Court of Appeals. Later, he petitioned Clay (through Crittenden) to get an appointment to West Point for his son, Humphrey Marshall. Crittenden's own son, George Bibb Crittenden, a friend of the younger Marshall, had already been accepted to the Military Academy. Marshall also convinced his uncle, Chief Justice John Marshall, to write a supporting letter. Apparently, the campaign succeeded; both young men graduated in 1832, served in the Mexican-American War, and were later brigadier generals in the Confederate army.

Marshall apparently returned to his home state fairly soon because in 1829 his name arose in a fight between Governor Thomas Metcalfe and the Kentucky legislature over the replacement of Bibb as chief justice of the Court of Appeals. Bibb had vacated the office upon his election to the US Senate, and Metcalfe had nominated George Robertson, a stalwart of the Old Court faction. The remaining New Court adherents had rejected this appointment, so Metcalfe appointed Marshall, who was also promptly rejected. The position remained open for much of the year (two other candidates were also rejected), until a second nomination of Robertson was finally accepted.[22]

In 1830 Marshall was appointed reporter of the Court of Appeals.[23] He served until at least 1833, publishing seven volumes from 1831 to 1834. His reports, along with those of his older cousin Alexander K. Marshall, were censured by George Robertson, who called the reports of "the Marshalls . . . signally incorrect and deficient in execution."[24] From a modern perspective, this seems an unfair assessment of John J. Marshall's reports, which appear to be consistent with those of his contemporaries. However, Robertson sat on the Court of Appeals when Marshall was reporter, so he certainly had an opportunity to observe his work firsthand.

As a conservative and a close friend of Crittenden, Marshall took his place in the National Republican (Whig) Party forming around Henry Clay. He served on the central committee set up to organize a state convention to be held in Frankfort in early 1831 to put forward Clay's name for the presidency. In December Marshall was a member of the Kentucky delegation to the national convention in Baltimore that named Clay the National Republican Party candidate for president in 1832; he was also one of the fourteen Clay electors in the Electoral College. In the wake of President Jackson's landslide victory, Clay's Kentucky supporters drew comfort from the election of James Morehead as lieutenant governor in 1832 (Morehead would become governor in 1834 when Democrat John Breathitt died in office) and from Marshall's election to the Kentucky house of representatives in 1833. In 1834 the renamed Whigs took over both houses of the Kentucky legislature. However, Marshall would not be part of that body; he had decided to return to the law full time to continue his lifelong struggle for financial solvency.

In 1836 Marshall moved to Louisville and, along with his son, James Birney Marshall, founded the *Daily City Gazette,* which supported the Whig Party and the presidential aspirations of Henry Clay.[25] But the newspaper had entered a crowded field, and it soon folded. James B. Marshall would go on to have a promising literary career and serve as an editor of newspapers in Ohio and Tennessee before dying from an accidental fall from the window of a Memphis hotel in 1870.[26] In 1837 Governor James Clark appointed the elder Marshall judge of the judicial circuit encompassing Jefferson County. He would serve as a leading member of the Louisville bench until 1846, alongside his old nemesis, chancellor George M. Bibb.[27]

Louisville was becoming one of the Upper South's leading commercial cities. In 1836 enthusiasm for Texas independence began to swell in Louisville, and Marshall was one of its earliest supporters. His home became a stop for traveling campaigners. Right after the declaration creating the Republic of Texas on March 2, he presided over a meeting in the Second Presbyterian Church where more than a thousand Louisvillians convened to condemn the actions of Mexican general Santa Anna and to welcome Texans "as brothers." His son Humphrey denounced the "military despotism and misrule" of Mexico and raised a company of volunteers to help defend the new republic. While marching to Texas, the Kentuckians heard news of Sam Houston's victory in the Battle of San Jacinto that ended the war. In July a meeting to promote emigration to the Republic of Texas was held, with the Marshalls listed as supporters. (Humphrey Marshall got an opportunity to prove his mettle in the Mexican-American War, serving as a colonel in the First Kentucky Cavalry at the Battle of Buena Vista in 1847.)

It is intriguing to imagine the conversations between the old Federalist Marshall and the old Democrat Bibb when they ran into each other in the Jefferson County courthouse. Perhaps the two able appellate lawyers discussed recent cases decided in the Court of Appeals. Certainly their views had converged over their shared opposition to President Jackson's bank policies, which ravaged the remaining wealth of both men. Standing as surety for their friends' debts, as public men often did, both would lose much property. In Marshall's case, his friends and family believe that "the trouble and anxiety" of his financial matters hastened his death, which occurred in 1846, before he ever managed to pull himself out of debt.[28]

9

THE EDITOR

James G. Dana (1785–1840)

James G. Dana, *Reports of Select Cases Decided in the Court of Appeals of Kentucky during the Year 1833 . . . to Spring Term 1840,* 9 vols. (Frankfort: Printed for the Reporter at His Print. Office, 1834–1840).

After the publication of John J. Marshall's last volume of reports in 1832, the General Assembly abolished the office of reporter of the court, and all prior acts prescribing his duties were repealed. The reasons for the legislature's dissatisfaction with the old act are not recorded, but perhaps the method of choosing a reporter—appointment by the governor and ratification by the legislature—was considered too cumbersome. Or, less likely, the lawmakers thought the prior laws infringed too much on the prerogatives of the judiciary. In any case, the new act gave the judges of the Court of Appeals the right to choose, by majority vote, a person to arrange for publication of its opinions. The new office was not formally titled reporter, and the individual served more as a contractor than an official. The law required that the reporter deliver 250 "lettered and well-bound" copies of each volume of reports to the secretary of state "for the use of the Commonwealth." He would be paid "one dollar for every page, including tables and indexes." The volumes were required to use "letter and paper of the same size and quality of *Hardin's Reports,*" and a majority of the judges of the Court of Appeals had to "certify [that] the work meets their approbation." The act also directed that the reports should contain "such decisions of the Court of Appeals as may not have been reported but which may in the opinion of the judges of said court establish some new or settle some doubtful point or be otherwise by them deemed important to be reported."[1] This sentence would ripen into Kentucky's practice of dividing opinions into "published" and "unpublished" decisions, with the former serving as mandatory precedent for future courts and the latter not being precedential. In fact, for much of Kentucky's legal history, unpublished decisions could not be cited or mentioned in state courts.

With the position of reporter becoming more analogous to that of a public printer, it was perhaps natural that the Court of Appeals turned to a politically attuned attorney and experienced newspaper editor, James G. Dana, whose paper had once had the contract to publish the acts and journals of the state legislature. Dana was one of many educated easterners who migrated to Kentucky to make their fortunes in the professions and in politics. Some set up legal practices; others edited newspapers, which sprouted like mushrooms in the fertile political environment of Kentucky's relief crisis and the development of its Democratic and Whig Parties. The passions of the Old Court–New Court controversy and the polarization of Kentuckians into the armed camps of Henry Clay and Andrew Jackson provided a ready market for sharp-tongued editors, and men like Amos Kendall (*Western Argus*), George Prentice (*Louisville Courier*), and Francis P. Blair (*Argus, Washington Globe*) cut their teeth in Kentucky before taking their editorial skills to the national stage. New Hampshire–born Dana tried his hand at both professions. While maintaining a law office in Frankfort, he edited the *Commentator,* the unabashed defender of the Old Court and of Henry Clay, the Great Compromiser. In 1833 Dana would combine his two professions and begin his service as reporter of the Court of Appeals, eventually producing nine high-quality volumes.

James Greene Dana was born on February 11, 1785, in Amherst, New Hampshire, the youngest son of the Reverend Samuel Dana and Anna Kendrick Dana. Samuel (1739–1798) was a Presbyterian minister who had been driven from the pulpit in 1775 by the Sons of Liberty because of his professed loyalty to the Crown. The former pastor turned his attentions to less sacred texts and was admitted to the Massachusetts bar in 1781, becoming a very successful lawyer. His former Tory sympathies did not prevent his election in 1783 to the Massachusetts constitutional convention and to the state senate in 1793.[2] His elder sons, Luther (1763–1832) and Samuel (1767–1835), were also successful lawyers, and Samuel followed his father into politics, serving briefly in the US Senate in 1814.[3]

James's early education is unrecorded, but he graduated from the prestigious Lawrence Academy in Groton, Massachusetts, where his father had settled after the Revolution. He then read law in his brother Samuel's law office in Boston, "in the Scollay's building on Court Street."[4] Samuel Dana was a leading Boston attorney and briefly partnered with Levi Woodbury, who would later serve in Andrew Jackson's cabinet as secretary of the navy and the treasury before being appointed to the US Supreme Court by James K. Polk. James Dana joined the Massachusetts bar, practiced law in Boston, and in 1810 was elected notary public for Suffolk County. He established an office near the new customhouse to take advantage of maritime business, and his advertised services included the accurate drafting of "ship's papers."[5]

However, perhaps tired of laboring in the shadow of his successful older brothers, he shuttered his Massachusetts law office in 1813 and moved to Frankfort, where "he established himself in his profession" in Kentucky's capital. When Dana arrived in Frankfort, he must have attracted some attention. Although there are no known portraits, he was later described as "prepossessing."[6] Well educated and with experience in the law and electoral politics, Dana was well suited to succeed. His first years in Frankfort are obscure, but his practice was apparently successful enough for him to purchase an interest in a newspaper and for L. F. Johnson to list him as one of the leading attorneys of the 1830s in his *History of Franklin County Bar*.[7]

It is in the field of journalism, however, that Dana would make his reputation. It is possible that he wrote editorials and political pieces anonymously soon after his relocation to Frankfort, but his official entry into the editorial pages occurred in 1824, when he bought a half interest in the *Frankfort Commentator* from Jacob Holeman and was named editor. Dana took the reins of the Old Court–leaning paper in the midst of the relief crisis and would guide the newspaper through that controversy and into the 1828 election and the creation of the Whig Party. Dana would also set his sights on the rival *Frankfort Argus* and its editor Amos Kendall, fighting over political and commercial ground.

When Dana assumed the editorship of the *Commentator* in April 1824, the cases of *Williams v. Blair* and *Lapsley v. Brashear* had already been decided, and the pro-relief faction was campaigning to take control of the legislature in the August elections and to elect Joseph Desha governor. Despite Dana's editorial efforts, the pro-relief party triumphed and, in December, abolished the old Court of Appeals and established a new one, with four members appointed by Desha. Around this time, Dana's partner Holeman decided to start a new publication, the *Spirit of '76*, to oppose the New Court. That decision apparently caused some financial friction between the two men. A later lawsuit between Holeman and Albert G. Hodges, who purchased a half interest in the newspaper in 1826, indicated that Dana had a significant lien on Holeman's interest due to a "divers sum" Dana had spent to carry on the business.[8] The strain may have increased after the new legislature stripped Holeman of the contract to print its acts and journals.[9] In any event, Holeman's establishment of the *Spirit of '76* left Dana in full editorial control of the *Commentator*.[10]

Although the *Commentator* published the serious speeches of Old Court advocates, Dana's editorials used ridicule as much as argument to attack the New Court, calling its judges the "fungus court," the "pretended" judges, or "the pensioners."[11] He tweaked them for decorating their courtrooms with expensive blue curtains and for other alleged plundering of public funds. When Thomas B. Monroe presented his second volume (containing opinions of the New Court) for payment, Dana employed his barbed wit with notable glee. "Sit down and count the cost," he implored, of a "queer little book" filed at the secretary of state's office that "contains Eighty-seven opinions (we do not say *decisions*) of the honors the Pensioners, upon certain matters of law, which they undertook to decide as though they were a court of appeals."[12]

Dana disclaimed any interest in the "fees of the New Court lawyers, who, with all their love of the dear people, don't work for nothing" (perhaps a jab at George M. Bibb) or the fees taken by James P. Blair "for writing New Court essays." That was private money. Dana's concern was with "hauls upon the Public Treasury." With sarcasm thicker than Kentucky sorghum syrup, Dana tallied the costs of the New Court, adding together the salaries of the judges, the cost of new equipment for the clerk's office that was more suited to Blair's "refined taste," monies spent to set up the courtroom (which Dana called the "school house") "to suit the complexions of their honor," and, of course, the cost of Monroe's "queer little book." In Dana's polemical method of calculation, the total amounted to $12,801. This, he calculated with mock horror, came to $147.13 for each opinion "paid by the yeomanry of the country who have no more interest in the sayings and doings of the Fungus Court than they have in the whim whams and opinions of Launcelot Longstaff gentleman."[13]

Dana's main editorial rival was Amos Kendall of the resolutely pro-relief *Frankfort Argus*. Both men were transplanted New Englanders and had markedly similar backgrounds. Kendall had been born in 1789 in Dunstable, in northern Massachusetts, just miles from the New Hampshire border. He had attended Dartmouth and migrated to Frankfort in 1816 (just three years after Dana), inspired by his support for Henry Clay. But Kendall's devotion to Clay had diverged, and by 1834 he was aligned with Clay's foes. Kendall and Dana had both studied law in New England, with Kendall reading law in Groton, the same Massachusetts town where Dana's father practiced. Both established law practices in Frankfort, although Dana's was apparently more successful. The New Englanders even shared certain physical similarities, with both men regularly described as tall and slender. The resemblance was superficial, however. While Dana had a "fair but blooming complexion, full blue eyes, fine teeth and soft light brown hair," Kendall's hair had turned white in his youth, and he was vividly described by one visitor as having such an "extreme sallowness of his complexion" that it was hard for the "superstitious to escape their dread" of seeing him.[14]

Fencing with their pens, Dana and Kendall fought the political battle of the 1820s with boldness and rhetorical vigor. However, the Frankfort pressmen's rivalry was also commercial, as they battled over newspaper circulation, book publishing, public printing contracts, and job printing. One area where the political and commercial converged was the coverage of two sensational murder cases with political overtones. As the rival editors strived for circulation dominance and publication revenue, they helped create a new and sensational crime journalism that would have national implications. The first of these murders occurred in Fleming County and would not have attracted much attention from the Frankfort press if not for the high position of the accused killer's father. In November 1824 Francis Baker, a Mississippi lawyer and newspaper editor, was killed near Blue Lick Springs while on the long trek to his wedding in New Jersey. Suspicion soon settled on Isaac B. Desha, who was seen in possession of Baker's fine gray mare and some of the unfortunate man's effects. The reports from Fleming County quickly inflamed the corridors of Frankfort: the accused man's father, Joseph Desha, had been elected Kentucky's governor that August. The governor's supporters intervened in the legislature, passing a bill to move the venue of his son's trial to his home county of Harrison. That measure did not prevent Isaac's conviction by a jury in January 1825, but it made the case political. Desha's trial and retrial in 1826 were covered with interest by Frankfort newspapers. He was once again convicted of murder in July 1826, and after a purported suicide attempt, his father the governor pardoned him on the eve of his execution.[15]

Both Dana and Kendall sent correspondents to the trials, and Dana prepared a pamphlet recording the testimony from the first murder trial. The trial pamphlet was that era's instant true-crime book, and Lexington's *Kentucky Reporter* advertised that "a full report of the trial is to be published by James G. Dana and James

Cowan, Esqrs."[16] However, for reasons not completely clear, Dana decided not to publish it. Judge George Shannon's decision to void the jury's verdict and order a new trial left the matter in a limbo, and Dana might have feared a libel suit from the powerful Deshas. In an 1826 editorial he took the high ground, noting that while the *Commentator* "took much pains and labor to obtain a report of the trial, . . . its publication, while the cause was pending would not be justifiable—and for that reason denied to the highly excited curiosity of our readers the newspaper summary of the trial we intended and to ourselves the large profit which would have resulted from a more minute account in pamphlet form."[17] In 1825 a Lexington publisher issued *A Statement of the Trial of Isaac B. Desha* by Robert S. Thomas and George W. Williams.[18] Since Thomas and Dana later collaborated on another trial pamphlet, it is possible that portions of this work were based on materials collected for Dana's advertised but never published Desha trial book.

Nonetheless, Dana was very critical of the governor's intervention in his son's case, as well as Kendall's pro-Desha coverage. As in all matters, the two editors went at each other personally. Dana mocked Kendall's efforts "in behalf of his friends the Deshas—*Joseph* the 'JUST' and Isaac the 'INNOCENT,'" calling his emotional editorials "bloated nonsense, fit only for ridicule."[19] Kendall accused Dana of a rush to judgment and was especially outraged when the *Commentator* tried to tally the cost of Desha's two trials. After Isaac Desha's attempted suicide, Kendall bitterly noted, "Mr. Dana may also console himself, that no more public money will be spent in the keeping of this young man. It has been industriously reported that he was living at his ease and faring sumptuously every day, while the Commonwealth was paying large sums for guards. It is now seen that he was not in a situation so comfortable but that he was willing to leave it and trust to the dread uncertainties of the external world." Kendall sneered that since Isaac Desha had been mortally injured, Dana "must now be exceedingly gratified."[20] Dana retorted that Kendall had neglected his purported duty as an "honest chronicler" by ignoring the "expenditure of public money" in the "*relief* of Isaac B. Desha, his connexions, and *their faction.*"[21] (The supposedly dying Isaac Desha left Kentucky, changed his name, and relocated to Texas, where he was charged with murdering a traveling companion. Recognized by other transplanted Kentuckians, he died of an "illness" the day before his trial.)[22]

While the Desha case slowly ground to its conclusion, another even more sensational murder engaged the two editors. On November 5, 1825, the Sunday before the Kentucky General Assembly was to begin its session, Solomon P. Sharp, the former attorney general and a presumptive favorite to become speaker of the Kentucky house of representatives, was brutally murdered in the doorway of his house on Madison Street, mere blocks from the capitol. Because Sharp supported the New Court, early suspicion fell on Old Court adherents, in particular, on hot-headed lawyer and newspaperman Patrick H. Darby, who had reportedly threatened Sharp's life during the previous election campaign. However, it soon became clear that the true culprit was Jereboam O. Beauchamp, a Bowling Green native who believed that his new wife, the former Ann Cook, had been ill treated by Sharp. Mrs. Beauchamp, who was sixteen years older than her eighteen-year-old husband, had accused Sharp of fathering her illegitimate child in 1821. Sharp had denied paternity, and Beauchamp's allies accused Sharp of spreading the rumor that the stillborn child was a mulatto. It was alleged that Cook had agreed to marry Beau-champ only after he promised to kill Sharp.

Darby, described by one account as a "noisy and mischief-making demagogue" with "more zeal than brains," did more than sigh in relief when Beauchamp was arrested; he made it his business to see that Beauchamp was convicted.[23] He traveled to western Kentucky and interviewed witnesses, where he found several who had heard the accused threaten to kill Sharp and collected a damning letter to that effect.

At some point, Dana agreed to use Darby (the soon-to-be owner of the *Con-stitutional Advocate*) as a correspondent in his reporting of the trial.[24] This led to an interesting early debate over the prejudicial effect of press coverage on criminal defendants. During Beauchamp's May arraignment (which Dana described as "A Novel Proceeding"), his attorney, John Pope, moved to hold Dana's *Commentator* and Kendall's *Argus* in contempt for unspecified articles that he claimed had injured his client and "deprive[d] him of his constitutional right to an impartial trial." The motion sought to gag press coverage for the duration of the trial. Darby, seated in the court, rose and claimed authorship of two of the articles in the *Commentator*, declaring that the claim should be against him, not the newspapers. With his typical combativeness, he stated that "he was ready now and at all times to defend himself." Pope objected, maintaining that the motion was aimed at the two newspapers. The prosecutor, Charles S. Bibb, declined to oppose the motion but asked that it be extended to all publications. The court decided that this was a separate matter and set a hearing date in July to decide the question.[25]

This may have temporarily restrained the publishers, but not Darby; he re-mained enmeshed in the case. He was called as a witness and testified that he had seen Beauchamp in Frankfort before the murder. He almost came to blows with Pope after a heated cross-examination. Amazingly, after Beauchamp was convicted and sentenced to death, he summoned Darby to his jail cell and threatened to name him as a coconspirator. Even in the shadow of the gallows, Darby was part of the story. As Beauchamp was conveyed to the scaffold in a cart, he called Darby over and said, "I wanted to acquit you to your face. . . . You are certainly innocent of participation in the murder of Col. Sharp; but you are guilty of base perjury at my trial." Then Beauchamp bravely went to his death. Darby, having threatened, fought, or made enemies of most members of both the New Court and Old Court factions (he was later indicted for attempting to cane law reporter Thomas B. Monroe), eventually returned to Meade County.[26]

The judge was perhaps prudent to limit press coverage of the trial (a decision that today would be considered unconstitutional prior restraint on the freedom of the press).[27] From its dramatic beginning, the case produced a profusion of strange rumors and absurd speculations. George M. Bibb went to the scene of the crime and measured the steps of the presumed assassin before declaring that Beauchamp could not possibly be the killer and that surely a conspiracy by the Old Court faction was to blame.

Dana and Thomas (author of the Desha trial account), "having taken down shorthand notes during the trial," published a transcript account of Beauchamp's trial, which likely sold out quickly.[28] Other accounts soon poured from Kentucky presses. The Beauchamp-Cook faction produced the *Confession of Jereboam O. Beauchamp Who Was Hanged at Frankfort, Ky. on the 7th Day of July 1826 for the Murder of Col. Solomon P. Sharp* and *Letters of Ann Cook, Late Mrs. Beauchamp, to Her Friend in Maryland Containing Short History of the Life of That Remarkable Woman.*[29] When *Confession of Jereboam O. Beauchamp* was registered for copyright purposes, Darby was listed as a coregistrant. "In zealous haste, Dr. Leander J. Sharp, who resided with his brother in the old Sharp home," published his maligned dead sibling's side of the story.[30]

The case, dubbed the "Kentucky Tragedy," had tapped into a deep melodramatic impulse in early-nineteenth-century America. With characters that included an allegedly dishonored maiden and her knight-errant husband, set against a dramatic political backdrop and involving a failed jailhouse suicide pact (the couple drank a vial of laudanum on the eve of Beauchamp's execution), the case was sensational. Reports from the *Commentator* and the *Argus* and the various books and pamphlets produced after the trial were reprinted all over the country, and the case became the subject of novels and plays from authors such as Edgar Allan Poe, the now forgotten but once lauded William Gilmore Simms, and Robert Penn Warren.[31] The topic is evergreen; two university presses released scholarly treatments of the case and its cultural significance in the last decade.[32]

The end of these trials and the restoration of the Old Court did not end the rivalry between Dana and Kendall and the political followers their newspapers represented. Murder and politics had been good for business, and the circulations of both the *Commentator* and the *Argus* had soared. That energy was soon directed into the 1828 presidential election. The New Court faction moved almost en masse into the camp of Andrew Jackson, while most of the Old Court faction followed Henry Clay in supporting the reelection of John Quincy Adams. Kendall, one of the most vigorous Jackson followers, would later form the center of the president's Kitchen Cabinet. He started the campaign by attacking the "corrupt bargain" whereby Clay had allegedly traded his support for Adams for his position as secretary of state. Clay had been an early mentor of Kendall, inviting him into his home and giving him a start in politics, so many Kentuckians found Kendall's attack especially underhanded—particularly when Kendall referred to private letters to make his case. Clay retaliated in December 1826 by transferring the contract to print the acts of Congress in Kentucky from the *Argus* to Dana's *Commentator*.[33] The war was on. The editorial columns of the *Argus* were soon filled with praise of Jackson and attacks on Clay (and occasionally President Adams).

Dana approached the battle against Jackson (and Kendall) with equal gusto. In May 1827 it turned very personal when Dana attacked Jackson's marriage to Rachel Robards. He started by focusing on the facts that were "*literally* correct." "This much is absolutely certain," he averred: "the woman who passes as the lady of Gen. Andrew Jackson . . . was once the wife of Lewis Robards of Kentucky." He drew attention to the "record of a suit [in Mercer County, Kentucky] in which Lewis Robards pled his bill, charging that Rachel, his wife (now called Mrs. Jackson) had *abandoned* him and was *living in adultery* with another man." He noted that the jury in the 1792 case had ruled in Robards's favor, "and a divorce was accordingly decreed to him."

Dana's attack then veered into shocking racism in an audacious attempt to breach the antebellum barrier surrounding the acknowledgment of sexual relations between masters and slaves and harness that horror and disgust to color readers' feelings about Jackson. In a section entitled "Illustration," he proposed: "Suppose some distinguished public character should happen to fall in love with the dirty, *black wench*, in his own, or his neighbor's kitchen, and suppose the gentleman, having fallen in love, with the *black wench*, should emancipate and marry her; and suppose, further, that he should attempt to make her . . . the associate of the respectable females of his neighborhood; and should, lastly, take her to the Federal City, and there introduce her, in a mask, to the ladies of the Presidents, Heads of Departments, Senators, &c. Would such conduct deserve to be exposed?"[34] The attack combined race, sex, and class in an explosive mixture. It is important to note, however, that such frank racism by a person presumably opposed to slavery was unremarkable for these times. What was shocking was Dana's act of ripping away the curtain that hid the slave owner's sordid predations in the bedsteads of his slaves.

The reaction was immediate; Jackson's partisans were enraged. Kendall responded with a spirited rejoinder in the *Argus*: "We do not recollect ever to have seen in a newspaper an article as utterly destitute of all decency as that in the last *Commentator*," Kendall sneered, "which compares the lady of General Jackson to a 'dirty, black wench!' Such attacks and such language . . . can only fill the public mind with disgust and indignation." Interestingly, even in his outrage over "these heartless and shameless attacks on an unoffending female," Kendall could not forget his loss of the contract "for printing the Laws of Congress," which "decency or respectability" required Dana to forfeit. Turning directly to his rival, Kendall observed: "We could almost imagine that Mr. Dana, in a moment of uncommon complacency, fancied himself a great man, and drew his 'illustrations' from what he knew might in truth be said of his own private habits!"[35] Kendall's reply to Dana was reprinted in the Jackson press. Ironically, since Kendall included the entirety of Dana's "Illustration" in his piece, he doubled the circulation of the attack on Mrs. Jackson. It is curious that after four years of vicious commercial and political competition and personal attacks suggesting something sordid about Dana's "private habits"—which could have been a throwaway line or could have been an allusion to a more specific rumor about the sexuality of the forty-two-year-old bachelor—the two men apparently never considered a resort to the field of honor. Perhaps it was merely their New England backgrounds, but it could well be that these near mirror images of the new fiercely partisan journalists considered such attacks "just business" and not worth dueling over.[36]

Despite Dana's efforts, Andrew Jackson won the election. He not only took Amos Kendall with him to Washington but also carried an abiding hatred of those who had impugned the honor of his wife. Without his rival, Dana's *Commentator* lost some of its edge. There was a great deal of readjustment in the anti-Jackson camp as the opposition gradually transformed itself into the Whig Party.[37] In 1826 Darby's *Constitutional Advocate* had been absorbed into the *Commentator* (and that July, Dana's partner Holeman had sold his half interest to Hodges).[38] For a brief period in 1831, Dana left his post as editor, but in October he bought out Hodges's interest and returned to the top of the masthead in 1832. Sometime in late 1832 or 1833, Hodges sued Holeman for default on notes issued for the 1826 sale, and the case went before the Court of Appeals in April 1833; Dana was not a party. In 1833 Hodges founded the *Frankfort Commonwealth,* a leading Whig paper that would bolster the Democratic opposition through the next three decades. (After the Whig Party dissolved in the wake of Clay's death, Hodges's *Commonwealth* first supported the Know-Nothings before becoming a Union/Republican Party organ. In 1864 he received a letter from Abraham Lincoln in which the president famously declared, "I am naturally anti-slavery. If slavery is not wrong, nothing is wrong.")[39]

While Hodges reentered the Frankfort market as a Whig, Dana's politics were evolving. At some point after Jackson's election, he developed an interest in the anti-Masonic movement. In 1826 William Morgan, a former Freemason who had written (but could not publish) an exposé of the order, disappeared and was feared dead. The Anti-Masonic Party was formed in upstate New York in 1828 by those who thought that politically powerful Masons had foiled attempts to solve the mystery of Morgan's disappearance. Sometime in 1830 Dana began editing an anti-Masonic newspaper in Louisville, *Lights and Shadows of Modern Times.* The paper survived until at least 1832.[40] Around the same time, he contributed to a small volume that attempted to expose the Masons, focusing heavily on the Morgan affair; in it, Dana is listed as the author of "A History of Anti-Masonry." As there are no other names associated with the book, it can safely be assumed that Dana edited it from various texts circulated by anti-Masons.[41]

As the anti-Mason movement became a national political party, problems arose with Dana's stance. The Masons had been very popular in pioneer Kentucky, and Clay had joined the Lexington lodge early in his career (although he was never a particularly active member). Clay was planning to run for president in 1832 as the candidate of the emerging National Republicans (commonly known as the Whig Party), the party of most of Dana's friends. While it appears that Dana remained a Whig (Kentucky had no Anti-Masonic Party), his loyalty might have been questioned. In May 1832 Thomas Metcalfe wrote to Clay and informed him of Dana's views: "Dana . . . concurs with Letcher in believing that Jackson cannot be elected. But he thinks [William] Wirt is to be the man." Metcalfe went on to report that Dana reads "many anti-Masonic papers" and is "the warmest & most zealous devotee to anti-masonry" in Kentucky, adding that "his prejudices, his jealousies & hatred of Masonry, exceeds anything of the kind that I have met with." Dana was enthusiastic about a coalition of Clay's Whigs and the Anti-Masonic Party to defeat Jackson. Metcalfe noted that Dana "shewed me [Charles] Hammond's paper [the *Cincinnati Gazette*] recommending the coalition which is so much dreaded by the Jackson Papers [viz] a united effort of the Calhoun & Clay parties, with the anti-masons— which in the end is to result to the benefit of the latter." Dana was wrong. President Jackson was reelected, and Wirt won only a single state, Vermont.[42]

From 1834 to 1840, Dana produced nine universally praised volumes of Kentucky law reports. Leading Kentucky jurist and Transylvania law professor George Robertson, in a sketch of the history of the Kentucky Court of Appeals, ranked Dana's reports among the "most accurate." He went on to say that "Dana's in execution and in the character of the cases are generally deemed the best. Of the decisions in Dana, it has been reported of Judge Story that he said they were the best in the Union—and of Chancellor Kent, that he said he knew no state decisions superior to them."[43] Legal historian Erwin C. Surrency echoes Robertson but qualifies that they are "deemed the best," and "tradition informs us" of Justice Story's and Chancellor Kent's high praise.[44] Robertson was a contemporary of Story and Kent, so his testimony is worthy of some respect, but the source of these quotes has been elusive.

Despite the high quality of his published work, the job of reporter was not so demanding that Dana could not practice law on the side. As often happened, accepting the position of law reporter rejuvenated Dana's appellate practice. He had appeared occasionally before the Court of Appeals since 1824, but of the fifty-nine reported cases in his career, twenty-seven were argued in the ten years before his appointment as law reporter, and thirty-two occurred during his six years in that position.[45]

On November 19, 1840, Dana died while still serving as law reporter. The newspaper notices are silent about the cause of death, but he was mourned as "a gentleman of talents and great personal worth." According to the Dana family history, he died unmarried.[46] A later historian of Frankfort, looking poetically at Dana's outsized shadow over the capital city, summed up his life: "A writer of more than ordinary ability this editor added lustre to the bright shield of the 'fourth estate' of his time in Frankfort. Today on a grassy slope shaded by lofty trees near the Louisville Pike overlooking the town, he sleeps unconcerned by the storms that for more than a century have swept across the valley below him, at rest in a grave beneath a great rectangular limestone slab on which appears only this name—DANA."[47]

10

THE PROFESSIONAL

Ben Monroe (1790–1860)

Ben Monroe, *Reports of Cases at Common Law and in Equity, Decided in the Court of Appeals of Kentucky,* 18 vols. (Frankfort: Printed for the Reporter by W. M. Todd, 1841–1858).

Benjamin Monroe (almost universally referred to as "Ben") is the most elusive member of the fraternity of law reporters. Though he is often praised for compiling one of the best sets of American law reports, there are no published biographies of him, and mentions in the historical literature are slight. Court records mark his service as a circuit court judge and tally Monroe's appearances before the Kentucky Court of Appeals. Even his familial associations are murky. A host of genealogical sources confirm that he was the older brother of Thomas B. Monroe, but so few biographies of Thomas mention this fact that it raises the question of whether the brothers were estranged. Ben Monroe and his brother's sons are buried in the same section of the Frankfort Cemetery, separated by a hundred yards—an apt metaphor for their relationship. One thing is clear: whereas Thomas was an enthusiastic supporter of the Confederacy and lost two sons in its defense, Ben supported emancipation and the African colonization movement (the quintessential expression of gentile southern opposition to slavery), and his son served in the Union army.

Family tradition holds that Ben was born in Albemarle County, Virginia, in 1790 and came to Woodford County, Kentucky, when his father, Andrew, relocated at the turn of the century.[1] Little is known of his early life, but given his later accomplishments, he could have studied at the Pisgah grammar school, founded in 1795, or even at the prestigious secondary school operated by Dr. Louis Marshall at his family estate, Buckpond (perhaps alongside the children of fellow reporter Alexander K. Marshall).[2] Like his brother, he moved to western Kentucky sometime in his youth. While his brother resided in Barren County, Ben settled in nearby Lincoln County. In 1813 he married Cynthia Montgomery, a member of a pioneer Kentucky family. Although the exact details of her ancestry are somewhat uncertain, Cynthia was the granddaughter of William Montgomery Sr., one of the settlers of Logan's Station, located near modern-day Stanford. Montgomery had immigrated to Kentucky from Augusta County, Virginia, in 1779, and he and Colonel Benjamin Logan had founded one of the state's earliest settlements. In 1781 William was killed by Indians at his home. As recounted by historian Thomas Marshall Green, "Jane, his daughter, quickly closed the door and defended the cabin from the intruders, while her sister, Betsey, 12 years of age, ran 2 miles to another cabin" to get help. His sons William Jr. and John (likely Cynthia's father) came to the rescue. The younger William was able to kill several of the attackers, but "John was killed by them, and his wife taken prisoner."[3]

In July 1812 Monroe placed an advertisement in Kentucky newspapers announcing that he would "practice law in the counties of Lincoln, Adair, Casey and Rockcastle." He promised that "strict attention will be paid to all business entrusted to his care" and reported his residence as Stanford.[4] While building his law practice, Monroe was an active citizen. An 1814 law enacted "for the better regulation of certain Towns" named Monroe a trustee of Stanford.[5] Newspaper stories also show his keen interest in the Green River Independent Bank, an important economic institution in the region.[6] Promoting an entirely different area of commerce, Monroe hosted traveling Cincinnati portraitist Edwin B. Smith in 1807.[7]

His aptitude as a lawyer must have drawn some attention because, when Christopher Tompkins resigned as circuit court judge for south-central Kentucky in early 1824, Governor John Adair appointed Monroe to replace him.[8] However, it may have helped that his brother Thomas was married to Adair's daughter and was currently serving as the secretary of state.[9] The sprawling district included the counties of Green, Adair, Cumberland, Monroe, Hart, Barren, and Edmonson. Monroe established his main judicial office in the Adair county seat of Columbia and rode the circuit as its judge for fourteen years until 1838.[10]

In 1840 Monroe was appointed reporter of the Court of Appeals.[11] He moved his family to Frankfort, where the 1850 census found him presiding over a large household, even though one son, William, had established a law practice in

Shelbyville and another, Andrew, had likely moved to Louisville.[12] He held the post of reporter until 1858, publishing eighteen volumes in all. His reports were well received, although reviewers of this era tended to focus on the content of the opinions rather than the execution of the reporter. In a notice of his ninth volume, covering cases from the winter 1848 and summer 1849 terms, the *American Law Journal* stated, "there is a freshness and vigor, and an adaption to the exigencies of a new country, in the decisions of the Western Courts, which elevate them far above the namby-pambyism of worn out minds, ever dealing in, and misunderstanding, and misapplying, obsolete technicalities."[13] In 1853 Monroe coauthored a widely used two-volume digest of Kentucky case law from 1792 to 1853 with James Harlan, the father of John Marshall Harlan.[14]

Like most of his predecessors, Monroe also practiced law during his time as reporter, both in the federal courts and before the Kentucky Court of Appeals.[15] In 1848 he participated in the celebrated Morse telegraph case filed in his brother Thomas's federal district court. Newspaper reports listed him as one of the attorneys for Samuel Morse at the hearing in September to enjoin Henry O'Reilly from infringing on Morse's patent for the "electro-magnetic telegraph," but he was not listed as counsel when the case was argued before the US Supreme Court.[16] Later, he published a pamphlet containing the judicial opinions rendered in this phase of the lawsuit, marketed with "The Great Telegraph Case" emblazoned on its cover.[17] Since most federal cases were not published in this era, the extent of Monroe's federal practice is unclear, but he argued one reported case before the US Supreme Court. *Waller's Lessee v. Best* involved the interpretation of the federal bankruptcy act of 1841 and turned on whether the delivery of a writ of fieri facias (writ of execution) to the sheriff created a lien on property that was superior to other claims under the act. Monroe's claim of a prior lien was endorsed by the Court.[18]

Having arrived in western Kentucky in the pioneer era, Monroe evinced a keen interest in Kentucky history in his later years. Lewis Collins, in his first edition of *Historical Sketches of Kentucky*, published in 1847, acknowledged his "indebtedness" to Monroe "for information concerning [his] counties, for incidents connected with the early settlement of the State, or for biographical sketches, &c."[19] Moreover, Monroe made himself available to the Reverend John D. Shane, who traveled the state from 1838 to 1864 interviewing pioneers for a history that was never published. Shane's material is a large part of the forty-seven volumes of Kentucky papers in the Draper Manuscript Collection at the Wisconsin Historical Society.[20]

Like his brother, Ben Monroe was caught up in the nation's and the state's agony over slavery, and their sons would fight in the Civil War. Many Kentuckians grappled with slavery's inevitable moral and political pull toward national division. Monroe was an elder in Frankfort's First Presbyterian Church and served as director of the Danville Theological Seminary in 1858, at a time when many American Presbyterians were philosophically opposed to slavery—and some were outright abolitionists. The northern and southern churches were heading toward a great schism in 1861.[21] Although the 1850 slave schedules for Franklin County show that Monroe owned five household slaves, he was active in the mainstream antislavery movement in Kentucky, which sought gradual emancipation rather than outright abolition.[22] In 1849 Monroe was elected president of the Kentucky Colonization Society, a position to which he would be reelected regularly over the next decade.[23] The group, founded in 1835, attempted to devise a way to end slavery through the gradual emancipation of slaves and their resettlement in Africa, specifically Liberia. The American colonization movement, which was most popular in border states like Kentucky, sought to balance the antislavery sentiments of persons in the slave states with their fear of a significant free black population. Despite the opposition of African American abolitionists, colonization was a fantasy of many Americans—including leaders such as Henry Clay and Abraham Lincoln—who wanted to end slavery without granting equal citizenship to free blacks. As a result, for many black Kentuckians, freedom was followed by a difficult and dangerous ocean voyage and, frequently, death by fever far from their Kentucky birthplaces.[24]

Promoting colonization was not the only way Monroe participated in the antislavery movement. In April 1849 he was a member of the Convention of Friends of Emancipation in Kentucky, which met in Frankfort to decide the group's official position in the upcoming August election of delegates to the state constitutional convention in October. Kentucky's first constitution of 1792 had, in Article IX, enshrined slavery in the state charter: "The Legislature shall have no power to pass laws for the emancipation of slaves without the consent of their owners, or without paying their owners, previous to such emancipation, a full equivalent in money for the slaves so emancipated." (Antislavery Kentuckians, led by Henry Clay, had failed to remove clause in the 1799 constitution.) Attending the Frankfort meeting were the Reverend Robert J. Breckinridge, a famed Presbyterian minister and educator from Lexington; his brother, the Reverend W. L. Breckinridge of Louisville; and the

"Lion of White Hall," Cassius Marcellus Clay of Madison County. Monroe chaired the platform committee, which hammered out a moderate draft resolution advising emancipationist delegates to the constitutional convention. "Believing that involuntary hereditary, as it exists in this state, is injurious to the prosperity of the commonwealth, inconsistent with the fundamental principles of free government, contrary to the natural rights of mankind, and injurious to a pure state of morals," it stated, "we are of the opinion that it ought not to be increased, and it ought not to be perpetuated." The draft promised that " no attempt ought be made . . . to set slaves free by compulsory emancipation without just compensation . . . and that the removal of the liberated slaves ought to form a part of any emancipation plan." The platform committee's draft then urged that the new constitution (1) mandate the "absolute prohibition" of any more new slaves in Kentucky and (2) give the "people of Kentucky" the "complete power" to enact a "system of gradual prospective emancipation."[25]

Radicals at the convention, led by the Jefferson County delegation, took exception to the draft as being "too indefinite." Earlier in the convention, one of its members had noted that "four-fifths" of the population of the "commercial metropolis" of Louisville was "ready and able" to "procure the extinction of slavery." W. L. Breckinridge offered an amendment demanding that the "slavery clause be removed [from] the new constitution" and replaced with a "scheme of gradual emancipation and colonization." This motion was amended by former US congressman W. P. Thomasson of Jefferson County to state: "provision shall be made for gradual prospective emancipation with colonization." Supporters of the Thomasson amendment decried a "half-way stand" that would "dishearten our friends by its timidity." Instead, they called for a "bold fight." The supporters of the platform committee's draft, led by Monroe, feared that a more far-reaching stance would not effectively engage the voters selecting the hundred delegates to the constitutional convention. "The gentlemen of Jefferson County may be far in advance of us," Monroe argued. "The amendment may suit them—[but] it would destroy us." "Our work must be done slowly," he urged, "and only after a radical change in public sentiment." The delegate elections will be lost "if we raise our banner too high." Surprisingly, Cassius M. Clay, whose defiantly antislavery newspaper the *True American* had been shut down by a mob in 1847, supported Monroe. That year, the pugilistic Clay had fought off six men with a Bowie knife, killing one of them, but here he struck a practical note. Stating that although his "whole feelings were with my Louisville friends," he had to "yield to the maturer judgment of the majority." In doing so, he argued, "we do not yield our principles—we still battle for them, if not in a straight line," then by choosing the "safest" and "best route." A compromise text was ultimately drafted that supported placing "complete power in the people of Kentucky to enforce and perfect, in or under the new Constitution, a system of gradual prospective emancipation of the slave."[26]

The majority's fear that getting too far ahead of the electorate would hurt in the upcoming elections was well-founded. A pro-slavery slate of delegates was sent to the October convention. They retained the slavery clause and added a new section to the Kentucky bill of rights, stating: "Absolute and arbitrary power over the lives, liberty and property of freemen exists nowhere in a republic, not even in the largest majority." (In a bit of historical irony, while section 2 was added "as an attempt to guarantee that no future legislative majority would emancipate Kentucky's slaves," Kentucky courts have found in its language "not only equal protection and procedural due process requirements" but also "substantive due process limitations" on government actions, similar to those found at the federal level in the Fourteenth Amendment—which was promulgated to protect the rights of former slaves emancipated by the Civil War.)[27]

It is unclear whether Monroe's emancipationist sentiments caused him to be estranged from his pro-southern brother and his family. He died in early 1860, before the die was cast for war. His son, George Wood Monroe, fought for the Union as commander of the 7th Kentucky Volunteer Infantry, and during Morgan's 1864 raid into the Bluegrass, Colonel Monroe took command of Frankfort's garrison and defended his hometown.[28] Ben Monroe was buried in the Frankfort Cemetery. He was survived by a large family with connections to the legal profession. One of his sons, Andrew, had been his law partner; another who predeceased him, William, had been a well-known lawyer in Shelbyville. His most prominent descendant was the product of his daughter Mary's marriage to Zachariah Wheat, a former judge on the Kentucky Court of Appeals. Their daughter, Cornelia Bush, "a most intelligent and spirited woman," would become the first woman in Kentucky history to hold state office when she was elected state librarian in 1876.[29]

However, Ben Monroe's lasting monument was his reports, which were well praised. The highly critical Judge George Robertson ranked them among the best, and they received good notices in the national legal press.[30] Vice President Adlai

E. Stevenson of Illinois, who had been schooled in the Bluegrass at Transylvania, provided perhaps their best tribute in his memoirs: in a humorous discussion of a certain hard and unsentimental judge, Stevenson noted that he was "more deeply versed in 'Blackstone' and 'Ben Monroe' than in theological lore."[31]

11

THE BANKER

James P. Metcalfe (1822–1889)

James P. Metcalfe, *Reports of Selected Civil and Criminal Cases, Decided in the Court of Appeals of Kentucky,* 4 vols. (Frankfort: Printed at the Kentucky Yeoman Office, 1859–1864).

The details of the life of James Parks Metcalfe are elusive, despite his success as a lawyer, banker, and civic leader. He thrived as a behind-the-scenes operator, advising both politicians and clients while quietly building a fortune that would take him from his widowed mother's home in rural Carlisle to an estate in the suburbs of Lexington. One cannot escape the impression that only faint traces of his life remain by design, and that privacy was key to his success.

Metcalfe's tombstone in the Frankfort Cemetery marks his birth on December 17, 1822.[1] He was raised in Nicholas County, Kentucky, by his mother, Isabella Parks Metcalfe (1798–1861), for whom he named his first daughter.[2] His father, Horace Metcalfe (1796–1829), was the son of Elias "Eli" F. Metcalfe, the half brother of Kentucky governor Thomas Metcalfe (1828–1832).[3] James grew up in the county seat, where his father served first as deputy clerk of the Nicholas County court and later as clerk in his own right.[4] Horace Metcalfe's untimely death in 1829 left his wife to raise young James on her own, perhaps in the distinctive brick house he built across from the courthouse and that still stands in historic Carlisle.[5]

Metcalfe's maternal uncle, John G. Parks (1788–1862), replaced his brother-in-law as clerk of the Nicholas County court; by the 1840s, he had appointed his nephew deputy clerk.[6] In 1841 Metcalfe was elected Carlisle city clerk.[7] At some point in this decade he read law and joined the Nicholas County bar; in the 1850 census his profession is listed as "lawyer," with real property valued at $1,000. Also around this time, Metcalfe joined the local Masonic lodge. He was apparently a popular and active member and was named senior warden of Dougherty Lodge No. 65 in 1850; in 1851 he was elected its master.[8]

In 1851 Metcalfe married Mary A. Drake in nearby Mason County. Miss Drake's father, Cornelius, was a prominent farmer and a relative of pioneering physician Daniel Drake; Cornelius's grandfather (also named Cornelius) was Daniel's paternal uncle. Dr. Drake graduated from the medical school of the University of Pennsylvania and became a medical researcher, writer, and educator. He founded the Medical College of Ohio in Cincinnati and taught at the medical schools of Transylvania University in Lexington and the University of Louisville; he was the founder of the *Western Journal of the Medical and Physical Sciences*.[9] The elder Cornelius Drake had moved his family from New Jersey to Mason County in the spring of 1788.[10] The move must have suited the family, which thrived in the Bluegrass. The younger Cornelius Drake reported owning $36,100 in real estate in the 1850 census.[11]

With municipal electoral experience, family and personal ties to courthouse officials, and a network of Masonic friends, young Metcalfe set his sights on the state legislature. In 1849 the twenty-seven-year-old Democrat was elected to represent Nicholas County in the Kentucky house of representatives.[12] This, along with his marriage into the wealthy Drake family, set the stage for Metcalfe's rise in state politics. He joined the legislature with a cadre of fellow Democratic politicians whom he would befriend, advise, and follow into the center of power. One was twenty-eight-year-old John C. Breckinridge, a resident of Lexington who had just stunned the Kentucky political world by winning a seat in the statehouse once held by Henry Clay and thought to be safely in the hands of Clay's Whig Party. The other was Lazarus W. Powell, a Henderson Democrat who had run unsuccessfully for governor in 1847; Metcalfe would help him win that prize in 1851. Metcalfe (who was distantly related to Clay's ally Thomas Metcalfe) entered the legislature at a time when the Whig Party was fading and his chosen Democratic Party was beginning to dominate state politics. With the new 1850 constitution extending the elective principle to county and judicial offices, Metcalfe would take full advantage of the opportunity it presented him.

Metcalfe befriended Breckinridge as soon as he entered the Kentucky house in late 1849. On his first day he joined in a quixotic attempt to elect Breckinridge as speaker and stuck with him through several rounds of voting. Metcalfe and Breckinridge later joined together to wind up the Whig majority by proposing a resolution supporting the right of settlers in US territories to allow slavery, just as Whig leader Henry Clay was trying to forge what would be the Compromise of 1850. A strong partisan, Metcalfe spent part of 1850 as an editor of the Democratic organ in the capital, the *Frankfort Yeoman*.[13]

Metcalfe would become one of Breckinridge's political advisers. In 1851 the two men attended the Democratic state convention that nominated mutual friend Lazarus Powell as the party's candidate for governor. One week later Breckinridge announced that he would run for US Congress in the "Ashland district," named for Clay's estate. The victory of the young and charismatic Lexington native shocked the political world. The extent of Metcalfe's work on this campaign is unknown, as he was also working hard to elect his friend Powell as governor. His role as an adviser is clearer in Breckinridge's 1853 reelection campaign against former governor Robert Letcher. In an April 15 letter, Metcalfe offered an assessment based on some early "opposition research." After reading all of Letcher's addresses as governor, Metcalfe advised Breckinridge that not "much, if any, capital can be made" over Letcher's management of state school bonds during his governorship; instead, he suggested attacking Letcher's support for borrowing money to make expensive internal improvements, especially efforts to erect dams to speed river traffic in becalmed or "slack water":

> You will see that he is great in national affairs—in every message [as governor] he eulogizes a National Bank and in his last message (in 1843) he says—"the slack water improvements, I think, must be acknowledged, as one of the most magnificent public works of the 'age'" (!). You see "fossil remains" sticking out every crevice. But don't be too hard on the old fellow, John. He has enough weight, in all conscience, to carry through the hot days, that come between this and August. I would like to see him defend the magnificence of slackwater if the Kentucky River did not wind its crooked way through the length of your district. A system which has cost the state originally over two millions, upon which we pay annually about $120,000 interest, and which yields annually to the state in net profits about fifteen or $20,000 a year—and which is so far behind every other description of "public works" not even excepting a common turnpike road, which is of

much more general use and importance, and pays a better dividend upon the investment.[14]

Later, on May 30, Metcalfe offered Breckinridge three key pieces of advice before the campaign kicked into high gear. First, he cautioned that while it was "important of course for the Democrats to be enthusiastic," Breckinridge should take care "that the Whigs, as a party, be not aroused more than can be avoided." He urged, "Give it to Old Bob [Letcher] like all the world," but do not "assail the Whig Party more than is absolutely necessary—not because they deserve forbearance, but policy requires that we do not offend Breckinridge Whigs, or do anything . . . which might arouse their old party feeling too much." Second, Metcalfe suggested that Breckinridge respond to charges that he was soft on the North (because of various emancipationists in his large and active family) by citing a speech Letcher had made in Indiana. In that speech, Metcalfe noted, Letcher had given the South a "more deadly stab by saying to the North at that critical period that if a contest arose between the North and South that the North would be safe by reason of the casting vote of Fillmore as Vice President." This, Metcalfe suggested, "would forever close the door of escape upon him." Finally, Metcalfe urged an attack on Letcher for not properly overseeing former treasurer James Davidson, who had been ac- cused—well after Letcher's term had ended—of defalcation (a quaint term for public embezzlement), noting, "You have only to read the report of the chairman of the Legislative Committee that the Governor in failing to take bond 'acted culpably' and of the report of the two Whig members of the committee that they felt 'driven to the conclusion that the Governor was guilty of a nonfeasance of office in not exacting bonds of the Treasurer.'"[15] This was a somewhat contrived issue—Davidson had been treasurer for many years before Letcher's governorship—but such issues were the grist of Kentucky campaigns. Newspaper accounts of Breckinridge's campaign indicate that he took all of Metcalfe's advice.

In 1852 newly elected Governor Powell appointed his friend James P. Metcalfe as secretary of state to replace David Meriwether, whom Powell had appointed to the US Senate after the death of Henry Clay. The office carried a salary of $750, and its light duties left more than enough time for political work.[16] The *Louisville Courier* voiced its approval of the appointment, calling Metcalfe a "high-toned Kentucky gentleman." Powell, a widower, was very fond of Metcalfe and his young wife, and he had the couple move into the governor's mansion with him in Frankfort. Mary

Drake Metcalfe served as Kentucky's first lady during Powell's term and organized lavish dinner parties on his behalf.[17] In addition to his ministerial duties as secretary of state, Metcalfe apparently handled some appellate work in his free time—a frequent sideline for Frankfort-based officials—appearing in four cases in 1852 and 1853. In 1854 he resigned his post. Although Metcalfe would never reenter public office, he remained behind the scenes as a member of the Central Committee of the Democratic Party, a party political adviser, and perhaps a campaign financier.

James Metcalfe remained in Frankfort and returned to private legal practice. He continued to appear occasionally before the Court of Appeals and was listed as counsel in three reported cases in the 1850s.[18] In 1858 he formed a partnership with former Frankfort police court judge Lysander Hord, establishing a law office on St. Clair Street, within eyeshot of the capitol.[19] His law practice (and perhaps his management of his wife's fortune) was apparently successful. The 1860 census shows him living on Wilkinson Street in the city's oldest and most prestigious district and owning real and personal property valued at $55,000 (more than $1 million in today's dollars).[20] Among his neighbors was Whig stalwart Orlando Brown; his father, John Brown, was a founder of Frankfort and one of its richest men. In 1835 John Brown had divided his property between his two sons, giving his historic home, Liberty Hall, to his older son, Mason, and commissioning architect Gideon Shryock to design a house for Orlando. Shryock had also designed the state capitol as well as the Bank of the United States building in Louisville, and his Orlando Brown House is still recognized as one of Kentucky's finest private homes.[21] Another neighbor was Dr. Hugh Rodman, a wealthy physician. Rodman's son, John, would later become the reporter for the state-run *Kentucky Reports*.

In 1859 Metcalfe was appointed reporter for the Kentucky Court of Appeals. He remained in that position through 1864, publishing four volumes that attracted neither criticism nor praise. After sending his fourth volume to press, Metcalfe resigned as reporter. He appeared before the Court of Appeals a few more times between 1867 and 1869, but sometime during this period he relocated to Fayette County, where he was listed in the 1870 census as a farmer with a sizable amount of money and movable property. The quintessential nineteenth-century dream was to acquire an estate, and it is possible that this property was the "magnificent farm of the Hon. J. P. Metcalfe" that was sold in 1871 to William Temple Withers, a former Confederate general who had returned to Kentucky after briefly practicing law in Mississippi. Withers renamed it Fairlawn and made it one of the leading breeding farms for trotting stock.[22] Metcalfe soon acquired a home in Lexington; the 1875 city directory has him living on the northeast corner of Maxwell and Limestone Streets, where he would remain until the last year of his life. That residence—perhaps lost to the expansion of the University of Kentucky hospital—was apparently impressive enough to deserve a news story when the "handsome building and very beautiful grounds" were sold in 1889 for the "pretty long sum" of $12,000. The reporter noted that the price "was cheap" because the house was "one of the most beautiful residences in the city."[23]

Though still occasionally referred to as a lawyer, Metcalfe spent the rest of his working life in banking and investment.[24] He was the founding president of the National Exchange Bank from 1878 until at least 1881.[25] The 1888 Lexington city directory gives him the picturesque designation "capitalist," and from all accounts, he was a successful one.[26] There is no evidence that Metcalfe was active in politics, but he did establish himself as an important civic leader. In 1880 he chaired a citizens' meeting to raise public contributions for a bid to attract the planned state agricultural and mechanical college to Lexington.[27] Metcalfe was part of the first Board of Visitors of the college—which would later be known as the University of Kentucky—along with Colonel W. C. P. Breckinridge (a cousin of his friend John). The cornerstone was laid in October 1880 by the Grand Lodge of Masons, something that no doubt pleased Metcalfe, who was described (perhaps inexactly) as a member of "one of Lexington's Masonic families."[28]

In 1888 Metcalfe sold his home on Limestone Street and moved to Detroit, Michigan, with his teenaged daughter Lillian. She would later shock society by participating in a "double runaway marriage" in Cincinnati in 1890. Along with another young couple, Lillian eloped with Joseph D. Armstrong, the son of the sheriff for Bourbon County, Kentucky. (Perhaps she was emulating her older sister, Elizabeth, who was married to Lexington police chief John McD. Ross. Ross would later be known as the police officer who arrested Caleb Powers, the presumed assassin of Governor William Goebel.) Metcalfe's sudden move north was likely health related; on July 15, 1889, Metcalfe died at the "residence of his son-in-law" in Detroit, leaving behind a substantial estate.[29] He was buried in the Frankfort Cemetery.[30]

12

THE COPPERHEAD

Alvin Duvall (1813–1891)

Alvin Duvall, *Reports of Selected Civil and Criminal Cases Decided in the Court of Appeals of Kentucky,* 2 vols. (Frankfort: Printed at the Public Printing Office, Osbourne & Co., 1865–1867).

In 1865 Alvin Duvall was appointed by the Court of Appeals as its law reporter. Duvall the man—lawyer, judge, and politician—would forever be dwarfed by Duvall the symbol—the martyr who was barred from running for a seat on the Court of Appeals in 1864 but returned as the triumphant figurehead of the pro-Confederate wing of the Democratic Party in 1866 when he was elected clerk of the Court of Appeals. That victory—the high point of his career—would inaugurate decades of control by former Confederates and, ironically, make it nearly impossible for men like Duvall, who had remained loyal to the Union during the war, to be elected to high office in Kentucky.

Duvall was born in 1813 to a lineage so prolific that both president Barack Obama and former vice president Dick Cheney can trace their ancestry to its pro-genitor, Mareen Duvall.[1] "The Emigrant," as he is known to the genealogists who encounter him in countless family trees, arrived from France in the seventeenth century, fleeing persecution as a Protestant. Although the early Duvalls settled in Maryland, Alvin's grandfather Cornelius (Mareen's grandson) and grandmother Keziah (a Mareen descendant through a collateral line) moved to Kentucky in 1791 and settled in Scott County. Cornelius became a successful farmer and entered the sparse county records as a surveyor and road builder; in 1792 he received a bounty for killing five wolves. When the Second Great Awakening arrived in Kentucky, he became a Baptist and served as a deacon in that denomination's first church in Scott County. Following the lineage's prolific nature, Cornelius and Keziah had at least five sons and three daughters. One of the sons, John, became a leading member of the Scott County gentry. During the War of 1812 he was commissioned a captain in the Kentucky militia and apparently saw combat; in 1850 he sought a land warrant for veterans. He is listed as a justice of the peace in records from 1833 (but could have been appointed earlier) and represented Scott County in the state house of representatives in 1827. In 1839 he became county sheriff. John and his wife, the former Jane Branham, had ten children; among them was Alvin, born just days before his father accepted his captain's commission.[2]

Young Duvall's early life in Scott County goes unremarked in the sources, but one can assume a traditional education in the common schools. He later graduated with honors in classics and English literature from Georgetown College, Kentucky's first Baptist institution of higher learning. Duvall read law with future governor James F. Robinson and entered Transylvania University, where he took courses in law and government. A dozen years older than Duvall, Robinson was a close friend and mentor. Robinson also graduated from the Transylvania Law Department and entered politics as a Whig in 1851, when he was elected to the state senate; he would return to that same body in 1861 as a Democrat. (The Civil War would influence Robinson's political life, as it did Duvall's. Robinson became governor in 1862 in a singular way. The sitting executive, Beriah Magoffin, was ill suited to be a wartime governor in a Unionist state, and the solidly pro-Union legislature thought him unduly sympathetic to the Confederacy and challenged him at every turn. Rendered ineffective, Magoffin agreed to resign, but only if his fellow Democrat Robinson—who was acceptable to all parties—took his place. The office of lieutenant governor was vacant, so the speaker of the senate—next in the line of succession—resigned, and Robinson was elected in his place. Magoffin then resigned, and Robinson took the oath as governor—likely from the chief justice of the Court of Appeals, Alvin Duvall.)

Upon graduating from Transylvania in 1840, Duvall was admitted to the bar. Although one writer claims he "began the practice of law in partnership with John C. Breckinridge," that is either confusion or mythology.[3] Breckinridge practiced in Georgetown only from 1844 to 1846, and always in partnership with William F. Bullock, who was based in Lexington.[4] It is possible that the two lawyers teamed up on some cases before the Scott circuit court. That kind of case-by-case fee splitting was fairly common and could have left the impression of a formal partnership. In any event, Duvall built up a strong legal reputation in Scott and the surrounding region.[5]

In 1850 Duvall won a special election to represent Scott County in the Kentucky house of representatives. It had been called after the death of the incumbent, Richard M. Johnson, a war hero and former vice president of the United States. Duvall took his seat in December, was appointed to the committees on federal relations and the code of practice, and spent much of his energy promoting a monument to the memory of his predecessor.[6] However, it soon became clear that Duvall's preference was for judicial, not legislative, office. When circuit judge Walker Reid of Washington died in 1852, Duvall was appointed to replace him. Although Reid had been a circuit court judge since 1832, the circuit he presided over was brand new, having been formed after ratification of the 1850 constitution. The 1851 legislature had divided the state into twelve districts, placing the counties of Campbell, Pendleton, Mason, Bracken, Nicholas, Harrison, Bourbon, and Scott into a new Ninth Circuit.[7] The change was fortunate for Duvall; the new circuit included the counties where he was most well known—Harrison, Bourbon, and Scott—and the new district seemed tailor-made for him. It was a challenging job, however; Duvall had to ride a circuit of the eight county seats twice a year, holding court each fall and spring in Georgetown, Paris, Carlisle, Maysville, Brooksville, Alexandria, Falmouth, and Cynthiana. But with the drudgery came great power. The circuit court had "original jurisdiction of all matters, both in law and equity," in the counties where it sat, and "all power necessary to carry into effect the jurisdiction given."[8] As one governor later said, "the powers conferred upon a circuit judge, both as a judge, and as a conservator of the public peace, are so unlimited that a firm and judicious discharge of his duties will almost invariably mould public sentiment in support of his judicial actions."[9]

Another benefit of the job presented itself in 1856 when Duvall won a seat on the Kentucky Court of Appeals—more than half of the twenty-three counties in the second appellate district were within the ambit of his old circuit court district or adjacent to his home county of Scott. Duvall became a workhorse on the Court of Appeals, writing opinions in 214 cases during his eight-year term. In 1860 he was named chief justice. At the start of the Civil War in Kentucky, Duvall remained at his post and apparently engaged in no overt acts that were inconsistent with support of the Union. However, as the war pressed on, federal military officials became very concerned about Confederate sympathizers, and Duvall, like many Democrats, drew their attention. Kentuckians, including prominent Unionists, were unhappy with the implication of the Emancipation Proclamation (which, while excluding Kentucky, left little doubt that slavery would not survive a Union victory), and they were increasingly upset with the actions of the military, which often treated the state like an occupied territory. Duvall, who had a number of relatives serving with the Confederates, was publicly loyal, but with spies from both sides listening, his private views were likely well known.[10] However, one opinion he wrote might have given federal authorities pause. In *Chrisman v. Bruce*, a Jessamine County man had been denied the right to vote in the August 1863 state elections because he would not swear loyalty to the Union to the satisfaction of a poll worker. That ruling had been based on a recent order by Major General Ambrose Burnside, who had declared martial law in Kentucky to "aid the constituted authorities of the State in the support of the laws and the purity of suffrage." Duvall ruled that the election judge's decision was contrary to Kentucky law—a decision that did not endear him to military officials.[11]

In 1864 President Lincoln was up for reelection, and the current military commander, General Stephen G. Burbridge, was determined to make sure there was no trouble. Burbridge, like Duvall, had been born in Scott County, and he had attended the Kentucky Military Institute (KMI) in Frankfort. After successfully leading troops at Shiloh and Vicksburg, Burbridge had been appointed to the Kentucky district in early 1864, with express orders from General William T. Sherman to bring order to the divided district, which had recently been subjected to the depredations of Morgan's Raiders. As a Kentuckian who had attended KMI with many of the men serving in the Confederate army, Burbridge was seen as an excellent candidate for the command, but any good feeling based on his local ties was mitigated by the tough measures he took to keep Kentucky from hampering the war effort.[12] In early 1864 Alvin Duvall had filed for reelection to his seat on the Court of Appeals. That summer, Burbridge ordered that Duvall's name be struck from the books on the grounds that he was a southern sympathizer. Fearing his arrest—not unreasonable, given that Burbridge had already arrested fellow judge Joshua F. Bullitt of Louisville—Duvall fled the state and eventually ended up in Canada. Burbridge perhaps expected the Unconditional Unionist candidate, Mortimer M. Benton, to win, but before the August 1 election, the Conservative Unionists nominated former chief justice George Robertson to replace Duvall. Despite the heavy presence of federal troops, Robertson won the election. Burbridge's actions were universally condemned as unconstitutional, and his name was vilified after the war; however, it is important to note that Congress had suspended habeas corpus, and Burbridge's commander, General Sherman, endorsed his actions. It was a civil war, after all, and the spate of postwar diaries and memoirs would confirm that sympathy for the rebels was as widespread as Burbridge feared.[13]

Duvall left Canada a few months after the election and returned to Georgetown, where he resumed the practice of law. In 1865, with the war nearly over and his persecution by Burbridge as a badge of honor, Duvall was appointed reporter by the Court of Appeals. He had published only one volume when he was asked to run for the office of clerk of the Court of Appeals in 1866. He would publish his second and last volume in 1867; the table of court personnel in its front matter listed him as both reporter and clerk.

As Duvall prepared his reports for the printer, the Civil War had entered its final phase. On April 9, 1865, Robert E. Lee surrendered the Northern Army of Virginia to Ulysses S. Grant at Appomattox Court House; less than a week later, President Lincoln was assassinated by John Wilkes Booth. Earlier, the two most anti-Republican factions in the Kentucky legislature, the Union Democrats and the Conservatives, had outmaneuvered the Unconditional Unionists and rejected ratification of the Thirteenth Amendment abolishing slavery. That same assembly dutifully passed resolutions of sorrow at the death of Lincoln, but after martial law in Kentucky was lifted in October, the legislature promptly removed all legal and electoral restrictions on former Confederates in its December session. As the new year dawned, all political factions began to focus on the 1866 elections. The only statewide office on the ballot was clerk of the Court of Appeals, and all parties realized it would be a key test of their strength in postwar politics.

The first faction to strike was the so-called southern Democrats, led mostly by returning Confederates. They were associated with the *Louisville Daily Courier,* which called for a "Democratic" convention on May 1. The group selected Alvin Duvall as its candidate for clerk. Duvall's status as the 1864 martyr of martial law clearly worked to his benefit; his election would be a symbolic negation of that act. Nonetheless, the party platform made a few nods toward acceptance of the war's verdict before turning into an attack on the radical Republicans in Congress. The speeches at the convention were more militant. The correspondent for the pro-Republican *New York Times* reported that "guerrilla looking fellows were conspicuous," and "no national flag was allowed" to fly over the hall; he noted that "all the speeches . . . including Judge Duvall's" promoted the Democratic Party as "the white man's party" and "the only party that can save the country from [the] Jacobin-nigger party."[14] The Union Democratic–leaning *Louisville Daily Journal* was only slightly less appalled by the proceeding, calling the "Courier-Rebel-Democratic" convention an example of the "particular kind of democracy that used to be popular in South Carolina" before it led the "Cotton States" into secession.[15] Perhaps the most important act of the convention was the creation of the State Central Committee; this body would help solidify the ex-Confederates' control over what would soon be simply the Democratic Party. After an abortive attempt at a unified ticket of the three wartime parties, the Unconditional Unionists went their own way (they would later evolve into Kentucky's Republican Party). The unified Conservative Union Democrats met on May 30 in Louisville and eventually selected Union general Edward H. Hobson as their candidate for Court of Appeals clerk.[16]

The campaign was unusually intense, given the office sought. Backed by the Democratic State Central Committee and the *Louisville Daily Courier,* Duvall barnstormed Kentucky, campaigning at traditional political barbecues from Scott County in the Bluegrass to Logan County in the west to Maysville in the north.[17] Meanwhile, opposition papers such as the *Daily Journal* hammered away, calling him a "thorough-going Radical of the Secession type" and floating rumors that Duvall had met with Confederate general Braxton Bragg during his brief invasion of Kentucky in 1862.[18] In July the paper warned, "Duvall men are preparing hot irons . . . to burn Duvallism into your flesh. Fight them with heated pokers."[19] As if the campaign were not heated enough, in August Duvall was called on to repudiate an ugly mob attack in his hometown of Georgetown. A Methodist minister had been severely beaten and almost drowned in mud for preaching in an African American church. (If Duvall did condemn this act, it was not conspicuous in state newspapers.)[20] On August 3 Duvall ended his campaign with a rally at Louisville's Fest Hall. Among the speakers was Clement Vallandingham, an Ohio "Copperhead" politician who had been arrested in 1863 for seditious speech and expelled across the battle lines to the Confederacy. Speaker after speaker "reviewed the history of Mr. Lincoln's Administration," accusing it of "violated pledges, tyrannical acts, and unconstitutional usurpations," as the *Daily Courier* approvingly reported.[21]

The 6,000 attendees at the rally reflected a trend, because on August 6 Duvall won the election handily, running up a 1,500-vote margin in Louisville and leading

General Hobson by more than 40,000 votes statewide.[22] The victory was clearly about more than whether Duvall was better qualified to be clerk of the Court of Appeals. It reflected a triumph of the "southern" element in the Democratic Party; soon, service in the Confederate army would become a de facto requirement for nomination by the party. It also reflected a triumph of the Democratic State Central Committee, which made each county's raw vote total for Duvall part of its formula for allocating delegates to the state conventions that would pick its candidates. The victory also led to the collapse of the Union and Conservative Democrats as recognized groups; they would soon join either the State Central Committee's Democratic Party or the Republicans. When Democrat John L. Helm won the governorship in 1867, his main opposition was Republican Sidney Barnes, with only a meager showing for the rump of the Union Conservative Democrats. By the next election, Kentucky was a two-party state.[23]

Clearly well qualified to be court clerk, Duvall also had time to finish his law reports and even take on a few cases in federal court (a practice then deemed compatible with service in the state's judicial branch). A faithful servant of the white supremacist cause, Duvall represented three men charged by federal officials with "having attacked and robbed five blacks near Georgetown." As described by the *Daily Courier*, "he kindly volunteered his services" to the three men in what the newspaper called an "outrage against white men's rights" by "a parcel of ignorant negroes." The paper was most upset that the "Jacobin legislation" had taken this matter from the state court system, which barred the testimony of African Americans (and thus would have thrown out the case), to the federal courts, which allowed blacks to swear out warrants and give evidence at trial.[24]

Duvall, the man, finished his term as clerk in 1871, perhaps without knowing that the moment of Duvall, the symbol, had passed. He made an unsuccessful bid to return to the clerk's office in 1874, and although his candidacy for the Court of Appeals was touted in 1880, he would never run for public office again. He stayed busy, however, serving as president of the Hope Insurance Company and as a member of the board of directors of Farmer's National Bank. And he remained in demand as a trial and appellate lawyer. He was counsel in 293 reported cases before the Court of Appeals (and 48 before the Superior Court, an experimental intermediate appellate court of the 1880s); he also represented the state before the US Supreme Court in 1885.[25] Duvall was a highly regarded trial lawyer; his name is regularly found in news coverage of celebrated cases. In 1887 he was listed as cocounsel in a legislative investigation of Rowan County circuit judge A. E. Cole, who was accused of colluding with one of the factions in the 1884–1887 "Rowan County War." The feud between the Democrats, led by Craig Tolliver, and the Republican Martin-Logan faction would produce countless deaths before it was over. Cole was accused of conspiring to ensure that no one from the Tolliver faction would be convicted of murder. Duvall's team was somewhat unsuccessful, as Cole was condemned by the investigating committee. However, the legislature adopted the committee's minority report, which exonerated Cole.[26]

Duvall was vigorous into his late seventies, when he suffered a paralytic stroke. He died in the care of his son, Dr. Alvin Duvall Jr., at his Frankfort home.[27] Alvin Jr. and several daughters survived to carry the Duvall bloodline into future generations. The pallbearers at his funeral were a who's who of the Democratic Party he had helped build. Among the ex-governors and judges were several men whose names were preceded by the military titles they had held in the Confederate army.[28]

Judge Duvall was a "small man, less than five feet in height," but he had an oversized reputation as a political speaker. Once while campaigning at one of the political barbecues that were ubiquitous in Kentucky until recently, a listener came up to the judge, perhaps as he ate from a tin of burgoo, eyed him up, and said, "Well I'll be darned, if you ain't the biggest man to be such a little man, that I ever seen."[29] Even more outsized was Duvall's role as a symbol of Kentucky's quick redemption of white supremacy by the southern wing of the Democratic Party. His election as clerk of the Court of Appeals in 1866 was a signal moment in the state's fabled secession from the Union after the Civil War. That tradition led to a Jim Crow regime in Kentucky that was as restrictive as in any of the former Confederate states. In 1906, when the Court of Appeals ruled in *Berea College v. Commonwealth* in support of a law banning the coeducation of whites and blacks at private colleges, the majority of its judges had been elected through a process that included nomination by the Democratic State Central Committee.[30]

13

THE LAST

W. P. D. Bush (1823–1904)

W. P. D. Bush, *Reports of Selected Civil and Criminal Cases Decided in the Court of Appeals of Kentucky,* 14 vols. (Frankfort: Printed at the Kentucky Yeoman Office, S. I. M. Major, 1868–1880).

Kentucky's last nominative reporter was a descendant of one of the state's earliest settlers and at least two veterans of the American Revolution.[1] A Democratic Party stalwart, he no doubt attained the position of law reporter at least partially through his political connections. Nonetheless, he was an accomplished lawyer, newspaperman, and businessman whose uniform and competent law reports would be a model for the official state reports of the future.

Born in Hardin County near Elizabethtown on March 14, 1823, William Pope Duval Bush (invariably shortened to W. P. D. Bush) carried connections to the state's past in that long name. His grandfather, Christopher Bush, had immigrated to Virginia from the Netherlands in 1750; he and Colonel John Hardin established the settlement of Hardinsburg in 1780. The Native Americans in the region contested the settlement of Europeans, and although "Christy" Bush lost at least one son to the fighting, a large family survived. One daughter, Sally, became the stepmother of Abraham Lincoln when she married his widowed father, Thomas. Christy's youngest son, Christopher Jr., was William's father. According to the historian of Elizabethtown, Samuel Haycraft, the younger Christopher Bush was a good citizen and successful farmer who "paid more attention to the education of his children than any other member of the family"; William's success proved "his labor wasn't in vain."[2]

William was named after William Pope Duval, a Virginia emigrant who settled in Bardstown, Kentucky. He was a congressman from 1812 to 1815, representing the region where the Bushes lived, and was likely a friend of Christopher Bush. Duval was a prominent Democratic-Republican and was appointed governor of Florida in 1822. (His son, Burr Harrison Duval, joined the First Regiment Volunteers, a group of Kentuckians who fought in the Texas War of Independence. Duval was killed in a famous battle at Goliad in 1836 that would have been avidly followed by thirteen-year-old William.)[3]

William received his early education in local common schools before enrolling in the Hardin Seminary, then under the direction of the highly respected educator Robert Hewitt. Hewitt was "a bright ornament of Elizabethtown" whose reputation was burnished by his many accomplished students and his successful sons. After graduating, Bush taught school for three years, either at the Hardin Seminary or at common schools in the area. In 1845 Bush was appointed deputy clerk in nearby Hancock County.[4] If he had not already done so, he settled in the county seat, Hawesville. Situated on the Ohio River, the city was younger than Bush, having been founded in 1829 by local landowner Richard Hawes to host the county government. By the mid-1850s, it was a coal-mining boomtown.

While working in the county and circuit courts, the twenty-two-year-old Bush read law and was awarded a license to practice. However, his budding legal career was soon interrupted. In July 1845 President James K. Polk sent General Zachary Taylor to Texas to try to force Mexico to accept the United States' claim that the Rio Grande was the border between the two nations. After talks to settle the issue failed, Polk asked Congress to declare war on Mexico. The start of war in May 1846 encouraged Americans to muster militias and recruit volunteers. In Kentucky, the raising of volunteer units was well under way. Perhaps inspired by his namesake's martyred son, Bush joined the Fourth Kentucky Infantry Regiment and became a second lieutenant in Company F, commanded by Captain Decius McCreary.[5] In early 1847 the Kentuckians were transported by boat down the Ohio and Mississippi Rivers to New Orleans. There, they boarded a ship to transport them across the Gulf of Mexico, but that vessel wrecked; the recruits had to be rescued and put on another ship that took them to Veracruz. Debarking, "they marched under General [Winfield] Scott through the swamps and over the mountains, constantly harassed by the foe, until the heights guarding Mexico City fell before them and they entered the gates of that ancient city."[6] Scott was installed as the military governor of Mexico

City as a final peace treaty was negotiated, and Bush remained for a year as part of the US garrison forces, perhaps using his newly acquired legal skills to assist in General Scott's pacification of Mexico City.[7]

Upon his return, Bush opened a law office in Hawesville and dabbled in "real estate dealing and developing coal mines." In 1849 the legislature approved Governor John J. Crittenden's appointment of Bush as police judge of Hawesville.[8] Later he served as Hancock County attorney.[9] In 1859 a dramatic incident happened in Hawesville that drew the attention of the *New York Times* and *Harper's Weekly*. It seems that a "difficulty occurred at a political meeting" in nearby Cloverport between Cicero Maxwell, the commonwealth attorney for the circuit that included Hancock County, and Thomas St. Clair Lowe, a merchant who had recently established a business in Hawesville. Lowe sent a note challenging Maxwell to a duel, which the attorney ignored. Recognizing this as an insult to his social standing, Lowe declared he would horsewhip Maxwell the next time he saw him. Maxwell was scheduled to appear in court in Hawesville in early March, and trouble was expected, so armed friends of both men attended court. A day after the court session began, Lowe entered the courthouse and started shouting invectives at Maxwell, who, at some point in the confrontation, drew a pistol and shot at Lowe. Lowe returned fire, and more than a hundred shots followed as friends of both men joined in. One man was killed and several were injured, including Lowe, who was captured and jailed. The next day a mob forced its way into the jail and opened fire on Lowe, "literally riddling his body" with bullets. A grand jury later found no grounds for indictment. While Bush apparently played no part in the "Hawesville Affray," it is hard to imagine he could have ignored this event occurring outside his workplace.[10]

In 1853 Bush was elected as a Whig to a two-year term in the Kentucky house of representatives; he served again from 1861 to 1863 as a Democrat. Bush's entry into politics brought him to Frankfort more often, but he retained his connection to Hancock County. In 1860 he purchased a 600-acre farm near Lewisport and continued to add to his real estate holdings in the county and elsewhere in western Kentucky. In 1863, after his term in the legislature ended, he purchased a home in Frankfort and apparently divided his time between Lewisport and the capital.

Sometime after the Whig Party collapsed in the 1850s, Bush began to ally himself with the Democratic Party. Nonetheless, when the Civil War began, Bush remained in the state, identifying as a Union Democrat. After being elected to the Kentucky house in 1861, he avoided controversy, serving on the relatively unexciting committees dealing with revised statutes and claims against the state. One issue that interested Bush was Union recruiting in his native county. Federal recruitment had gone well in Kentucky at the beginning of the war, but by 1862, the flow of volunteers had stagnated. In July Congress passed an act threatening a draft for states that fell short of their quotas of volunteers. As he told the *Hancock Messenger* in 1866, Bush had discovered duplicate names on the rolls of eligible men for Hancock County, as well as the names of dead men and those who had already enlisted in the Union or rebel army. He decided to go to Washington with George H. Yeaman of neighboring Daviess County to try to get the rolls corrected (thus reducing Hancock's share of the quota). According to later accounts, Bush met with President Lincoln and "showed the injustice and proved that Kentucky had already given its proper quota." This was a bit of exaggeration, as Bush was representing only his region, not the whole state.[11]

As the war ground on, the former Whig became a Democratic Party leader, serving as an officer of the 1863 state Democratic convention.[12] As Kentucky prepared for elections in August 1865, feelings were running high because of heavy-handed actions by military officials during the war. General John M. Palmer, the military governor of Kentucky, warned that "some of the bitterest 'stay-at-home rebels'" were being run for office in Hancock" and other counties.[13] Among these "rebels" was Bush, who won another term as Hancock's representative in an election that swept Democrats and their allies into power, to the dismay of Palmer and Unionists in Kentucky. Led by former governor John L. Helm, who had been elected to the state senate as a Democrat, Bush and his friends in the legislature set about removing all impediments to former rebels and passed resolutions opposing the application of the newly ratified Thirteenth Amendment to Kentucky.

Later Bush became involved in contentious struggles to reorganize the Democratic Party. Its ranks had swelled with former Confederates, which troubled those in the party who had remained loyal. In an 1866 letter to the *Louisville Courier,* Bush supported the May convention called by the pro-Confederacy *Courier* and called on the Union and Conservatives to scrap their planned convention later in the month.[14] Bush offered himself as a candidate for clerk of the Court of Appeals but came in a distant second to Alvin Duvall in the balloting. In 1867 Bush's name was floated at the Democratic state convention as a candidate for lieutenant governor, but the delegates eventually nominated John W. Stevenson as Helm's running mate. That was fortunate for Stevenson, as Helm died five days into his term. Ultimately, the pro-Confederate faction took control of the party, and with the exception of "stay-at-home rebels" like Bush, Helm, and Stevenson, the future of the Democratic Party rested with veterans of the Lost Cause.

In 1868 Bush was appointed the law reporter of the Court of Appeals, replacing the newly elected clerk of the court, Alvin Duvall. Politically well connected and with substantial business experience, the Hancock County lawyer was a good choice for what had evolved into a position that was as much management as editorial. The fourteen volumes of reports he published were uniform, well printed, and accurate. In fact, the high quality of *Bush's Reports* might have marked the death knell of the nominative law reporter, as they demonstrated how a system of official state reporting should operate. When viewed on a library shelf, the transition from *Bush's Reports* to the state-published *Kentucky Reports* is seamless. And, given the variety of other business activities Bush carried on during his decade as law reporter, the position had become a part-time job at best and a sinecure at worst when held by a competent manager. After publishing five volumes in Frankfort, in 1870 Bush moved printing operations to the John P. Morton Company in Louisville, the first time law reports were printed in Kentucky's largest city.

While working as reporter, Bush built up a healthy law practice in Frankfort. Although he appeared only once before the Court of Appeals before 1868, in his twelve years as reporter, Bush argued at least 68 reported cases before the court (out of a career total of 154 high court appearances and another 41 before the Superior Court, a short-lived intermediate appellate court).[15] The 1870 census revealed a wealthy man with a large household. Bush's real estate was valued at $50,000, and he had a personal fortune of $8,000. His wife, Carrie, had reported real estate valued at $2,000. In addition to seven children ranging in age from eight months to twelve years, Carrie's two younger sisters lived with the family (both women reported $2,000 in real property and $1,500 in personal property). The family employed four servants: a black couple, Jack and Sarah Bryant, and two Irish maids, teenagers Alice and Mary Connor. The family lived in a large Greek Revival house on the corner of Washington and Main Streets that had once been owned by Jacob Swigert. Bush had purchased the house from E. H. Taylor Jr., founder of the Old Taylor Distillery. The house now serves as headquarters of the Kentucky Heritage Council.[16] Among Bush's assets were landholdings near Uniontown that had grown to 400 acres. In 1899 he would sell the property to the new Kentucky Coal, Coke

& Mining Company for $60,000 in cash in what was described as the "biggest land sale made in Kentucky in recent years."[17]

While Bush was serving as reporter, the Court of Appeals suffered its greatest tragedy: the assassination of a sitting member of the court. On March 26, 1879, Judge Milton Elliott and fellow jurist Thomas Hines had just left the Old State House on Broadway and were walking down Ann Street in front of the Capitol Hotel, where they encountered Thomas Buford. Elliott had ruled against Buford's late sister in a case involving the sale of her property to satisfy a debt of $20,000. Buford shot Elliott in the chest with a double-barreled shotgun; he died instantly. In the trial that followed, Buford was found not guilty by reason of insanity and was sent to the Central Kentucky Insane Asylum in Anchorage (he escaped briefly to Indiana in 1882 but died in the asylum in 1885). Bush was a pallbearer at Elliott's funeral and helped arrange for all Frankfort shops to be closed that day.[18] Apparently, a question later arose over whether the normally four-judge Court of Appeals could sit with only three judges. Bush published a scholarly article in the *Courier-Journal* in which he demonstrated that this had actually happened three times since the 1850 constitution (although once it had occurred during a recess). He also carefully counted the reported decisions issued by the three-judge panels, noting that no one had ever doubted the authority of these opinions. Finally, he analyzed the judicial article of the state constitution, showing conclusively that a quorum of three judges was a valid court.[19]

Bush ended his service as law reporter in 1880. The legislature had eliminated the position of reporter of the Court of Appeals in 1878, but out of deference, the law became effective only after Bush retired. He returned to the practice of law and joined his son, Finlay F. Bush, on the editorial board of the *Kentucky Law Reporter*. The publication described itself as a "Monthly Magazine, Devoted to the Interests of the Legal Profession at Large and Particularly of the Kentucky Bar," but it acted mainly as an "advance sheet," reporting leading cases of the Court of Appeals and the unpublished opinions of other Kentucky courts. In 1888 or 1889 Bush moved to Louisville. Finlay had already relocated there in 1883 to practice law in the state's commercial center.

In the winter of 1899 Bush's health was seriously endangered by a "case of the grip . . . from which he never fully recovered and which forced him to abandon the practice of law." Influenza, or the grippe, was pandemic in Europe that year, and Bush may have contracted an unusually deadly strain. The *Courier-Journal* posted a short notice in 1901 to report that Bush was improving from a near-fatal illness. In June 1904 he succumbed at age eighty-one to the "infirmities of age" at his home on Sixth Street. He was surrounded by his large family, which had been assembled during his decline. Bush's funeral took place at the Broadway Methodist Church, and he was buried alongside his wife, who had died seven years earlier, in the large family plot at Louisville's Cave Hill Cemetery.[20]

CONCLUSION

By the late 1870s, Kentucky legislators recognized that the system developed by the nominative law reporters had become so regularized that it could be absorbed into the (still undersized) machinery of state government. In 1878 a new law was passed that put the printing of the reports in the hands of the public printer and retained copyright for the state. The Court of Appeals was still empowered to name a court reporter to collect and index the decisions, but he was paid a fixed salary of $1,800, and his duties were confined to preparing the manuscript for the state printer. Perhaps out of deference to Bush, the law took effect "from and after the term of office of the present Reporter of the Court of Appeals."[1] In 1893 additional legislation further regularized the printing and distribution of reports.[2] The era of the independent nominative reporter was over.

The existing nominative reports (including the much-criticized *Sneed's Decisions* and the legally questionable second volume produced by Thomas B. Monroe) were renumbered volumes 1–77 of the new *Kentucky Reports*. As the bindings of circulating copies of older volumes such as "1 Bibb" and "3 B. Mon." wore out, they were frequently rebound with only the *Kentucky Reports* name and number on the spine. Although the name of the person presiding over the new official state reports appeared in small print on the labels of the first few printed volumes, *Kentucky Reports* soon assumed the nature of anonymous government documents like *Kentucky Acts*.

By this time, copies of the first editions of the early volumes had become rare, and reprint editions were already on the market. In 1850 H. W. Derby & Company of Cincinnati issued a new edition of the first thirty-five reports, which received "well-deserved praise" by reviewers. The new edition was "printed in the best style," without abridgment, and "bound in a superior manner." Advertisements touted that the price was one-third that of the first edition, "which for some time has been out of print."[3] Derby's successor, Robert Clarke & Company, reissued the reports in the 1870s, and in 1898 it announced a joint venture with Louisville's John P. Morton

Company and Geo. C. Fetter Printing Company to issue a "complete standard set of the Kentucky Reports up to Vol. 100 limited to 250 sets." The "century edition," as it was known, would be "uniform in size and appearance," with "many of the volumes printed from the original copyright plates owned by the John P. Morton Co. and the Robert Clarke Co."[4] These new editions smoothed out variations between the reports; for instance, the unusual quarto volume of *Hughes's Reports* was reset in a more standard octavo size, and its beautiful plats were plainly redrawn. The new editions of Hughes and Hardin sometimes condensed the type, leaving page citations slightly out of skew with earlier editions.

As the nineteenth century waned, the regional legal publishing industry experienced pressure from national publishers. John P. Morton, which had printed *Bush's Reports* and reprint editions of *Kentucky Reports,* as well as legal digests and treatises, began to retreat from the legal field, concentrating instead on the literary and education markets.[5] (It nonetheless kept up its job-printing business, and its descendant, Westerfield-Bonte, is one of the last places in Kentucky that prints legal briefs in the old six-by-nine-inch format.)[6] The law publishing activities of Robert Clarke & Company took a similar course.[7] The industrial age was beginning, and it demanded a new kind of reporter. As state appellate courts began to see new kinds of lawsuits spawned by the rise of the factory, the railroad, and big capital, they increasingly looked to other states to see how they dealt with these novel cases of tort and nuisance. The national and regional reporters filled this need. One such work was the "Trinity Series" by San Francisco law publisher Bancroft-Whitney Company, which included *American Decisions* (covering opinions from 1760 to 1869), *American Reports* (1868–1887), and *American State Reports* (1886–1911). The series' creators carefully selected leading state court decisions from around the country. In 1888 the Rochester, New York–based Lawyers Co-operative Publishing Company continued the tradition of publishing selected decisions from state appellate courts with its *Lawyer's Reports Annotated.* In 1919 it was renamed the *American Law Reports* and ultimately became known as the *ALR.* In addition, regional reporters that published opinions of adjacent states entered the market. Bancroft published a *West Coast Reporter;* Lawyers Co-operative had the *New England, Central,* and *Western Reporters;* and Wm. Gould & Company published the *Eastern Reporter.*

But John B. West had a different idea: he wanted to publish the decisions of *all* American appellate courts in one service and provide lawyers with the tools they needed to find precedents. In less than two decades he would do so, rendering all other reporters superfluous. West's career in legal publishing began quietly in St. Paul, Minnesota, with the 1876 publication of *The Syllabi,* a work designed to solve a problem common to all state and commercial reporters: their slow publication schedules. The weekly news sheet gave lawyers "prompt and reliable intelligence" on the legal precedents decided in a jurisdiction.[8] The success of the *Syllabi* spurred the creation of the *North Western Reporter,* which published all current decisions from Iowa, Minnesota, Michigan, Nebraska, Wisconsin, and the Dakota Territory; its bound volumes were regularly updated with "advance sheets" of recent decisions. It was followed by the *Federal Reporter* and *Supreme Court Reports* covering federal appellate decisions. But this was only the beginning. In 1885 West's company "made a bold move: it simultaneously announced the tentative publication of four new regional reporters which, along with its current reporters, would give it nationwide coverage." Meanwhile, West either bought out or ruthlessly competed against rival regionals published by Bancroft and Lawyer's Co-op.[9] As one historian noted, "by 1888, the war was over; West had won all." The "National Reporter System," as the West Publishing Corporation called it, had driven all other regional and selective reporters out of the market, and its so-called blanket-method of case reporting had triumphed. The only selective reporter that remained was *Lawyer's Reports Annotated–American Law Reports,* and it increasingly focused on analytical articles (or "annotations"); providing access to cases became a distant afterthought. In Kentucky, West's *South Western Reporter,* established in 1886, was increasingly preferred over the official *Kentucky Reports.*[10]

However, John B. West did not stop with creating a national system of reporters. Building on the indexing scheme of Benjamin Vaughn Abbott, which West's company acquired (along with Abbott's valuable services) when it purchased the *United States Digest,* West created the trademarked and patented Topic–Key Number system, which integrated the headnotes (short statements of the legal rule in a decision) in West reporters into new sets of state and regional digests. Using this system, legal researchers could find a pertinent headnote in a case and use its Topic–Key Number to find similar cases from every appellate court in America; they could also look up Topic–Key Numbers in West digests to do the same thing. The result was a marvel of pre–computer search technology.[11] (Incorporated into the DNA of its algorithms, this system still drives searching in its linear descendant, the Westlaw database.)

With its powerful advertising and sales staff and the era's tendency toward monopolies, West Publishing Company soon absorbed or drove out all its commercial competitors. It also slowly drained the oxygen sustaining the state reports. Heavily subsidized by state governments, the state reports survived in some jurisdictions, but Kentucky lawyers clearly preferred the West reporters and their integration with the West state digests. A 1905 review in the *Louisville Courier-Journal* opined that the new *West's Kentucky Digest* "will render it useless and unnecessary for any lawyer in Kentucky to attempt a similar work for a similar purpose and object for the next twenty or thirty years."[12] West had driven all the Kentucky publishers out of the digest business by 1912.[13] In 1951 the *Kentucky Reports* gave up the ghost, ending 148 years of Kentucky case reporting.

When online legal research tools first appeared in the 1980s, they were severely constrained by the storage and bandwidth limitations of the mainframe computer and telephone modem era. As a result, the back files of case law in the early Westlaw and Lexis legal database services barely scratched the surface of cases published in the West regional reporters since the 1880s, much less those from the nominative law reporter era. Well into the mid-1990s, coverage of state case law went back only to the 1940s. Then, in 1996, Lexis threatened not to renew West's contract to offer the Shepard's case citator database (which Lexis was in the process of purchasing) on Westlaw. West had a problem. Case law citators are vital to case law research. They collect citations in reported decisions, analyze how other courts have treated particular precedents in judicial decisions, and tell researchers whether that precedent has been reversed, overruled, or otherwise diminished in its authority. A legal research service without a citator would be at significant commercial disadvantage, so West decided to embrace the challenge and create its own sophisticated computer program to analyze all the cases in the database, identify citation relationships, and deliver them in an understandable report. The programmers knew that to be competitive with Shepard's, the new service, named KeyCite, had to analyze all American law, and all the reporters—including the nominative reporters—had to be digitized.[14] (Once Lexis discovered that Westlaw was scanning all case law from the founding of the republic, it had to do the same to keep up.) Through this necessity of invention, all Kentucky case law from Hughes through the *Kentucky Reports* to the *South Western Reporter* entered the digital age.[15]

As the second decade of the twenty-first century continues, the triumphant *South Western Reporters* are still being published—even though most lawyers see them only in database versions or neatly arranged in bookcases as background for law firm promotional photographs. The nominative reporters are usually relegated to an occasional footnote or comment in a case or old treatise, but given the twists and turns of Kentucky common law, they occasionally turn up at the top of a results list to a query on Lexis Advance or Westlaw, making yet another generation of Kentucky lawyers wonder: Just who was Bibb?

ACKNOWLEDGMENTS

I would like to acknowledge my dean at the Louis D. Brandeis School of Law, Susan Duncan, who provided both encouragement and research grants; the University of Louisville, which approved a sabbatical that was very valuable in bringing this project to fruition; and especially my colleagues at the Law Library, present and past, including director David Ensign, who has been supportive in countless ways, and Robin Harris, Scott Campbell, Will Hilyerd, Michael Whiteman, and Virginia Mattingly, who patiently listened to me talk about this arcane subject for years.

I also want to thank all the librarians and curators who have been helpful over the years, including the staff of the Kentucky Historical Society; the Filson Historical Society, especially Jim Holmberg; the Kentucky Department for Library and Archives; the Kentucky Gateway Museum Center; and the electronic reference staff of the Library of Congress. I would also like to thank my friends and colleagues in the Legal History and Rare Books section of the American Association of Law Libraries, especially Mark Podvia, Joel Fishman, and Laura Ray, my collaborators in so many projects. It would be remiss not to acknowledge the staff of my writing haven, Nancy's Bagel Grounds.

I am also grateful to the wonderful library research assistants who helped me and read various chapters, including Sarah Johnstone, Kim Balkcom, Helen Vawter Cooper, and Bailey Schrupp, and especially my library fellow and friend Leah Rupp Smith. I must also express appreciation to the peer reviewers of the manuscript and Ashley Runyon of the University Press of Kentucky. Constructive criticism is the rarest and richest gift any writer can receive, and I am genuinely thankful for it.

But my greatest thanks go to my wife, Beth Haendiges. Not only did she provide loving support during the book's gestation; she also made immeasurable concrete contributions to the project. As I researched the book, she tramped with me through cemeteries, explored historic Frankfort and Lexington to locate scenes of the book's dramas, and tolerated diversions to libraries disguised as day trips. When the writing was under way, she applied her well-honed professional editorial skills to every chapter, reading some more than twice.

It goes without saying that all the flaws of this book are mine—some stubbornly persisted in despite the good counsel of all those acknowledged above.

NOTES

Introduction

1. Austin first published his critique as a series of letters to the Boston press from "Honestus"; it was later released as the widely circulated *Observations on the Pernicious Practice of Law* (Boston: True & Weston, 1819).

2. James Wilson, *The Works of the Honourable James Wilson, L.L.D., Late One of the Associate Justices of the Supreme Court of the United States, and Professor of Law in the College of Philadelphia* (Philadelphia: Lorenzo Press, Bronson & Chauncey, 1804), 199–200.

3. Denis P. Duffey Jr., "Genre and Authority: The Rise of Case Reporting in the Early United States," *Chi.-Kent L. Rev.* 74 (1998–2000): 263–75. See also George S. Grossman, *Legal Research: Historical Foundations of the Electronic Age* (New York: Oxford University Press, 1994), and Erwin C. Surrency, *A History of American Law Publishing* (New York: Oceana Publications, 1990), 37–60.

4. Ky. Acts, ch. 7 (February 12, 1808).

5. *Hickman v. Boffman,* Hard. 356, 372–73 (1808).

6. Ibid.

7. Thomas J. Young Jr., "A Look at American Law Reporting in the 19th Century," *Law Libr. J.* 68 (1975): 294–306. See also Shackelford Miller, "The Value of Precedent," *Proc. Ky. St. Bar Assoc.* (1911): 269–91; Richard Priest Dietzman, "Kentucky Law Reports and Reporters," *Ky. L. J.* 16 (1927–1928): 16–27.

8. James Iredell, *Reports of Cases at Law Argued and Determined in the Supreme Court of North Carolina* (Raleigh, NC: Turner & Hughes, 1841); Thomas Bee, *Reports of Cases Adjudged in the District Court of South Carolina* (Philadelphia: William P. Farrand & Co., Fry & Krammerer, Printers, 1810).

9. John Bradford and Thomas D. Clark, *The Voice of the Frontier: John Bradford's Notes on Kentucky* (Lexington: University Press of Kentucky, 1993), 167.

10. Paul Brand and Joshua Getzler, *Judges and Judging in the History of the Common Law and Civil Law: From Antiquity to Modern Times* (Cambridge: Cambridge University Press, 2012).

11. See John William Wallace, *The Reporters Arranged and Characterized with Incidental Remarks* (Boston: Soule & Bugbee, 1882); C. G. Moran, *The Heralds of the Law*

(London: Stevens, 1948); L. W. Abbott, *Law Reporting in England 1485–1585* (London: Athlone Press, 1973); Chantal Stebbings, *Law Reporting in Britain: Selected Papers of the 11th British Legal History Conference* (London: Hambledon, 1995).

12. Wallace, *Reporters*, 11–12.

13. James Oldham, *English Common Law in the Age of Mansfield* (Chapel Hill: University of North Carolina Press, 2004); Norman S. Poser, *Lord Mansfield: Justice in the Age of Reason* (Montreal: McGill-Queen's University Press, 2013).

14. James Burrow, *Reports of Cases Adjudged in the Court of King's Bench*, 5 vols. (London: 1766–1780).

15. Mike Widener, "Landmarks of Law Reporting 10—Burrow's Reports: Works of Art," Lillian Goldman Law Library, Yale Law School, http://library.law.yale.edu/news/landmarks-law-reporting-1-introduction/ (accessed August 7, 2015).

16. Wallace, *Reporters*, 449.

17. *Somerset v. Stewart*, 98 ER 499 (1772). See William M. Wiecek, "Somerset: Lord Mansfield and the Legitimacy of Slavery in the Anglo-American World," *U. Chi. L. Rev.* 42 (1974): 86–146; Poser, *Lord Mansfield*.

18. *Barwell v. Brooks*, 3 Doug. 371 (1784).

19. English law reports were an important part of a lawyer's library in 1789, as shown in studies of the eighteenth-century law book trade and surveys of probate inventories. See Herbert Alan Johnson, *Imported Eighteenth-Century Law Treatises in American Libraries, 1700–1799* (Knoxville: University of Tennessee Press, 1978); Michael H. Hoeflich, *Legal Publishing in Antebellum America* (Cambridge: Cambridge University Press, 2010); William Hamilton Bryson, *Census of Law Books in Colonial Virginia* (Charlottesville: University Press of Virginia, 1978) (some of the books listed in Bryson's work were likely later carried to the Kentucky Territory). On the desire for native reports in the early republic, see Erwin C. Surrency, "Law Reports in the United States," *Am. J. Legal Hist.* 25 (1981): 48–66, 54. See, generally, Wallace, *Reporters;* William Hamilton Bryson, *The Virginia Law Reporters before 1880* (Charlottesville: University Press of Virginia, 1977); Morris L. Cohen and Sharon Hamby O'Connor, *A Guide to the Early Reports of the Supreme Court of the United States* (Littleton, CO: F. B. Rothman, 1995).

20. Conn. Acts, sec. 41, 129 (1785); Surrency, "Law Reports," 54.

21. T. Jefferson, *Reports of Case Determined in the General Court of Virginia* (n.p., 1829); Surrency, "Law Reports," 50. See also W. Hamilton Bryson, "Virginia Manuscript Law Reports," *Law Libr. J.* 82 (1990): 305–11.

22. Surrency, "Law Reports," 52.

23. Ibid., 54.

24. Ibid., 53.

25. Ephraim Kirby, *Reports of Cases Adjudged in the Superior Court of Connecticut with Some Determinations in the Supreme Court of Errors* (Litchfield, CT: Collier & Adam, 1789), iii–iv.

26. Joel Fishman, "The Reports of the Supreme Court of Pennsylvania," *Law Libr.*

J. 87 (1995): 643–93; Wilfred J. Ritz, *American Judicial Proceedings First Printed before 1801: An Analytical Bibliography* (Westport, CT: Greenwood Press, 1984), 111 (citing Kirby's ownership of a copy of Chipman's reports); M. Leigh Harrison, "A Study of the Earliest Reported Decisions of the South Carolina Courts of Law," *Am. J. Legal Hist.* 16 (1972): 51–70.

27. Elizabeth Gaspar Brown, "Frontier Justice: Wayne County 1796–1836," in *Essays in Nineteenth-Century American Legal History,* ed. Wythe Holt (Westport, CT: Greenwood Press, 1976), 686.

28. Ky. Const. Art. IV, secs. 3–4 (1792).

29. *Russ v. Hart,* Sneed (2 Ky.) 308, 308–9 (1804); *Whitledge v. Wait's Heirs,* Sneed (2 Ky.) 335, 336–37 (1804); "Rules of Practice of the Court of Appeals of Kentucky," 1 B. Mon. (40 Ky.) iii–viii, vi (1840).

30. Jennifer Frazier, "The History of the Kentucky State Law Library," *Ky. Libr.* 77 (2013): 12–23.

31. Ky. Acts, ch. 251 (December 19, 1804).

32. "An Act to Procure Reports of the Decisions of the Court of Appeals," Ky. Acts, ch. 487 (February 20, 1808).

33. Ky. Acts, ch. 256 (1815).

34. "Letter from Frankfort—Further Particulars of the Destructive Fire at the State Capitol," *Cincinnati Daily Enquirer,* November 24, 1865; Leslie Combs, Clerk of the Court of Appeals, to Thomas E. Bramlette, Governor of Kentucky, Ky. Senate Journal (1865), 28–29.

35. Lewis N. Dembitz, *Kentucky Jurisprudence* (Louisville: J. P. Morton, 1890), 20.

36. Ibid., 19.

37. "Rules of Practice," 1 B. Mon. vi (1840). An 1810 rule required written briefs in chancery cases.

38. "Extract of a Letter from Kentucky, Dated December 25," *New Hampshire Gazette,* March 10, 1790.

39. The rise of Kentucky book culture is well documented. The spread of literacy, book publishing, and libraries is surveyed in W. H. Venable, *Beginnings of Literary Culture in the Ohio Valley* (Cincinnati: Robert Clarke & Co., 1891), and Howard H. Peckham, "Books and Reading on the Ohio Valley Frontier," *Miss. Valley Hist. Rev.* 44 (1958): 649. The nascent publishing industry is treated generally in William Henry Perrin, *The Pioneer Press of Kentucky: From the Printing of the First West of the Alleghanies, August 11, 1787, to the Establishment of the Daily Press in 1830* (Louisville: J. P. Morton & Co., 1888); Willard Rouse Jillson, *The First Printing in Kentucky; Some Account of Thomas Parvin and John Bradford and the Establishment of the* Kentucky Gazette *in Lexington in the Year 1787, with a Bibliography of Seventy Titles* (Louisville: C. T. Dearing Print. Co., 1936); and Douglas C. McMurtrie, *John Bradford, Pioneer Printer of Kentucky: An Account of How Public Necessity Affected the Career of a Kentuckian Who, without Previous Experience in Printing, Brought the First Press to Lexington during 1787 and*

There Established the Kentucky Gazette (Springfield, IL: privately printed, 1931). A keen eyewitness to the birth of the book business in Kentucky was William A. Leavy, whose father moved the family's mercantile business to Lexington from Philadelphia in the 1780s. See William Leavy, "Memoir of Lexington and Its Vicinity: With Some Notice of Many Prominent Citizens and Its Institutions of Education and Religion," *Reg. Ky. Hist. Soc.* 41 (1943): 310, 319–22. An example of the breadth of legal offerings available in Kentucky is the probate record of James Harlan, the father of Justice John M. Harlan. See Kurt X. Metzmeier and Peter Scott Campbell, "Nursery of a Supreme Court Justice: The Library of James Harlan of Kentucky, Father of John Marshall Harlan," *Law Libr. J.* 100 (2008): 639–73.

40. Robert M. Ireland, *Kentucky State Constitution* (Oxford: Oxford University Press, 2000), 6–7; *The Address of George Muter and Benjamin Sebastian: Two of the Judges of the Court of Appeals: To the Free Men of Kentucky* (Lexington: Printed by John Bradford, 1795).

41. Robert M. Ireland, "George Robertson," in *Kentucky Encyclopedia*, ed. John E. Kleber (Lexington: University Press of Kentucky, 1992), 776. See also Peter Karsten, *Heart versus Head: Judge-Made Law in Nineteenth-Century America* (Chapel Hill: University of North Carolina Press, 1997).

42. Although many Kentucky cases mentioned slaves as property, few truly grappled with slavery as an institution. Perhaps recognizing it as offensive to the common law, the legislature took care to enshrine it in the positive law. In most of the legal cases involving slaves, they were treated as property that was being devised or used as collateral; others dealt with their manumission under increasingly strict state statutes. "Kentucky," in *Judicial Cases Concerning Slavery and the Negro* (1926; reprint, New York: Octagon Books, 1968), 1:269–469.

1. The Barrister: James Hughes (d. 1818)

A version of this chapter was published as "James Hughes: Kentucky's First Nominative Reporter," *Unbound: Annual Review of Legal History and Rare Books* 1 (2008): 25–32.

1. "Communicated: Obituary Notice," *Kentucky Gazette*, August 28, 1818.

2. E. Alfred Jones, *American Members of the Inns of Court* (London: Saint Catherine Press, 1924). See also J. G. de Roulhac Hamilton, "Southern Members of the Inns of Court," *N.C. Hist. Rev.* 10 (1933): 273–86.

3. Lucien Beckner, "History of the County Court of Lincoln County, Va.," *Reg. Ky. State Hist. Soc.* 20 (1922): 120–90.

4. James Rood Robertson, *Petitions of the Early Inhabitants of Kentucky to the General Assembly of Virginia, 1769 to 1792* (Baltimore: Genealogical Pub. Co., 1998), 164–65.

5. George Washington Ranck, *History of Lexington, Kentucky: Its Early Annals and Recent Progress, Including Biographical Sketches and Personal Reminiscences of the Pioneer Settlers, Notices of Prominent Citizens, Etc., Etc.* (Cincinnati: Robert Clarke & Co., 1872), 155–61.

6. "Elections," *Kentucky Gazette*, January 24, 1795; "Elections," *Kentucky Gazette*, January 9, 1796.

7. Hughes was a supporter of Lexington's first library and a trustee of Transylvania University. See *Kentucky Gazette*, February 18, 1812; Lewis Collins and Richard H. Collins, *Collins' Historical Sketches of Kentucky: History of Kentucky*, 2 vols. (Frankfort: Kentucky Historical Society, 1966), 2:511. First published by Lewis Collins as *Historical Sketches of Kentucky* (Maysville, KY: L. Collins; Cincinnati: J. A. & U. P. James, 1847), this work went through a number of editions, including several versions substantially enlarged by his son, Richard H. Collins, and titled *History of Kentucky*. Unless otherwise noted, all subsequent references are to the 1966 two-volume edition and are cited as Collins, *History of Kentucky*.

8. Collins, *History of Kentucky*, 1:170.

9. Ky. House Journal (1796), 6–7.

10. "A Collection of the Acts and Parts of Acts of the Virginia Assembly, Concerning the Titles to Lands in This Commonwealth," Ky. Acts, ch. 261 (1796).

11. Ky. House Journal (1801), 16.

12. Samuel M. Wilson, *The "Kentucky Gazette" and John Bradford, Its Founder* (Chicago: The Society, 1937).

13. Joan Wells Coward, *Kentucky in the New Republic: The Process of Constitution Making* (Lexington: University Press of Kentucky, 1979), 188, 121; *Kentucky Gazette*, November 2 and 7, 1793.

14. Westlaw searches indicate eight appearances before the Court of Appeals in Hughes's reports, seventeen in Hardin's, and twenty in A. K. Marshall's. Westlaw is a powerful database of case law that reflects all printed law reports from 1785 to the present. Searches can be limited to cases in a particular time frame and to those in which a particular attorney appeared. For example, the search DA(AFT 1802 & BEF 1859) & AT(BIBB) in the Kentucky cases database finds all cases after 1802 and before 1859 in which a Bibb is listed as appearing for a party. In this case, "Bibb" would be George M. Bibb because, in early case reports, the most senior person with that surname is designated by last name only (the more junior Charles S. Bibb appears as "C. S. Bibb"). In all cases in this book, searches were carefully reviewed for false positives. This method, however, provides only an approximation of the extent of an attorney's appellate practice; law reports covered only selected cases, and some reports, such as those of Sneed and Bibb, did not list the attorneys.

15. *Kentucky Gazette*, October 15, 1811.

16. Willard Rouse Jillson, *Old Kentucky Entries and Deeds: Complete Index to All of the Earliest Land Entries, Military Warrants, Deeds, and Wills of the Commonwealth of Kentucky* (Baltimore: Genealogical Pub. Co., 1969), 1–9.

17. "Obituary," *Kentucky Gazette*, August 28, 1818.

18. A survey of Willard Rose Jillson's *Old Kentucky Entries and Deeds* and his *Kentucky Land Grants: A Systematic Index to All of the Land Grants Recorded in the State*

Land Office at Frankfort, Kentucky, 1782–1924 (Baltimore: Genealogical Pub. Co., 1971), finds Hughes's name widely represented.

19. James Hughes, "Preface," in *A Report of the Causes Determined by the Late Supreme Court for the District of Kentucky, and by the Court of Appeals, in Which the Titles to Land Were in Dispute* (Lexington: Printed by John Bradford, 1803).

20. Woodford L. Gardner Jr., "Kentucky Justices on the U.S. Supreme Court," *Reg. Ky. Hist. Soc.* 70 (1972): 121–42.

21. Martin D. Hardin, "Preface," in *Reports of Cases Argued and Adjudged in the Court of Appeals of Kentucky, from Spring Term 1805, to Spring Term 1808, Inclusive* (Frankfort: Printed by Johnston & Pleasants for the author, 1810).

22. A crown quarto book measures about ten inches by eight inches; it was the size favored by some early publishers of Shakespeare. For more on Humphreys, see Charles Richard Staples, *The History of Pioneer Lexington, Kentucky, 1779–1806* (Lexington: Transylvania Press, 1939), 63.

23. "An Act to Provide a Seal for This Commonwealth," Ky. Acts, ch. 37 (December 20, 1792).

24. "Kentucky Can't Make up Its Mind What the State Seal Should Show," *Louisville Courier-Journal*, August 28, 1952.

25. Robert B. McAfee, *History of the Late War in the Western Country Comprising a Full Account of All the Transactions in that Quarter, from the Commencement of Hostilities at Tippecanoe, to the Termination of the Contest at New Orleans on the Return of Peace* (Lexington: Worsley & Smith, 1816).

26. Noble W. Hiatt and Lucy F. Hiatt, *The Silversmiths of Kentucky; Together with Watchmakers and Jewelers, 1785–1850* (Louisville: Standard Print. Co., 1954).

27. Douglas C. McMurtrie, *John Bradford, Pioneer Printer of Kentucky: An Account of How Public Necessity Affected the Career of a Kentuckian Who, without Previous Experience in Printing, Brought the First Press to Lexington during 1787 and There Established the* Kentucky Gazette (Springfield, IL: privately printed, 1931). See also Willard Rouse Jillson, *The First Printing in Kentucky; Some Account of Thomas Parvin and John Bradford and the Establishment of the* Kentucky Gazette *in Lexington in the Year 1787, with a Bibliography of Seventy Titles* (Louisville: C. T. Dearing Print. Co., 1936).

28. Early legal works by Bradford include John Bradford, *The General Instructor, or, The Office, Duty, and Authority of Justices of the Peace, Sheriffs, Coroners and Constables, in the State of Kentucky* (Lexington: Printed by John Bradford on Main Street, 1800), and *Laws of Kentucky Comprehending Those of a General Nature Now in Force and Which Have Been Acted on by the Legislature Thereof: Together with a Copious Index and a List of Local or Private Acts, with the Dates of the Sessions at Which They Were Passed* (Lexington: Printed by John Bradford, 1799–1817). See also G. Glenn Clift, *John Bradford, "The Caxton of Kentucky": A Bibliography* (New York: American Notes & Queries, 1975).

29. *Decisions of the Court of Appeals of the State of Kentucky* (Cincinnati: Robert Clarke & Co., 1869).

30. Henry Julian Abraham, *Justices, Presidents, and Senators: A History of the U.S. Supreme Court Appointments from Washington to Clinton* (Lanham, MD: Rowman & Littlefield, 1999), 64–65.

31. Charles Warren, *History of the Supreme Court* (Boston: Little, Brown, 1922), 1:305.

32. Henry Clay was a notoriously proficient cardplayer, so this could have been a risky venture. See Steven Lubet, *Lawyers' Poker: 52 Lessons that Lawyers Can Learn from Card Players* (New York: Oxford University Press, 2006), 213–15.

33. "The Late Mr. Hughes," *Kentucky Gazette,* August 28, 1818.

2. The Reporter Who Was Not: Achilles Sneed (1772–1825)

1. "Act Concerning the Promulgation of the Opinions of Court of Appeals," Ky. Acts, ch. 251, 3 Litt. 236 (December 19, 1804). "Be it enacted by the general assembly, that it shall be lawful for the court of appeals to procure reports to be made of all such decisions of the court since its establishment, as shall be deemed useful, and to certify to the succeeding general assembly what they shall deem a reasonable allowance, to be made to any person engaged therein, for the purpose of aiding the legislature making due compensation."

2. Ermina Jett Darnell, *Forks of Elkhorn Church* (Louisville: n.p., 1946), 264–67.

3. *Kentucky Gazette,* February 25, 1797.

4. G. Glenn Clift, *Kentucky 1800 Census: "Second Census" of Kentucky, 1800* (Baltimore: Genealogical Pub. Co., 1993).

5. Darnell, *Forks of Elkhorn Church,* 264–67.

6. "An Ode from the Poet to Rhadamanthus Alias W. W. Cooke," *Frankfort Western World,* August 23, 1806.

7. [Julia] Ardery, *Kentucky Court and Other Records* (Baltimore: Genealogical Pub. Co., 1979), 2:132 (Sneed is listed as an attorney in an 1801 deed); *Kentucky Gazette,* April 16, 1806.

8. For the original shareholders of the Kentucky Vineyard Society, see https://web.archive.org/web/20071220123620/http://www.kyvineyardsociety.org/Shareholders.htm (accessed October 19, 2015).

9. *Kentucky Gazette,* January 23, 1800.

10. Collins, *History of Kentucky,* 2:200. See also John E. Kleber, ed., *Kentucky Encyclopedia* (Lexington: University Press of Kentucky, 1992), 47.

11. Ky. Acts, ch. 251 (December 19, 1804).

12. Ky. Acts, ch. 1 (December 20, 1802).

13. Wendell Holmes Rone, *An Historical Atlas of Kentucky and Her Counties* (Owensboro, KY: Mayfield Printing Co., 1965).

14. This estimate was determined using the purchasing power calculator and historic standard of living calculators on MeasuringWorth.com, a nonprofit website managed by a board of historical economists: http://www.measuringworth.com/uscompare/ (accessed October 19, 2015).

15. Ky. Acts, ch. 307 (January 6, 1812).

16. Collins, *History of Kentucky,* 2:200.

17. The definitive account is Arndt M. Stickles, *The Critical Court Struggle in Kentucky, 1819–1829* (Bloomington: Indiana University Press, 1929). See also W. H. Mackey, "The Old and New Court Struggle," in *Lawyers and Lawmakers of Kentucky* (Easley, SC: Southern Historical Press, 1982), 304–18.

18. *Blair v. Williams* and *Lapsley v. Brashear,* 4 Litt. (14 Ky.) 34 (1823).

19. Achilles Sneed, *Address to the People of Kentucky* (Frankfort: Holeman, 1825). Unless otherwise noted, the account of Sneed's activities comes from this work, which was derived from documents included in Sneed's contempt trial and is written mostly in his plain-spoken style. It also includes polemical introductory and concluding passages in a different style that were likely provided by an Old Court partisan.

20. William Ernest Smith, *The Francis Preston Blair Family in Politics* (New York: Macmillan, 1933), 1:24–28.

21. Stickles, *Critical Court Struggle,* 69.

22. Ibid., 37.

23. "Domestic Intelligence," *Boston Weekly Messenger,* April 14, 1825, which reprinted Blair's indictment.

24. Stickles, *Critical Court Struggle,* 70.

25. Ky. Acts, ch. 8 (December 30, 1826).

3. The Soldier: Martin D. Hardin (1780–1823)

1. Ky. Acts, ch. 15 (February 20, 1808).

2. Lucius P. Little, *Ben Hardin, His Times and Contemporaries, with Selections from His Speeches* (Louisville: Courier-Journal, 1887).

3. Robert B. McAfee, *History of the Late War in the Western Country* (reprint, Bowling Green, OH: Historical Publications Co., 1919).

4. Robert B. McAfee, "The Life and Times of Robert B. McAfee and His Family and Connections," *Reg. Ky. State Hist. Soc.* 25 (1927): 134.

5. According to early sources, and based on an honestly held but inaccurate Nicholas family tradition, Nicholas was the recipient of Jefferson's draft resolutions, not Breckinridge; this has been debunked. Ethelbert Dudley Warfield, *The Kentucky Resolutions of 1798: An Historical Study* (New York: G. P. Putnam's Sons, 1887), 142–44.

6. Ky. Acts, ch. 71 (December 19, 1804).

7. Martin D. Hardin, "Preface," in *Reports of Cases Argued and Adjudged in the Court of Appeals of Kentucky, from Spring Term 1805, to Spring Term 1808, Inclusive* (Frankfort: Printed by Johnston & Pleasants for the author, 1810), iii.

8. Ibid.

9. Ibid., iv.

10. *Owens v. Owens,* 1 Hard. (3 Ky.) 154 (1807).

11. Hardin, *Reports,* 158.

12. The legislature was primarily concerned about cost, but there was also some fear that the counsels' arguments would dilute the authoritativeness of the court's decision.

13. Hardin, *Reports,* iii–iv.

14. Ibid., iv.

15. Ky. Acts, ch. 142 (January 25, 1810).

16. Collins, *History of Kentucky,* 2:241.

17. Westlaw search: DA(BEF 1823) & AT(HARDIN). Hardin took precedence over his nephew, Benjamin Hardin, on the appellate rolls.

18. *Argus of Western America* (Frankfort), May 30, 1813, quoted in G. Glenn Clift, *Remember the Raisin! Kentucky and Kentuckians in the Battles and Massacre at French-town, Michigan Territory, in the War of 1812* (Frankfort: Kentucky Historical Society, 1961), 15.

19. McAfee, *History of the Late War,* 146–47.

20. Clift, *Remember the Raisin!,* 87.

21. Orval W. Baylor, *John Pope, Kentuckian; His Life and Times, 1770–1845; a Saga of Kentucky Politics from 1792 to 1850* (Cynthiana, KY: Hobson Press, 1943).

4. The Jurist: George M. Bibb (1776–1859)

1. Ky. Acts, ch. 256, sec. 2 (February 8, 1815).

2. Ibid., sec. 3.

3. Ibid., secs. 3–4.

4. Ky. Senate Journal (1814), 201.

5. Pattie Burnley, "Bibb," *Reg. Ky. Hist. Soc.* 1 (1903): 43–44; Charles William Bibb, *The Bibb Family in America, 1640–1940* (n.p., 1941) (accessed via Ancestry.com).

6. Samuel L. Webb and Margaret E. Armbrester, *Alabama Governors: A Political History of the State* (Tuscaloosa: University of Alabama Press, 2001), 11–17.

7. John S. Goff, "The Last Leaf: George Mortimer Bibb," *Reg. Ky. Hist. Soc.* 59 (1961): 331–42. Goff's is the only full biographical treatment of Bibb, but there are many short entries for Bibb in larger works, including E. Merton Coulter, "George Mortimer Bibb," in *Dictionary of American Biography* (Detroit: Gale Research, 1974), 1:235; John C. Doolan, "The Court of Appeals of Kentucky," *Green Bag* 12 (1900): 348–50; Sallie E. Marshall Hardy, "Some Kentucky Lawyers of the Past and Present," *Green Bag* 9 (1897): 260–61; H. Levin, *Lawyers and Lawmakers of Kentucky* (Chicago: Lewis Publishing Co., 1897), 76.

8. Goff, "Last Leaf," 333.

9. "Trustees of Hampden-Sydney College," *Virginia Magazine of History and Biography* 6 (1898): 174–84.

10. Samuel D. Alexander, *Princeton College during the Eighteenth Century* (New York: D. F. Randolph & Co., 1872), 257–59.

11. Goff, "Last Leaf," 333, citing a letter from the Princeton University archivist; Charles Richard Williams, *The Cliosophic Society, Princeton University: A Study of Its*

History in Commemoration of Its Sesquicentennial Anniversary (Princeton, NJ: Princeton University Press, 1916), 34.

12. "Notable Alumni," https://alumni.wm.edu/notable_alumni/ (accessed November 28, 2015), does not list a graduation year; *A Provisional List of Alumni, Grammar School Students, Members of the Faculty, and Members of the Board of Visitors of the College of William and Mary in Virginia, from 1693 to 1888* (College of William & Mary, 1941). Coulter omits Princeton from Bibb's CV in the *Dictionary of American Biography* but says that in later years he held the "sentimental distinction" of being William and Mary's oldest living graduate. (An e-mail inquiry to the William and Mary archives returned citations to these same sources.)

13. Imogene E. Brown, *American Aristides: A Biography of George Wythe* (Rutherford, NJ: Fairleigh Dickinson University Press, 1981).

14. "Trustees of Hampden-Sydney College," 174–84.

15. John S. Goff, *Bibb Family in America, 1640–1940* (n.p., 1941).

16. Lucius P. Little, *Ben Hardin: His Times and Contemporaries, 1784–1852* (Louisville: Courier-Journal Job Printing Co., 1887), 26–27, 472.

17. This was just the first time Bibb's and Thruston's careers would be entwined. Bibb later served in the Senate with Thruston and would practice before him after Thruston was appointed judge of the US Circuit Court for the District of Columbia. In 1837, while Bibb was once again in the Senate, the House considered impeachment charges against Thruston, but the matter died, sparing Bibb the decision of whether to vote to impeach.

18. Tufts University Digital Collections and Archives, "A New Nation Votes: American Election Returns 1787–1825" (elections.lib.tufts.edu/), citing *Western World* (Frankfort), November 22, 1806; *Palladium* (Frankfort), November 20, 1806.

19. Levin, *Lawyers and Lawmakers,* 76. See also Grand Lodge of Kentucky Free and Accepted Masons website, http://www.grandlodgeofkentucky.org/grand_officers/past_grandmasters.htm. Bibb's biography in William R. Denslow et al., *10,000 Famous Freemasons* (Richmond, VA: Macoy Publishing, 2004), lists a number of other Masonic titles he accumulated: master of Lexington Lodge No. 1, master of Russellville Lodge No. 17, master of Hiram Lodge No. 4 Frankfort, and high priest of Frankfort Chapter No. 3.

20. Mary K. Bonsteel Tachau, *Federal Courts in the Early Republic, Kentucky 1789–1816* (Princeton, NJ: Princeton University Press, 1978), 75.

21. The Westlaw database was searched to determine Bibb's appellate practice. For example, the search DA(AFT 1802 & BEF 1859) & AT(BIBB) in the Kentucky cases database found all cases between 1802 and 1859 in which a Bibb was listed as appearing for a party. Searches in this chapter were run against the Kentucky, Federal Circuit (which includes the DC courts), and US Supreme Court databases.

22. Collins, *History of Kentucky,* 2:772.

23. Goff, *Bibb Family in America.*

24. Perry M. Goldman and James S. Young, eds., *The United States Congressional Directories, 1789–1840* (New York: Columbia University Press, 1974), 51.

25. George M. Bibb to John J. Crittenden, May 12, 1812, Crittenden Manuscripts, Library of Congress; Charles M. Wiltse, "The Authorship of the War Report of 1812," *Am. Hist. Rev.* 49 (1944): 253–59.

26. George M. Bibb to John J. Crittenden, April 16, 1812, as quoted in Irving Brant, *James Madison, the President, 1809–1812* (Indianapolis: Bobbs-Merrill, 1956), 473.

27. Glenn Tucker, *Poltroons and Patriots: A Popular Account of the War of 1812* (Indianapolis: Bobbs-Merrill, 1954), 1:20–21.

28. George M. Bibb, "Dedication to the People of Kentucky," in *Reports of Cases at Common Law and in Chancery, Argued and Decided in the Court of Appeals of the Commonwealth of Kentucky, from Fall Term 1808 to Spring Term 1817* (Frankfort: Printed for the author by Johnston & Buchanan, 1815), 3–8.

29. Ibid.

30. Westlaw search.

31. Robert V. Remini, *Henry Clay: Statesman for the Union* (New York: W. W. Norton, 1993), 208.

32. *Green v. Biddle,* 21 U.S. 1 (1823).

33. In 1818 and 1819 the legislature tried to impose a state tax on operations of the Bank of the United States in Kentucky; the later measure set a rate of $5,000 a month. The Supreme Court's March 6, 1819, decision in a similar case, *McColloch v. Maryland,* 17 U.S. 316 (1819), did not end the legal wrangling over the tax.

34. Ky. House Journal (1819), 249.

35. Arndt M. Stickles, *The Critical Court Struggle in Kentucky, 1819–1829* (Bloomington: Indiana University Press, 1929), provides an excellent, well-researched time line of events in the court controversy.

36. Britain would not abolish debtors' prison until 1860—as any reader of Charles Dickens's novels would know. Marshalsea Prison, where Dickens's father was jailed, is central to *Little Dorrit,* but it is not the only one of his novels to feature the odious institution.

37. Stickles, *Critical Court Struggle,* 22–23.

38. During the Great Depression states offered moratoriums on debt executions. The measure by Minnesota survived a challenge before the Supreme Court in the case of *Home Building & Loan Assoc. v. Blaisdell,* 290 U.S. 398 (1934). See Joseph V. Heffernan, "The Minnesota Mortgage Moratorium Case," *Ind. L. J.* 9 (1934): 337–56. After the subprime lending crisis of 2008, a moratorium on foreclosures was proposed. See Alex Abella, "A Simple Solution: A National Debt Moratorium," May 20, 2009, http://www.huffingtonpost.com/alex-abella/a-simple-solution-a-natio_b_188634.html. A similar solution has been proposed for residents of Detroit. See Laura Gottesdiener, "Detroit's Debt Crisis: Everything Must Go," *Rolling Stone,* June 20, 2013.

39. *Blair v. Williams,* 3 Litt. (14 Ky.) 34 (1823).

40. "James Clark," in Lowell H. Harrison, *Kentucky's Governors* (Lexington: University Press of Kentucky, 2004), 47–50.

41. *Lapsley v. Brashear,* 3 Litt. (14 Ky.) 47 (1823).

42. George M. Bibb, *An Exposition of the Meaning of the Clause in the Constitution of the United States that "No State Shall Pass Any Ex Post Facto Law, or Law Impairing the Obligation of Contracts": An Examination of the Opinions of the Court of Appeals of Kentucky, in the Cases of Blair vs. Williams and Lapsley vs. Brashear, in Petition for Re-hearing* (Frankfort: Printed by order of the senate, by Amos Kendall & Co., 1824).

43. Stickles, *Critical Court Struggle,* 51.

44. L. F. Johnson, *Famous Kentucky Tragedies and Trials* (Cleveland, OH: Baldwin Law Pub. Co., 1922), 7–15.

45. Stickles, *Critical Court Struggle,* 58.

46. Westlaw search: AT(BIBB) & DA(BEF 1827 & AFT 1822).

47. Remini, *Henry Clay,* 199.

48. Hardy, "Some Kentucky Lawyers of Past and Present," 261.

49. John Steele Gordon, "An Inauguration for the People," *Wall Street Journal,* January 20, 2009.

50. Robert V. Remini, *Andrew Jackson & His Indian Wars* (New York: Viking, 2001).

51. "Messrs. Moore and Bibb, of the Senate," *Niles' Weekly Register,* June 2, 1832, 261–62.

52. *Register of Debates,* May 3, 1833, 898.

53. Joseph Howard Parks, *Felix Grundy, Champion of Democracy* (Baton Rouge: Louisiana State University Press, 1940), 243–68.

54. John Campbell to David Campbell, May 23, 1832, Campbell Family Papers, Duke University Library, Durham, NC.

55. *Register of Debates,* July 10, 1832, 1219.

56. Ibid., March 1, 1833, 807–8.

57. Ibid., January 21, 1833, 263–312.

58. Ibid., February 21, 1833, 688–89.

59. Westlaw search of the US Supreme Court, Federal Circuit, and Kentucky cases databases.

60. Francis P. Blair to Martin Van Buren, April 25, 1859, Van Buren Papers, Library of Congress.

61. George M. Bibb to John B. Bibb, February 24, 1839, Filson Historical Society, Louisville, KY.

62. George H. Yater, *Two Hundred Years at the Falls of the Ohio: A History of Louisville and Jefferson County* (Louisville: Heritage Corp. of Louisville & Jefferson County, 1979), 25.

63. *Haldeman's Picture of Louisville, Directory and Business Advertiser, for 1844–1845* (Louisville: W. N. Haldeman, 1844).

64. "An Oration Commemorative of Laying the Corner Stone of the College Edifice of the Louisville Medical Institute," *Louisville J. Med. Surg.,* January 1838, 1–25.

65. "Mr. Webster," *Louisville Daily Journal,* May 31, 1837.

66. George M. Bibb to John B. Bibb, February 24, 1839, Filson Historical Society.

67. Robert V. Remini, *Andrew Jackson and the Course of American Democracy, 1833–1845* (New York: Harper & Row, 1984), 522–23. The 1859 letter from Blair to Van Buren (see note 60) appears to contain an oblique echo of Jackson's claim, but nothing about Bibb's finances indicates such a windfall.

68. "Died," *Washington (DC) Constitution,* April 15, 1859.

69. Kevin T. McGuire, *The Supreme Court Bar: Legal Elites in the Washington Community* (Charlottesville: University Press of Virginia, 1993), 16–17.

70. Joseph Story, *Life and Letters of Joseph Story* (London: J. Chapman, 1851), 2:631.

71. Westlaw shows about a dozen such cases, but the law reports of this era covered the lower federal courts only minimally. A number of cases that Bibb was associated with in newspapers are not found in Westlaw databases.

72. "George M. Bibb," *Louisville Morning Courier,* December 7, 1847, quoting the *Philadelphia Sun.*

73. For example, Bibb represented the government in *United States v. Heirs of Rillieux,* 55 U.S. 189 (1852). It appears that Bibb was able to represent private parties as well, as long as their interests were not adverse to the United States. In *Tremlett v. Adams,* 54 U.S. 295 (1851), Bibb represented the federal collector of the port of New Bedford, while Attorney General Crittenden represented the allied but broader interests of the federal government—a role for which the office of solicitor general was established in 1870.

74. *Letters of Jessie Benton Fremont* (Champaign: University of Illinois Press, 1993), 82–83.

75. *Louisville Daily Courier,* March 8, 1855, quoting the *Buffalo Democracy; Fremont v. United States,* 58 U.S. 542 (1854), overturning 25 Fed. Cas. 1214, Case No. 15,164 (N.D. Calif. 1853).

76. "A Tribute to Judge Bibb," *National Intelligencer,* April 18, 1859; "The Late Chancellor Bibb," *Washington (DC) Constitution,* April 17, 1859.

77. "Correspondence of the Mercury," *Charleston Mercury,* April 22, 1859.

78. See entry for George M. Bibb in *Biographical Directory of the United States Congress* (Washington, DC: Government Printing Office, 2005), 651; internment records, Congressional Cemetery, http://www.congressionalcemetery.org/search-interment-records.asp. Although the Frankfort Cemetery might be his final resting place (his first wife is buried there), the Kentucky Genealogical Society's comprehensive index, *The Frankfort Cemetery in Kentucky* (Frankfort: Kentucky Genealogical Society, 1988), does not list his burial there.

5. The Brother: Alexander K. Marshall (1770–1825)

1. Ky. Senate Journal (1817), 55, 61.

2. William McClung Paxton, *The Marshall Family, or a Genealogical Chart of the Descendants of John Marshall and Elizabeth Markham, His Wife, Sketches of Individuals and Notices of Families Connected with Them* (Cincinnati: Robert Clarke & Co., 1885).

See also "Alexander K. Marshall," in H. Levin, *Lawyers and Lawmakers of Kentucky* (Chicago: Lewis Publishing Co., 1897), 182.

3. Thomas Marshall Green, *Historic Families of Kentucky* (Cincinnati: Robert Clarke & Co., 1889), 104.

4. Albert J. Beveridge, *The Life of John Marshall*, vol. 1 (Boston: Houghton Mifflin, 1919), 18. See also Sallie E. Marshall Hardy, "John Marshall: Third Chief Justice of the United States, as Son, Brother, Husband, and Friend," *Green Bag* 8 (1896): 479–80.

5. Elizabeth Patterson Thomas, *Old Kentucky Homes and Gardens* (Louisville: Standard Print. Co., 1939), 62.

6. Green, *Historic Families*, 103–16. June Lee Mefford Kinkead, *Our Kentucky Pioneer Ancestry: A History of the Kinkead and McDowell Families of Kentucky, and Those Families Associated by Marriage* (Baltimore: Gateway Press, 1992).

7. Thomas Marshall House, US Highway 68, Old Washington, Mason County, KY, Historic American Buildings Survey HABS KY, 81-WASH1 (1933), reproduced at http://www.loc.gov/rr/print/res/114_habs.html; Thomas, *Old Kentucky Homes and Gardens*, 63. For more on early Washington and Mason County, see G. Glenn Clift, *History of Maysville and Mason County* (Lexington: Transylvania Printing Co., 1936); Edna H. Best, *The Historic Past of Washington, Mason County, Kentucky* (Cynthiana, KY: Hobson Book Press, 1944).

8. "Meffords's Fort," in Dianne Wells, Melba Porter Hay, and Thomas H. Appleton, *Roadside History: A Guide to Kentucky Highway Markers* (Frankfort: Kentucky Historical Society, 2002), 7.

9. Mary Augusta Rodgers, "Old Kentucky Towns," *New York Times*, October 5, 1986, http://www.nytimes.com/1986/10/05/travel/old-kentucky-towns.html.

10. Levin, *Lawyers and Lawmakers*, 182; Lucy C. Lee, "Historic Places of Mason County, Kentucky," *Reg. Ky. State Hist. Soc.* 7 (1909): 45–47.

11. Lucy Marshall Bentley, "Recollections" (1930), in collections of Kentucky Gateway Museum Center, Maysville, KY. Lucy was a descendant of Colonel Thomas Marshall through her mother, Phoebe A. Paxton, who was a granddaughter of Alexander K. Marshall, and through her father, Charles A. Marshall, who was a grandson of Captain Thomas Marshall. Paxton, *Marshall Family*, 132–38, 244.

12. Randall Capps, *The Rowan Story: From Federal Hill to My Old Kentucky Home* (Bowling Green, KY: Homestead Press, 1976); Lou Delle McIntosh, My Old Kentucky Home NRHP Nomination Form (Kentucky Department of State Parks, 1971).

13. All census information is from the US Census databases on Ancestry.com.

14. Bruce Fehn, "Thomas Jefferson and Slaves: Teaching an American Paradox," *OAH Magazine of History* 14 (2000): 24–28.

15. Levin, *Lawyers and Lawmakers*, 182.

16. Collins, *History of Kentucky*, 2:576; Green, *Historic Families*, 105.

17. E. Polk Johnson, *History of Kentucky and Kentuckians* (Chicago: Lewis Publishing Co., 1912), 2:839.

18. "An Act Establishing Franklin Academy," Ky. Acts, ch. 52 (December 15, 1795); "An Act to Establish a Town on the Lands of George Lewis," Ky. Acts, ch. 50 (December 17, 1795).

19. "Humphrey Marshall," in *Dictionary of American Biography* (Detroit: Gale Research, 1974), 6:310–11.

20. "James Markham Marshall," ibid., 313–14; "Louis Marshall," ibid., 325–26.

21. David O. Stewart, *American Emperor: Aaron Burr's Challenge to Jefferson's America* (New York: Simon & Schuster, 2011), 145–46.

22. James F. Hopkins, ed., *Papers of Henry Clay* (Lexington: University Press of Kentucky, 1959), 1:244–46.

23. Westlaw search: AT(A. K. MARSHALL) & DA(BEF 1825).

24. Collins, *History of Kentucky,* 1:499.

25. Clarence S. Brigham, *History and Bibliography of American Newspapers, 1690–1820* (Worcester, MA: American Antiquarian Society, 1947), 1:163, 166; Hopkins, *Papers of Henry Clay,* 2:160–61.

26. Josephine L. Harper, ed., *The Draper Manuscript Collection* (Chicago: University of Chicago, 1980), 6 CC 107b.

27. Green, *Historic Families,* 103–16; "Marshall, Alexander Keith," in *Biographical Directory of the United States Congress, 1774–2005* (108th Congress, 2nd session, House, no. 108-222), 1503–4.

28. Karl Raitz and Nancy O'Malley, *Kentucky's Frontier Highway: Historical Landscapes along the Maysville Road* (Lexington: University Press of Kentucky, 2012), 25.

29. Green, *Historic Families,* 111–12. See also "Col. Charles A. Marshall," in *Biographical Encyclopædia of Kentucky of the Dead and Living Men of the Nineteenth Century* (Cincinnati: J. M. Armstrong, 1878), 311–12; Johnson, *History of Kentucky and Kentuckians,* 837–41, esp. 840–41; William E. Connelley, *History of Kentucky* (Chicago: American Historical Society, 1922), 585–86.

30. I have to thank the late Tom Fryman for taking the time to show me Federal Hill and explain its relationship to Walnut Grove.

6. The Poet: William Littell (1768–1824)

1. Collins, *History of Kentucky,* 1:412; L. F. Johnson, *History of Franklin County Bar, 1786–1931* (Frankfort: F. K. Kavanaugh, 1932), 31; Willard Rouse Jillson, *Literary Haunts and Personalities of Old Frankfort, 1791–1941* (Frankfort: Kentucky Historical Society, 1941), 9; "William Littell," in *Dictionary of American Biography* (Detroit: Gale Research, 1974), 6:296–97; Edwin Anderson Alderman and Joel Chandler Harris, eds., *Library of Southern Literature* (New Orleans: Martin & Hoyt, 1910), 7:260–61. Many of the vaguer details have been corrected by Robert S. Cotterill, "William Littell," *Filson Club Historical Quarterly* 25 (1951): 295–99, and various articles in the Littell Families of America newsletter, including "William Littell of Kentucky," *Littell's Living Age* 3, no. 2 (Spring 1981): 11–17. See also Kurt X. Metzmeier, "William Littell," in *The Yale*

Biographical Dictionary of American Law, ed. Roger K. Newman (New Haven, CT: Yale University Press, 2009), 342–43.

2. His obituary is the most reliable source, as it was clearly based on information from the family; it lists his age at death as fifty-six. "Communicated, Died," *Frankfort Argus,* September 29, 1824.

3. "William Littell of Kentucky," 11–17.

4. Ibid. James Pyle Wickersham's *A History of Education in Pennsylvania, Private and Public, Elementary and Higher from the Time the Swedes Settled on the Delaware to the Present Day* (Lancaster, PA: Inquirer Pub. Co., 1886), offers several options.

5. Interview with William Sudduth by John D. Shane, Draper Manuscripts, Kentucky Papers, 1768–1892, 12 CC 64 (microfilm edition, 1949), State Historical Society of Wisconsin.

6. *Festoons of Fancy, Consisting of Compositions Amatory, Sentimental, and Humorous, in Verse and Prose* (1940; reprint, University of Kentucky Publications Committee, Margaret Vorhies Haggin Trust, 1976), 3.

7. James Veech, *The Monongahela of Old, or Historical Sketches of South-Western Pennsylvania to the Year 1800* (Pittsburgh, 1910), 105.

8. Cotterill, "William Littell."

9. The process is described in Donald B. Cole, *A Jackson Man: Amos Kendall and the Rise of American Democracy* (Baton Rouge: Louisiana State University Press, 2010), 47.

10. Cotterill, "William Littell."

11. *Laws of Kentucky: Comprehending Those of a General Nature Now in Force, and Which Have Been Acted on by the Legislature Thereof. Together with a Copious Index and a List of Local or Private Acts, with the Dates of the Sessions at Which They Were Passed. To Which Is Prefixed the Constitution of the United States, with the Amendments, the Act of Separation from the State of Virginia, and the Constitution of Kentucky* (Lexington: Printed by John Bradford, 1799).

12. William Littell, *The Statute Law of Kentucky; With Notes, Praelections, and Observations on the Public Acts: In Three Volumes* (Frankfort: Printed for William Hunter, by Johnston & Pleasants, 1809–1811). Volumes 4 and 5, published in 1814 and 1819, extended the coverage.

13. William Littell, *Reprints of Littell's Political Transactions in and Concerning Kentucky* (Louisville: Filson Club, 1926).

14. At least one historian has suggested that Littell was provided forged documents. Thomas Marshall Green, *The Spanish Conspiracy: A Review of Early Spanish Movements in the South-West. Containing Proofs of the Intrigues of James Wilkinson and John Brown; of the Complicity Therewith of Judges Sebastian, Wallace, and Innes; the Early Struggles of Kentucky for Autonomy; the Intrigues of Sebastian in 1795–7, and the Legislative Investigation of His Corruption* (Cincinnati: Robert Clarke & Co., 1891), 353–56.

15. A modern edition was published by the University of Kentucky Publications Committee, Margaret Vorhies Haggin Trust, in 1940 and reprinted in 1976; see note 6.

16. Thomas Johnson and Burton Milward, *The Kentucky Miscellany* (1821; reprint, Lexington: University of Kentucky Libraries, 1995).

17. *Festoons of Fancy* (1976 ed.), 15–18.

18. Karen Mauer Green, *Kentucky Gazette: Genealogical and Historical Abstracts, 1797–1820* (Baltimore: Gateway Press, 1983). See also Ebenezer Hiram Stedman, Frances L. S. Dugan, and Jacqueline Bull, *Bluegrass Craftsman: Being the Reminiscences of Ebenezer Hiram Stedman, Papermaker, 1808–1885* (Lexington: University Press of Kentucky, 2015).

19. *Festoons of Fancy* (1976 ed.), 18–23.

20. Honor R. Sachs, "The Myth of the Abandoned Wife: Married. Women's Agency and the Legal Narrative of Gender in Eighteenth-Century Kentucky," *Ohio Valley History* 3 (2003): 3–20.

21. Ky. House Journal (November 12, 1805), 25–26.

22. Ky. House Journal (1805), 41, 45, 103–4, 108–9: first reading on November 19, second reading on November 20, bill killed on a motion to table it on December 12, motion to reconsider it failed on December 13.

23. *Festoons of Fancy* (1976 ed.), 29–33.

24. Ibid., 33–37; Ky. House Journal (1805), 4, 64, 76–77, 152: first reading on November 28, second reading and amended on December 3, tabled and killed on December 25.

25. William Littell and Jacob Swigert, *A Digest of the Statute Law of Kentucky: Being a Collection of All the Acts of the General Assembly, of a Public and Permanent Nature, from the Commencement of the Government to May Session, 1822, Also, the English and Virginia Statutes, Yet in Force; Together with Several Acts of Congress* (Frankfort: Kendall & Russell, Printers for the State, 1822).

26. William Littell, *Principles of Law and Equity, Recognised and Established by the Court of Appeals of Kentucky, in the Various Cases Determined in that Court Commencing with Its First Existence, and Concluding with the Close of the October Term, One Thousand Eight Hundred and Six (Except the Land Cases Published by James Hughes): Digested and Arranged in Alphabetical Order* (Frankfort: From the Press of William Gerard, 1808).

27. Kurt X. Metzmeier, "Blazing Trails in a New Kentucky Wilderness: Early Kentucky Case Law Digests," *Law Libr. J.* 93 (Winter 2001): 93–108.

28. "Wm Littell of Frankfort," *Cincinnati Liberty Hall*, January 25, 1808.

29. "William Littell, Esq.," *Louisville Correspondent*, May 11, 1814.

30. "William Littell," *Louisville Correspondent*, September 23, 1816.

31. "Gig for Sale," *Louisville Correspondent*, January 8, 1816.

32. "William Littell," *Frankfort Commentator*, June 25, 1819; "William Littell," *St. Louis Enquirer*, June 2, 1819.

33. "Uriel B. Chambers & Wm. Littell," *Frankfort Argus*, July 28, 1824.

34. Westlaw search: AT(LITTELL) & DA(BEF 1825).

35. Interview with Ben Monroe by John D. Shane, Draper Manuscripts, Kentucky Papers, 1768–1892, 11 CC 291 (microfilm edition, 1949), State Historical Society of Wisconsin.

36. Ky. Acts, ch. 536 (December 11, 1822).

37. Ky. Acts, ch. 643 (December 29, 1823).

38. This is based on copyright dates. The "publication" dates—1822 for volumes 1 and 2, 1823 for volumes 3 and 4, and 1824 for volume 5—do not jibe and appear to be based on Littell's plan before the problem of the missing decisions arose.

39. Ky. Acts, ch. 682 (January 7, 1824).

40. Ibid.

41. "Communicated, Died," *Frankfort Argus,* September 29, 1824. In a small coda to Littell's early career, the death of Humphrey Marshall's widow was reported in the same column.

42. "Sickness in Kentucky," *Boston Commercial Gazette,* August 25, 1823.

43. J. P. Harrison, "Remarks on the Epidemic Bilious Fever Which Prevailed in Louisville, Kentucky, in the Summer and Autumn of 1821–2," *Medical Recorder* 7 (1822): 597–600. The newspapers of this era recognized yellow fever and scarlet fever but did not identify this particular illness as such.

44. "I, William Littell attorney and counsellor at law of Frankfort, Kentucky, do hereby make my last Will and Testament in manner and form following. First, I declare my two sons Philander Littell and William Littell my sole heirs at law and give and bequeath to them and the survivor of them and his heirs forever all my estate real personal or mixed whatsoever; to William all the estate which came by his mother and one moiety of the residue of my estate; and to Philander the other moiety of my estate independent of what was received through William's mother. Secondly, I hereby appoint the Rev. George T. Chapman of Lexington and the Rev. William Holeman of Frankfort guardians to my two children, and Thirdly, I constitute and appoint my friend Jacob Swigert of Frankfort sole Executor of this my last will and testament. In Witness thereof I have hereto set my hand and seal this—of Aug't 1824." "William Littell," *Littell's Living Age* (1981): 15. The Reverend George T. Chapman, DD, was the rector of Lexington's Christ Church from 1820 to 1830 and the leading figure behind the creation of the Kentucky Episcopal Diocese. The scholarly Chapman was also a professor of history and antiquity at Transylvania University.

45. Ky. Acts, ch. 91 (January 6, 1825).

46. "Communicated, Died," *Frankfort Argus,* September 29, 1824.

47. Collins, *History of Kentucky,* 1:412.

48. Robert S. Cotterill, "William Littell," in *Dictionary of American Biography,* 297. Cotterill, a great historian, was a cofounder of the Southern Historical Association in the 1930s and shared some of the sympathy for the Old South prevalent in the early association. John David Smith and J. Vincent Lowery, eds., *The Dunning School: Historians, Race, and the Meaning of Reconstruction* (Lexington: University Press of Kentucky, 2013).

7. The Rebel: Thomas Bell Monroe (1791–1865)

1. Richard Priest Dietzman, "Kentucky Law Reports and Reporters," *Ky. L. J.* 16 (1927–1928): 16–27.

2. Biographies of Monroe include the following: "Thomas Bell Monroe," in Judicial Conference of the United States, *History of the Sixth Circuit: A Bicentennial Project* (Washington, DC: The Committee, 1977), 172; Collins, *History of Kentucky*, 1:409; H. Levin, *Lawyers and Lawmakers of Kentucky* (Chicago: Lewis Publishing Co., 1897), 158; *Biographical Encyclopædia of Kentucky of the Dead and Living Men of the Nineteenth Century* (Cincinnati: J. M. Armstrong, 1878), 547–48. Perhaps the survey that is closest to the man himself is that of Edwin Porter Thompson, *History of the First Kentucky Brigade* (Cincinnati: Caxton Publishing House, 1868), 509–24. Thompson was a family friend and served with Monroe's sons during the Civil War.

3. In matters of family history, I have drawn on the resources of the oldest Monroe family organization, the Clan Munro Association USA, a national subsidiary of the international Clan Munro Association. Its website (http://clanmunrousa.org) has a comprehensive database of Munro/Monroe family history resources. Each person has a data sheet with source notes that I occasionally cite directly. Joan S. Guilford McGuire, *Monroe Book: Being the History of the Munro Clan from Its Origins in Scotland to Settlement in New England and Migration to the West, 1652–1850 and Beyond* (Franklin, NC: Genealogy Publishing Service, 1993).

4. "James Monroe," in *American Presidential Families*, ed. Charles Mosley (New York: Macmillan, 1993), 259–71.

5. "Individual Report for Maj. Andrew Munro," Clan Munro USA.

6. Ibid.

7. "Individual Report for Col. William [Gent] Monroe, Jr.," Clan Munro USA.

8. All Monroe genealogies show Thomas and Benjamin as brothers, although few sources say so explicitly. My conclusion is that they were brothers, based on the universal support from genealogical charts, the fact that both of them started their careers in the same place, and the fact that Andrew—universally regarded as Thomas's father—is buried next to Benjamin. Nonetheless, the absence of any discussion of their family relationship suggests the brothers were not close or had fallen out for some reason.

9. "John Adair," in Lowell H. Harrison, *Kentucky's Governors* (Lexington: University Press of Kentucky, 2004).

10. Collins, *History of Kentucky*.

11. Ibid. At least one lawyer, Caswell Bennett, was known to have "had as his preceptor in law Judge Underwood." John C. Doolan, "Court of Appeals of Kentucky (Part III)," *Green Bag* 12 (1900): 465.

12. Collins, *History of Kentucky*.

13. Patrick H. Darby, "To the Public, No. 7," *Spirit of '76*, August 4, 1826, 378–80; William Henry Perrin, *The Pioneer Press of Kentucky: From the Printing of the First West of the Alleghanies, August 11, 1787, to the Establishment of the Daily Press in 1830* (Louisville: J. P. Morton & Co., 1888), 43.

14. "The Occupant," *Spirit of '76*, March 10, 1826, 7–9.

15. "The Lawyer Faction," *Spirit of '76*, March 10, 1826, 7–9.

16. Ibid.

17. "Fungus Court Business," *Frankfort Commentator,* May 12, 1826, 3.

18. *Smith et al. v. Overstreet's Adm'r.,* 81 S.W. 2d 571, 573 (1935).

19. Judicial Conference, *History of the Sixth Circuit.*

20. Russell R. Wheeler and Cynthia Harrison, *Creating the Federal Judicial System,* 3rd ed. (Washington, DC: Federal Judicial Center, 2005); Joshua W. Caldwell, *Sketches of the Bench and Bar of Tennessee* (Knoxville, TN: Ogden Brothers & Co., 1898); Melvin I. Urofsky, *The Supreme Court Justices: A Biographical Dictionary* (New York: Garland, 1994); Steven P. Brown, *John McKinley and the Antebellum Supreme Court Circuit Riding in the Old Southwest* (Tuscaloosa: University of Alabama Press, 2012).

21. *O'Reilly v. Morse,* 56 U.S. 62, 109 (1854).

22. Ibid., 112–13.

23. "Act to Incorporate the Montrose Law College of Kentucky," Ky. Acts, ch. 68 (1854).

24. James W. Raab, *J. Patton Anderson, Confederate General: A Biography* (Jefferson, NC: McFarland, 2004). Anderson's mother was Monroe's sister-in-law, Margaret L. Adair.

25. "Henry J. Leovy: The Distinguished Soldier, Citizen, Editor and Jurist, Passes Away Suddenly after Long Life of Honor and Usefulness," *New Orleans Times-Picayune,* October 4, 1902.

26. *Bulletin of the Tulane University of Louisiana* (1905): 7–9, 173–80. His grandson Frank Adair Monroe also taught in Tulane's Law Department for twenty years (and served almost forty on the Supreme Court of Louisiana). Herman de Bachellé Seebold, *Old Louisiana Plantation Homes and Family Trees* (New Orleans: Pelican Press, 1941), 77–79.

27. "Historical Notice of the Western Military Institute," *South-Western Monthly* 2 (September 1852): 131–33; R. T. Durrett, "Famous Old Drennon Springs," *Reg. Ky. Hist. Soc.* 15 (1907): 87–90; Linda M. Roberts, History of Drennon Springs, Henry County Historical Society, http://www.history.henrycountyky.com/drennon/drenhist.htm.

28. Westlaw search: DA(BEF 1865) & AT(MONROE).

29. Lowell H. Harrison, *Civil War in Kentucky* (Lexington: University Press of Kentucky, 1975).

30. *Richmond Daily Dispatch,* October 8, 1861.

31. Judicial Conference, *History of the Sixth Circuit.*

32. Thompson, *History of the First Kentucky Brigade,* 459–66.

33. "Judge Monroe," *New Orleans Daily True Delta,* October 6, 1861; "Interesting Scene at the Confederate States Court in Nashville," *New Orleans Times-Picayune,* October 8, 1861.

34. "Items," *New York Times,* October 22, 1861.

35. Kenneth C. Martis, *Historical Atlas of the Congresses of the Confederate States of America: 1861–1865* (New York: Simon & Schuster, 1994).

36. *Charleston Mercury,* December 2, 1861.

37. "From Richmond," *New York Times,* April 20, 1862.

38. William M. Robinson, *Justice in Grey: A History of the Judicial System of the Confederate States of America* (Cambridge, MA: Harvard University Press, 1941); G. Edward White, "Recovering the Legal History of the Confederacy," *Wash. & Lee L. Rev.* 68 (2011): 467–554.

39. Halyburton (1803–1879) was nominated by John Tyler on June 15, 1844, to the US District Court, Eastern District of Virginia, and was confirmed by the Senate. He resigned on April 24, 1861, and was immediately appointed judge of the Confederate District Court, Eastern District of Virginia, where he served until the end of the war. He was considered a senior member of the Confederate bench and swore in Jefferson Davis at his second inaugural.

40. The lack of a court of last resort was a notable problem and a frequent subject in opinions of the attorney general of the Confederacy. In a September 24, 1861, letter outlining the areas in which his office could not opine, assistant attorney general Wade Keyes specifically noted matters that might come up "for argument before the Supreme Court," likely assuming that the court would be established soon. Years later, on August 18, 1864, a letter to attorney general George Davis complained that the District Court of Virginia was in error, but because no supreme court had been established, losing parties were denied their right to appeal. Davis responded that he could not "defeat a judicial sentence by the interposition of special Executive authority." In the midst of this vacuum, the opinions of senior judges like Halyburton were highly esteemed. Rembert W. Patrick, ed., *Opinions of the Confederate Attorneys General* (Buffalo, NY: William S. Hein & Co., 2005), 37–39, 495; see also 277–80, 538–43.

41. *Decisions of Hon. James D. Halyburton, Judge of the Confederate States District Court for the Eastern District of Virginia, in the Cases of John B. Lane and John H. Leftwich, in Relation to Their Exemption, as Mail Contractors, from the Performance of Military Service* (Richmond, VA: Ritchie & Dunnavant, Printers, 1864).

42. "Important Decision—Constitutionality of the Habeas Corpus Suspension," *Richmond Daily Dispatch*, April 19, 1864; "Important Decision in the Confederate States District Court," *Richmond Sentinel*, April 19, 1864. For a copy of the decision, see "Judge Halyburton's Opinion in the Habeas Corpus Case," *Richmond Daily Enquirer*, April 28, 1864. For more context, see D. J. Flook, "Civil Liberties in Virginia during the Civil War," in *Encyclopedia Virginia*, Virginia Foundation for the Humanities, http://www.encyclopediavirginia.org/Civil_Liberties_in_Virginia_during_the_Civil_War (accessed May 17, 2015).

43. "From Kentucky," *New York Times*, September 3, 1861; Thompson, *History of the First Kentucky Brigade*, 459–66.

44. Dee Alexander Brown, *Morgan's Raiders* (New York: Konecky & Konecky, 1959), 193–94, 301–20 (this book was also released by Lippincott the same year under the title *The Bold Cavaliers: Morgan's 2nd Kentucky Cavalry Raiders*); George Levy, *To Die in Chicago: Confederate Prisoners at Camp Douglas, 1862–65* (Gretna, LA: Pelican, 1999), 245.

45. "Henry J. Leovy: The Distinguished Soldier, Citizen, Editor and Jurist," *New*

Orleans Times-Picayune, October 4, 1902; Lawrence L. Hewitt and Arthur W. Bergeron, *Louisianans in the Civil War* (Columbia: University of Missouri Press, 2002), 82.

46. Brown, *Morgan's Raiders,* 303.

47. "Confederate Treasure," *Augusta (GA) Chronicle,* January 6, 1882.

48. Dan A. Ellis, *Trinity and Live Oak* (Pass Christian, MS: CreateSpace, 2010). See also Ellis's *Pass Christian Historic District* (Pass Christian, MS: CreateSpace, 2011). Ellis is a local historian from the area who was displaced by Katrina; he has documented much of the region's lost history through websites and publications.

8. The Scion: John James Marshall (1785–1846)

1. There is some dispute among sources over whether his middle initial stands for Jay or James, but his marriage license has the latter. Lucy Kate McGhee, *Mercer County Kentucky Marriages, 1785 to 1852* (Washington, DC: L. K. McGhee, 1950), 93. Biographical sketches can be found in H. Levin, *Lawyers and Lawmakers of Kentucky* (Chicago: Lewis Publishing Co., 1897), 173, and William McClung Paxton, *The Marshall Family, or a Genealogical Chart of the Descendants of John Marshall and Elizabeth Markham, His Wife, Sketches of Individuals and Notices of Families Connected with Them* (Cincinnati: Robert Clarke & Co., 1885), 184.

2. E. Merton Coulter, "Humphrey Marshall," in *Dictionary of American Biography* (Detroit: Gale Research, 1974), 1:309–10.

3. J. Winston Coleman and John Lyde Wilson, *Famous Kentucky Duels* (Lexington: Henry Clay Press, 1969).

4. Humphrey Marshall, *The History of Kentucky: Exhibiting an Account of the Modern Discovery; Settlement; Progressive Improvement; Civil and Military Transactions; and the Present State of the Country* (Frankfort, KY: G. S. Robinson, Printer, 1824).

5. "Obituary [John James Marshall]," *Daily National Intelligencer,* July 3, 1846.

6. *Catalogue of the Officers and Alumni of Washington and Lee University* (Lexington, VA: J. Murphy & Co., 1888), 56.

7. "Obituary," *Daily National Intelligencer,* July 3, 1846; Levin, *Lawyers and Lawmakers,* 173; *General Catalogue of Princeton University 1746–1906* (Princeton University, 1908), 118.

8. *General Catalogue of Princeton,* 118–19.

9. "Obituary," *Daily National Intelligencer,* July 3, 1846.

10. *Dictionary of American Biography,* 2:291–94; William Birney, *James G. Birney and His Times: The Genesis of the Republican Party with Some Account of Abolition Movements in the South before 1828* (New York: D. Appleton & Co., 1890); Betty Fladeland, *James Gillespie Birney Slaveholder to Abolitionist* (Ithaca, NY: Cornell University Press, 1955).

11. J. Freeman Clark, *Anti-Slavery Days* (New York: R. Worthington, 1884), 23, quoted in Norman Barton Wood, *The White Side of a Black Subject: A Vindication of the Afro-American Race, from the Landing of Slaves at St. Augustine, Florida, in 1565, to the Present Time* (Chicago: American Pub. House, 1897), 293–94.

12. Russell Hatter and Gene Burch, *A Walking Tour of Historic Frankfort* (Frankfort: R. Hatter, 2002), 26.

13. The firm is also listed as drawers and endorsers in 1821 and 1822 in Reports of Committees of House of Representatives, Rep. No. 460, Bank of U.S. (April 30, 1832), 4:237.

14. Brenham later moved to Shelbyville, operated a tavern, and served as postmaster in 1828. *Stage-Coach Days in the Bluegrass; Being an Account of Stage-Coach Travel and Tavern Days in Lexington and Central Kentucky, 1800–1900* (Louisville: Standard Press, 1935); "Mr. Robert Brenham," *Baltimore Patriot*, April 16, 1830, 3; "The Late R. Brenham," *New Orleans Times-Picayune*, October 8, 1843.

15. Hatter and Burch, *Walking Tour of Historic Frankfort*, 7.

16. Levin, *Lawyers and Lawmakers*, 173.

17. Ky. Senate Journal (December 20, 1828), 107, (December 22, 1828), 110–12, (January 16, 1829), 224–25, (January 17, 1829), 230–31, (January 22, 1829), 262–63, (January 24, 1829), 275 (John J. Marshall nominated), (January 26, 1829), 301 (Marshall rejected).

18. Levin, *Lawyers and Lawmakers*, 173.

19. James F. Hopkins, ed., *Papers of Henry Clay* (Lexington: University Press of Kentucky, 1959), 7:429–31. The entire transaction is discussed in varying degrees of specificity in ibid., 3:133, 233, 287, 331–32, 348, 386, 389.

20. "Obituary," *Daily National Intelligencer*, July 3, 1846.

21. Lucy C. Lee, "Historic Places of Mason County," *Filson Club Historical Quarterly* 7 (1928): 85.

22. George Robertson and Alexander Hamilton Robertson, *An Outline of the Life of George Robertson: Written by Himself* (Lexington: n.p., 1876), 58–59.

23. *Kentucky Gazette*, November 25, 1830.

24. Collins, *History of Kentucky*, 1:499.

25. Josiah Stoddard Johnston, *Memorial History of Louisville from Its First Settlement to the Year 1896* (Louisville: American Biographical Publishing Co., 1896), 67.

26. "Death of James Birney Marshall," *Louisville Courier-Journal*, September 5, 1870; "Mortuary Notice," *Cincinnati Daily Enquirer*, September 7, 1870.

27. "Kentucky," in *American Almanac and Repository of Useful Knowledge* (Boston: Crosby, Nichols, Lee & Co., 1837–1842).

28. "Obituary," *Daily National Intelligencer*, July 3, 1846.

9. The Editor: James G. Dana (1785–1840)

1. "An Act to Change the Mode of Publishing the Decisions of the Court of Appeals," Ky. Acts, ch. 52 (January 4, 1833).

2. Rossiter Johnson and John Howard Brown, *The Twentieth Century Biographical Dictionary of Notable Americans* (Boston: Biographical Society, 1904), 3:1898; A. Egerton Ryerson, *The Loyalists of America and Their Times: From 1620 to 1816* (Toronto: Briggs, 1880), 1:92–93.

3. James Dana and James Freeman Dana, *Memoir of the Late Hon. Samuel Dana* (Cambridge, MA: John Wilson, 1877).

4. Ibid., 13–14.

5. "Notary's Office," *Boston Gazette,* January 10, 1811.

6. Dana and Dana, *Memoir of Samuel Dana,* 28.

7. L. F. Johnson, *History of Franklin County Bar, 1786–1931* (Frankfort: F. K. Kavanaugh, 1932).

8. *Hodges v. Holeman,* 1 Dana (31 Ky.) 50 (1833).

9. Jacob Harrod Holeman and James Greene Dana, *The Case of the Public Printer, with Some Brief Illustrations of the Testimony* (Lexington: n.p., 1828).

10. Willard Rouse Jillson, *Newspapers and Periodicals of Frankfort, Kentucky, 1795–1945* (Frankfort: Kentucky State Historical Society, 1945).

11. "Fungus Court Business," *Frankfort Commentator,* May 12, 1826.

12. Ibid.

13. Ibid.

14. Dana and Dana, *Memoir of Samuel Dana.* Kendall's appearance is described by Harriett Martineau in "Amos Kendall's Letter," *Memphis Daily Enquirer,* September 27, 1860, quoted in Amos Kendall and William Stickney, *Autobiography of Amos Kendall* (Boston: Lee & Shepard, 1872), 585–86. See also Donald B. Cole, *A Jackson Man: Amos Kendall and the Rise of American Democracy* (Baton Rouge: Louisiana State University Press, 2010).

15. L. F. Johnson, *Famous Kentucky Tragedies and Trials: A Collection of Important and Interesting Tragedies and Criminal Trials Which Have Taken Place in Kentucky* (New York: Classic Publishers, 1916), 34–43.

16. *Kentucky Reporter,* January 31, 1825, quoted in *Saturday Evening Post,* February 15, 1825, 2.

17. *Frankfort Commentator,* July 22, 1826.

18. Robert S. Thomas and George W. Williams, *A Statement of the Trial of Isaac B. Desha Indicted for the Murder of Francis Baker, Late of Natchez, Miss., Held at Cynthiana, Ky.* (Lexington: T. T. Bradford, 1825).

19. *Frankfort Commentator,* July 22, 1826.

20. *Frankfort Argus* quoting *Frankfort Commentator,* July 22, 1826. See also Amos Kendall, "The Governor's Son," *Frankfort Patriot,* July 17, 1826.

21. *Frankfort Commentator,* July 22, 1826.

22. Andrew Forest Muir, "Isaac Desha, Fact and Fancy," *Filson Club Historical Quarterly* 30 (1956): 319–23.

23. A. C. Quisenberry, *Life and Times of Humphrey Marshall* (Winchester, KY: n.p., 1892), 114–17; William Henry Perrin, *The Pioneer Press of Kentucky* (Louisville: John P. Morton Co., 1884), 43. See also Jillson, *Newspapers and Periodicals of Frankfort.*

24. "A Novel Proceeding," *Frankfort Commentator,* May 13, 1826.

25. Ibid.

26. Leander J. Sharp, *Vindication of the Character of the Late Col. Solomon P. Sharp from the Calumnies Published against Him since His Murder, by Patrick Darby and Jereboam O. Beauchamp* (Frankfort: Printed by A. Kendall, 1827). See also Perrin, *Pioneer Press*, 43, 115.

27. *Near v. Minnesota*, 283 U.S. 697 (1931).

28. Robert S. Thomas and James G. Dana, *Beauchamp's Trial: A Report of the Trial of Jereboam O. Beauchamp before the Franklin Circuit Court in May 1826* (Frankfort: Albert G. Hodges at the Commentator Office, 1826). Portions are reproduced in Loren Kallsen, *The Kentucky Tragedy: A Problem in Romantic Attitudes* (Indianapolis: Bobbs-Merrill, 1963).

29. The publication details of Beauchamp's *Confession* are confused (even his authorship is in doubt), but according to Willard Rouse Jillson, it was likely published in Bloomfield, Kentucky. Ann's undated letters were purportedly sent to a friend in Baltimore, and the collection was published in Washington, DC. Both Beauchamp accounts were merged, with new material, in *The Kentucky Tragedy: A Full and Particular Account of the Lives and Tragical Deaths, of Jereboam O. Beauchamp and Ann, His Wife, the Murderers of Colonel Sharp: With Their Trial for the Same, Their Conduct in Prison, Confession, and Last Words: Epitaph on Both, Written by Mrs. Beauchamp: and Other Authentic Particulars, Never before Published* (Philadelphia: T. Town, Printer, 1826). Details about all these publications are from noted antiquarian Willard Rouse Jillson's *Literary Haunts and Personalities of Old Frankfort 1791–1941* (Frankfort: Kentucky Historical Society, 1941), 29–30.

30. Sharp, *Vindication of the Character.*

31. "Politian" (1835), in *Collected Works of Edgar Allan Poe: Poems,* ed. Thomas Ollive Mabbott (Cambridge, MA: Belknap Press of Harvard University Press, 1969); William Gilmore Simms, *Beauchampe, or, the Kentucky Tragedy: A Sequel to Charlemont* (Philadelphia: Lea & Blanchard, 1842); Robert Penn Warren, *World Enough and Time: A Romantic Novel* (New York: Random House, 1950).

32. Matthew G. Schoenbachler, *Murder & Madness: The Myth of the Kentucky Tragedy* (Lexington: University Press of Kentucky, 2009); Dickson D. Bruce, *The Kentucky Tragedy: A Story of Conflict and Change in Antebellum America* (Baton Rouge: Louisiana State University Press, 2006).

33. James D. Daniels, "Amos Kendall: Kentucky Journalist, 1815–1829," *Filson Club Historical Quarterly* 52 (1978): 55.

34. "Andrew Jackson's Private Character," *Frankfort Commentator,* April 14, 1827.

35. "Dana vrs. Mrs. Jackson," *Frankfort Argus,* April 18, 1827. See also Daniels, "Amos Kendall," 56.

36. Dana's attack was not without parallel. Jackson was also attacked as a slave trader, and his marriage was repeatedly under fire. See Mark R. Cheathem, "Slavery, Kinship, and Andrew Jackson's Presidential Campaign of 1828," paper presented at the 2011 Southern Historical Association meeting and posted at https://mcheathem.files.wordpress.

com/2011/10/paper-submitted-draft_sha-2011.pdf; Norma Basch, "Marriage, Morals, and Politics in the Election of 1828," *Journal of American History* 80 (1993): 890–918.

37. Jillson, *Newspapers and Periodicals of Frankfort*.

38. *Hodges v. Holeman*, 1 Dana (31 Ky.) 50 (1833).

39. President Abraham Lincoln to Albert G. Hodges, editor of the *Frankfort Commonwealth*, April 4, 1864, Robert Todd Lincoln Family Papers, Library of Congress, Manuscript Division.

40. Only a single issue of *Lights and Shadows of Modern Times* survives; the September 18, 1832, edition of the paper is owned by the American Antiquarian Society.

41. *A Manual of Masonry and Anti-Masonry, Containing a View of the Secrets, Principles and Practices of the Order, with a Collection of Documents, Explaining the Grounds of Opposition, Assumed by the Anti-Masons—Moral and Political* (Louisville: Printed for the People, 1833).

42. Thomas Metcalfe to Henry Clay, Frankfort, Ky., May 7, 1832, in *Papers of Henry Clay: Candidate, Compromiser, Whig, March 5, 1829–December 31, 1836*, ed. Robert Seager II (Lexington: University Press of Kentucky, 1984), 506; William Preston Vaughn, *The Antimasonic Party in the United States, 1826–1843* (Lexington: University Press of Kentucky, 1983).

43. Collins, *History of Kentucky*, 1:499.

44. Erwin C. Surrency, *A History of American Law Publishing* (New York: Oceana Publications, 1990), 44.

45. Westlaw search: DA(BEF 1845) & AT(DANA).

46. *Kentucky Gazette*, November 26, 1840; "Died," *(Philadelphia) North American*, December 10, 1840. The family memoir misstates his year of death as 1841. Dana and Dana, *Memoir of Samuel Dana*.

47. Jillson, *Literary Haunts and Personalities*, 30.

10. The Professional: Ben Monroe (1790–1860)

1. One source suggests Westmoreland County as his birthplace, but Benjamin was only a year or two older than Thomas, whose headstone in a Pass Christian cemetery clearly notes an Albemarle County birthplace. It is likely the two brothers were born in the same place.

2. William E. Rainey, "Woodford County (Concluded)," *Reg. Ky. Hist. Soc.* 19 (1921): 30.

3. Thomas Marshall Green, *Historic Families of Kentucky* (Cincinnati: Robert Clarke & Co., 1889), 133. It is reasonably certain that Cynthia was a granddaughter of the elder William; some private family trees list John as her father, but others do not. Green describes Anne Montgomery Logan, a daughter of William Sr., as Cynthia's aunt, so the connection is not completely fanciful.

4. "Advertisement," *Lexington Reporter*, August 1, 1812.

5. Kentucky Acts, ch. 196 (January 10, 1815).

6. *Kentucky Gazette,* April 10 and December 11, 1818.

7. *Kentucky Gazette,* November 3, 1807; Robert Bishop, *Folk Painters of America* (New York: E. P. Dutton, 1979).

8. "Christopher Tompkins Resigned," *Frankfort Argus,* April 7, 1824.

9. Thomas B. Monroe Sr. served as Kentucky's fourteenth secretary of state from September 1823 to September 1824, having replaced Joseph Cabell Breckinridge, who died of fever. See Kentucky Office of Secretary of State, http://apps.sos.ky.gov/secdesk/sosinfo/default.aspx?id=14.

10. Kurt X. Metzmeier, "Circuit Court Judges Listed in the Kentucky Law Reports, 1825–1903," *Kentucky Ancestors* (2013): 141–56; Kurt X. Metzmeier, "Judges of the Kentucky Circuit Courts, 1831–1861," *Kentucky Ancestors* (2008): 151–60.

11. Richard Priest Dietzman, "Kentucky Law Reports and Reporters," *Ky. L. J.* 16 (1927–1928): 16–27.

12. Andrew had certainly done so by 1856, when his wife, the former Julia Bull, gave birth to a son, the future Andrew Leight Monroe, MD. William Harvey King, ed., *History of Homeopathy* (Chicago: Lewis Publishing Co., 1905), 4:361. Andrew Monroe is listed as a judge of the Jefferson County court in 1859–1860 in the Louisville city directory.

13. "Monroe's Reports," *Am. L. J.* 9 (1850): 428.

14. Ben Monroe and James Harlan, *Digest of Cases at Common Law and in Equity, Decided by the Court of Appeals of Kentucky, from Its Organization in 1792, to the Close of the Winter Term of 1852–3* (Frankfort: A. G. Hodges, 1853). See Kurt X. Metzmeier, "Blazing Trails in a New Kentucky Wilderness: Early Kentucky Case Law Digests," *Law Libr. J.* 93 (Winter 2001): 93–108.

15. Westlaw searches DA(BEF 1865) & AT(B. MONROE) and DA(BEF 1865) & AT(B. AND A. MONROE) show 173 Kentucky cases argued by Monroe alone or with his son Andrew.

16. "The Great Telegraph Suit," *Baltimore Sun,* September 19, 1848; "Louisville and New Orleans Telegraph," *New Orleans Times-Picayune,* June 29, 1849. See chapter 7 for more about this case.

17. Ben Monroe, *Reports of Selected Cases Argued and Decided in the Circuit and District Courts of the United States for the Kentucky District* (Frankfort: Printed by Cavins & Holeman, 1848).

18. *Waller's Lessee v. Best,* 44 U.S. 111 (1845).

19. Lewis Collins, *Historical Sketches of Kentucky* (Maysville, KY: L. Collins, 1847).

20. Mabel Clare Weaks. *Calendar of the Kentucky Papers of the Draper Collection of Manuscripts* (Madison, WI: The Society, 1925), 11 CC 289–91.

21. W. H. Averill, *A History of the First Presbyterian Church, Frankfort, Kentucky, Together with the Churches in Franklin County, in Connection with the Presbyterian Church in the United States of America* (Frankfort: First Presbyterian Church, 1901), 73; J. B. Adger, "Danville Theological Seminary," in "The General Assembly of MDCCCLVII," *Southern Presbyterian Review* 10 (1858): 309.

22. The survey is from residential Frankfort, and the five slaves ranged in age from three to fifty years. Obviously domestics, they included one adult male, one adult female, and three juveniles. The official census taker, or "assistant marshall," was Ben's nephew, John A. Monroe. "Franklin County, Kentucky," 1850 US Federal Census—Slave Schedules, Ancestry.com.

23. Harold D. Tallant, *Evil Necessity: Slavery and Political Culture in Antebellum Kentucky* (Lexington: University Press of Kentucky, 2003); "Annual Meeting of Kentucky Colonization Society," *African Repository* 28 (July 1852): 214; "Item," *New Orleans Times-Picayune,* February 26, 1856; "Liberia: An Opinion of the Kentucky Colonization Society of Liberia," *African Repository* 34 (December 1858): 378.

24. Tallant, *Evil Necessity;* Jeffrey B. Allen, "'All of Us Are Highly Pleased with the Country': Black and White Kentuckians on Liberian Colonization," *Phylon* 43 (1982): 97–109.

25. "Convention of the Friends of Emancipation in Kentucky," *National Era (DC),* May 5, 2010, reprinting the *Frankfort Commentator.*

26. Ibid. See also Tallant, *Evil Necessity,* 143–45; "An Interesting Letter from Kentucky," *Worcester (MA) National Aegis,* June 20, 1849.

27. Robert M. Ireland, *The Kentucky State Constitution: A Reference Guide* (Westport, CT: Greenwood, 1999), 25–26.

28. Tim Talbott, "1864 Attack on Frankfort," *ExploreKYHistory,* http://explorekyhistory.ky.gov/items/show/497 (accessed July 23, 2015). George Wood Monroe was appointed quartermaster general of the Kentucky militia by Governor Thomas E. Bramlette and served from 1866 to 1868.

29. Jennifer Frazier, "The History of the Kentucky State Law Library," *Ky. Libr.* 77 (2013): 12–23. Cornelia was the grandmother of George Franklin Berry, a prominent whiskey distiller and the builder of Berry Hill, a famous mansion located on the grounds of her great-uncle Thomas B. Monroe's Montrose estate.

30. George Robertson, "Sketch of the Court of Appeals," in Collins, *History of Kentucky,* 1:499; "New Publications," *Am. L. J.* 9 (1849–1850): 430.

31. Adlai E. Stevenson, *Something of Men I Have Known: With Some Papers of a General Nature, Political, Historical, and Retrospective* (Chicago: A. C. McClurg, 1909), 403.

11. The Banker: James P. Metcalfe (1822–1889)

1. See *The Frankfort Cemetery in Kentucky* (Frankfort: Kentucky Genealogical Society, 1988).

2. Howard Hurtig Metcalfe, *Metcalfe Lineages* (Decorah, IA: Anundsen Publishing Co., 1990), 70.

3. Frank F. Mathias, "Thomas Metcalfe," in Lowell H. Harrison, *Kentucky's Governors* (Lexington: University Press of Kentucky, 2004).

4. William Perrin, *History of Bourbon, Scott, Harrison and Nicholas Counties, Kentucky* (Chicago: O. L. Baskin & Co., 1882), 399, 412–13.

5. Carlisle-Nicholas County Tourism, Inc., "Walking Tour of Carlisle, Kentucky," http://www.carlisle-nicholascounty.org/tours/walking/index.htm (accessed 2010).

6. James P. Metcalfe appears as "deputy for J. G. Parks clerk of the Nicholas County court" in deed and will books in 1841.

7. Perrin, *History of Bourbon*, 417.

8. In 1850 Dougherty Lodge No. 65 listed "Officers, Willis Sims, M[aster]., James P. Metcalfe, S[enior]. W[arden].'; in 1851 it listed "James P. Metcalfe, M[aster]." For the years 1852–1855, Metcalfe was listed as "past master."

9. *Memoirs of the Life and Services of Daniel Drake* (New York: D. Appleton & Co., 1860).

10. Daniel Drake, *Pioneer Life in Kentucky* (Cincinnati: Robert Clarke & Co., 1870), 3–4, 6–8. See also Ancestry.com tree for Jacob Drake.

11. The 2010 value of this real estate is estimated at between $600,000 and $1.75 million; see http://www.measuringworth.com. Cornelius Drake later appeared in the 1860 census as part of James P. Metcalfe's household and was listed as owning $30,000 in real and personal property, which was dwarfed by his son-in-law's $55,000. However, it is possible the census taker failed to take into account Drake's remaining property in Nicholas County.

12. Collins, *History of Kentucky*, 2:651.

13. Ibid., 562.

14. James P. Metcalfe to John C. Breckinridge, April 15, 1853, Breckinridge Papers, Library of Congress.

15. James P. Metcalfe to John C. Breckinridge, May 30, 1853, Breckinridge Papers.

16. "Kentucky," in *American Almanac and Repository of Useful Knowledge* (Boston: C. C. Little & J. Brown, 1851), 292.

17. Office of First Lady Glenna Fletcher, Mary A. Drake Metcalfe (1831–1900, 19th First Lady), in "First Lady Dolls," firstlady.ky.ov/first+lady+dolls/First-Ladies+-+13th+-+22nd/pic7.htm (accessed January 6, 2007; discontinued).

18. Westlaw search: AT(METCALFE) & DA(BEF 1890).

19. See *Tri-Weekly Kentucky Yeoman*, July 8, 1858. Hord was elected police judge of Frankfort in 1845 and was later elected Franklin County judge. A Democrat, he served in the General Assembly in the early 1850s and was elected again in 1879. J. H. Battle, William Henry Perrin, and G. C. Kniffin, *Kentucky: A History of the State* (Chicago: F. A. Battey Publishing Co., 1887).

20. Calculated at http://www.measuringworth.com.

21. Clay Lancaster, *Antebellum Architecture of Kentucky* (Lexington: University Press of Kentucky, 1991). Liberty Hall and the Orlando Brown House still survive as exquisite representations of Frankfort in its heyday. They are managed by Liberty Hall Historic Site, which operates as a "learning center that engages the public in exploring the history, politics, social and cultural life in early Kentucky" (http://www.libertyhall.org).

22. *History of Fayette County, Kentucky* (Chicago: O. L. Baskin & Co., 1882), 822–24.

Fairlawn was in the northern suburbs of Lexington; the main house at 904 North Broadway still stands. There is evidence that Metcalfe owned another estate in southeastern Fayette County, so it is unclear to which property the 1870 census refers.

23. "Metcalfe Residence Sold," *Kentucky (Lexington) Leader,* May 24, 1889. This is probably the former residence of James Orlando Harrison depicted on the Hart & Mapother map of the City of Lexington (Fayette County, KY, 1855).

24. "James P. Metcalfe, a Prominent Former Lexingtonian, Dies in Detroit," *Kentucky (Lexington) Leader,* July 16, 1889.

25. Benjamin Homans, ed., *1881 Banker's Almanac & Register* (New York: Bankers Magazine, 1881), 54; *Williams Lexington City Directory for 1881–82* (Lexington: Williams & Co., 1881).

26. *Prather & Snyders's Directory of Lexington, Ky. 1888* (Lexington, 1888).

27. J. W. Norwood, "Builders of Lexington VIII: The Pivot Year 1880," *Lexington Herald,* December 31, 1911; "First Buildings at University 40 Years Old," *Lexington Herald,* February 12, 1922.

28. "Board of Visitors, 1878–79," in *Biennial Report of the Superintendent of Public Instruction of Kentucky for the Years, Ending June 30, 1913* (Frankfort: Kentucky Department of Education, 1913), 635; *Fiftieth Anniversary of the University of Kentucky, 1866–1916* (Lexington: University of Kentucky, 1916).

29. "James P. Metcalfe," *Kentucky (Lexington) Leader,* July 16, 1889.

30. *Frankfort Cemetery in Kentucky.* A "leaf" of Metcalfe's family drifted west in the years following his death. The marriage of Lillian Metcalfe and Joseph D. Armstrong endured, and they relocated to California. Lillian Metcalfe Armstrong died in 1955; she and her husband were buried in Hollywood Memorial Cemetery—alongside giants of the movie business such as Cecil B. DeMille—far from rural Kentucky where her father began his rise.

12. The Copperhead: Alvin Duvall (1813–1891)

1. Anne E. Kornblut, "Obama and Cheney, Making Connections," *Washington Post,* October 17, 2007.

2. Harry Wright Newman, *Mareen Duvall of Middle Plantation: A Genealogical History of Mareen Duvall, Gent., of the Province of Maryland and His Descendants, with Histories of the Allied Families of Tyler, Clarke, Poole, Hall, and Merriken* (Washington, DC: n.p., 1952).

3. "Wouldn't Work His Way," *Ky. L. J.* 2.1 (July 1882): 51.

4. William C. Davis, *Breckinridge: Statesman, Soldier, Symbol* (Lexington: University Press of Kentucky, 2010).

5. H. Levin, *Lawyers and Lawmakers of Kentucky* (Chicago: Lewis Publishing Co., 1897), 86; *Biographical Encyclopedia of Kentucky of the Dead and Living Men of the Nineteenth Century* (Cincinnati: J. M. Armstrong & Co., 1878), 163–64; L. F. Johnson, *History of Franklin County Bar, 1786–1931* (Frankfort: F. K. Kavanaugh, 1932), 215; John

C. Doolan, "Court of Appeals of Kentucky," *Green Bag* 12 (1900): 408, 416–17; "Alvin Duvall," in Newman, *Mareen Duvall,* 136–37.

6. Ky. House Journal (1806), 147, 168, 255.

7. Ky. Acts, ch. 22, art. 10 (January 7, 1852).

8. "Courts," art. 8, sec. 1, in *Revised Statutes of Kentucky* (Frankfort: Hodges, 1852).

9. Simon B. Buckner to Circuit Judge Lilly, December 14, 1988, in Charles G. Mutzenberg, *Kentucky's Famous Feuds and Tragedies* (New York: R. F. Fenno & Co., 1917).

10. Five Kentuckians from Scott County—William Duvall, Dr. Ben Duvall, Cornelius Duvall, William H. Duvall, and Mareen Duvall—served in either the 9th Kentucky Cavalry or 4th Kentucky Infantry. All appear to be sons of Alvin's uncle Cornelius.

11. *Chrisman v. Bruce,* 1 Duv. (62 Ky.) 63 (1863); "Kentucky under Martial Law," *Harper's Weekly,* August 15, 1863, 51.

12. "Stephen G. Burbridge," in *Dictionary of American Biography* (Detroit: Gale Research, 1974), 1:270–71. A modern example of the animus against Burbridge is Bryan S. Bush, *Butcher Burbridge: Union General Stephen Burbridge and His Reign of Terror over Kentucky* (Morley, MO: Acclaim Press, 2008).

13. Ross A. Webb, "Kentucky: Pariah among the Elect," in Richard O. Curry, *Radicalism, Racism, and Party Realignment: The Border States during Reconstruction* (Baltimore: Johns Hopkins University Press, 1969), 105–45. See also E. Merton Coulter, *The Civil War and Readjustment in Kentucky* (Gloucester, MA: P. Smith, 1966), 184–85.

14. "Sketch of the Proceedings and Character of Democratic State Convention," *New York Times,* May 7, 1866.

15. "The Courier's 'Democracy,'" *Louisville Daily Journal,* June 6, 1866.

16. Ezra J. Warner, *Generals in Blue: Lives of the Union Commanders* (Baton Rouge: Louisiana State University Press, 1964), 231–32.

17. "Letter from Georgetown," *Louisville Daily Courier,* June 23, 1866; "Great Barbecue at Middletown," *Louisville Daily Courier,* July 9, 1866; "Item," *Louisville Daily Courier,* June 20, 1866.

18. "Duvall a Radical," *Louisville Daily Journal,* June 9, 1866; "Duvall and Bragg—Raid on Camp Dick Robinson," *Louisville Daily Journal,* July 16, 1866.

19. "The Question Settled," *Louisville Daily Journal,* July 13, 1866.

20. "A Brutal and Scandalous Outrage," *Louisville Daily Journal,* August 1, 1866.

21. "The Great Meeting of Saturday Night: Six Thousand Democrats in Council," *Louisville Daily Courier,* August 6, 1866.

22. "Victory," *Louisville Daily Courier,* August 7, 1866.

23. Coulter, *Civil War and Readjustment,* 257–311, esp. 303–9; Thomas L. Connelly, "Neo-Confederatism or Power Vacuum: Post-war Kentucky Politics Reappraised," *Reg. Ky. Hist. Soc.* 64 (1966): 257–69.

24. "Civil Rights Case," *Louisville Daily Courier,* September 6, 1866.

25. Westlaw search: DA(BEF 1892) & AT(DUVALL).

26. "Bloody Rowan: Craig Tolliver Violates the Truce and Morehead Is Again Ter-

rorized," *Maysville Republican,* January 8, 1887. See, generally, Mutzenberg, *Kentucky's Famous Feuds and Tragedies.*

27. "Death's Relief: Judge Alvin Duvall Passes Away after a Long Suffering," *Louisville Courier-Journal,* November 18, 1891.

28. "The Dead Honored: The Court of Appeals Adjourns and the Executive Offices to Be Closed," *Louisville Courier-Journal,* November 19, 1891; "Judge Duvall's Death: Suitable Action Taken by the Bar at Frankfort," *Louisville Courier-Journal,* November 20, 1891.

29. Doolan, "Court of Appeals of Kentucky," 408, 417.

30. *Berea College v. Commonwealth,* 94 S.W. 623 (1906).

13. The Last: W. P. D. Bush (1823–1904)

1. Henry Hall, *Year Book of the Societies Composed of Descendants of the Men of the Revolution, 1890* (New York: Republic Press, 1891), 138.

2. Samuel Haycraft, *History of Elizabethtown, Kentucky, and Its Surroundings* (Elizabethtown: Woman's Club of Elizabethtown, Kentucky, 1921).

3. Elizabeth J. E. Hardin, "Kentucky Mustangs," *Handbook of Texas Online,* http://www.tshaonline.org/handbook/online/articles/qjk01 (accessed March 27, 2015).

4. "William P. D. Bush," in H. Levin, *Lawyers and Lawmakers of Kentucky* (Chicago: Lewis Publishing Co., 1897).

5. *History of Daviess County, Kentucky* (Chicago: Inter-State Pub. Co., 1883), 299; Anderson Chenault Quisenberry, *General Zachary Taylor and the Mexican War* (Kentucky Historical Society, 1911).

6. R. D. W. Connor, William K. Boyd, and Joseph Grégoire de Roulhac Hamilton, *History of North Carolina* (Chicago: Lewis Publishing Co., 1919), 247.

7. James W. Chichetto, "General Winfield Scott's Policy of Pacification in the Mexican American War of 1846–1848," *Combat Literary Journal* 5 (2007): 4–5.

8. Ky. Senate Journal (February 9, 1849), 243.

9. Levin, *Lawyers and Lawmakers.*

10. "A Bloody Affray at Hawesville, Ky.," *New York Times,* March 7, 1859; *Harper's Weekly,* March 26, 1859, 196.

11. *Louisville Daily Courier,* January 12, 1866, quoting the *Hancock Messenger.* The impetus for the *Messenger* article was to keep Yeaman from claiming all the credit. See also Levin, *Lawyers and Lawmakers,* 287–89; Connor et al., *History of North Carolina,* 246–47.

12. Collins, *History of Kentucky,* 1:119.

13. E. Merton Coulter, *The Civil War and Readjustment in Kentucky* (Gloucester, MA: P. Smith, 1966), 283, citing the *Cincinnati Gazette,* August 15, 1865.

14. "A New Dodge," *Louisville Daily Courier,* April 2, 1866.

15. Westlaw search: AT(W. P. D. BUSH) & DA(BEF 1904).

16. Elizabeth Patterson Thomas, *Old Kentucky Homes and Gardens* (Louisville:

Standard Print. Co., 1939), 42. In 1891 Bush sold the house to Union army major William Edward Bradley, who had moved to Frankfort to manage his distillery holdings. The house was listed on the National Register of Historic Places in 1971.

17. "Coal Lands: Bought for a Louisville Syndicate Four Hundred Acres," *Louisville Courier-Journal,* September 13, 1899.

18. L. F. Johnson, *Famous Kentucky Tragedies and Trials: A Collection of Important and Interesting Tragedies and Criminal Trials Which Have Taken Place in Kentucky* (New York: Classic Publishers, 1916), 205–23.

19. "The Big Court: Can Three Judges Constitute a Constitutional Court of Appeals?" *Louisville Courier-Journal,* April 28, 1879.

20. His death certificate lists "senility" (old age) as the cause of death. "Judge Bush Is Better," *Louisville Courier-Journal,* February 14, 1901; "Death's Hand Laid upon Judge William P. D. Bush," *Louisville Courier-Journal,* June 24, 1904; "Distinguished Lawyer and Former Citizen of Frankfort Dies in Louisville," *Frankfort Roundabout,* July 3, 1904.

Conclusion

1. J. F. Bullitt and John Feland, *General Statutes of Kentucky* (Lexington, KY: James E. Hughes, 1879), 279–80.

2. L. Russell, *Statutes of Kentucky* (Frankfort: Major, Johnson & Barrett, 1909), §§495–507 (printing and distribution), §2794 (salary).

3. "New Books," *Western L. J.* 8 (1850–1851): 191. See also *Western L. J.* 9 (1852): 255, and advertisement in *Literary World* 9 (1851): 300.

4. Notice, *Albany L. J.* 58 (1898): 342.

5. Based on an analysis of John P. Morton Company imprints in OCLC WorldCat global book catalog. See also "Guide to John P. Morton & Company Records, 1852–1943," University of Kentucky.

6. "Westerfield-Bonte History," http://www.westerfieldbonte.com/history.html (accessed July 21, 2015).

7. Charles Haynes McMullen, "The Publishing Activities of Robert Clarke & Co., of Cincinnati, 1858–1909," *Papers of the Bibliographical Society of America* 34 (1840): 315–26.

8. Volume 1 of this seminal work has been republished in facsimile in *The Syllabi: Genesis of the National Reporter System* (Clark, NJ: Lawbook Exchange Co., 2011). See, especially, Michael H. Hoeflich, "Preface," and W. E. Butler, "Introduction: John Briggs West and the Transformation of the American Law Reports," ibid.

9. W. W. Marvin, *West Publishing Company: Origin, Growth, Leadership* (St. Paul, MN: West, 1969), 46–49. See also Erwin C. Surrency, *A History of American Law Publishing* (New York: Oceana Publications, 1990).

10. Robert M. Jarvis, "John B. West: Founder of the West Publishing Company," *Am. J. Legal Hist.* 50 (2008): 1–22; Thomas A. Woxland, "Forever Associated with the Practice of Law: The Early Years of the West Publishing Company," *Legal Reference Services*

Quarterly 5 (1985): 115–24; Ross E. Davies, "How West Law Was Made: The Company, Its Products, and Its Promotions," *Charleston L. Rev.* 6 (2012): 231–82.

11. John Doyle, "WESTLAW and the American Digest Classification Scheme," *Law Libr. J.* 84 (1992): 229–58; Patti Ogden, "Mastering the Lawless Science of Our Law: A Story of Legal Citation Indexes," *Law Libr. J.* 85 (1993): 1–47.

12. "Kentucky Decisions," *Louisville Courier-Journal,* March 18, 1905.

13. Kurt X. Metzmeier, "Blazing Trails in a New Kentucky Wilderness: Early Kentucky Case Law Digests," *Law Libr. J.* 93 (Winter 2001): 93–108.

14. Patrick Lee, "Times Mirror to Boost Its Legal Publishing Unit with Shepard's," *Los Angeles Times,* July 4, 1996; Elizabeth M. McKenzie, "Comparing KeyCite with Shepard's Online," *Legal Reference Services Quarterly* 17 (1999): 85–99; William L. Taylor, "Comparing KeyCite and Shepard's for Completeness, Currency, and Accuracy," *Law Libr. J.* 92 (2000): 127–41.

15. Since then, HeinOnline, which publishes older legal materials as they looked in their original format, has replicated the old reports as part of its State Reports: A Historical Archive database.

Index